# PRISON DAYS

THE FIRST SIX MONTHS

SIMON KING

# CONTENTS

ISBN: 9781698877358

## ALSO BY SIMON KING

Prison Days

(Books 1 to 12)

Prison Days: Inmates

(Books 1 to 5)

The Lawson Chronicles

(Books 1 to 3)

MAX

(Books 1 to 6)

The Sam Rader Thriller Series

(Books 1 to 5)

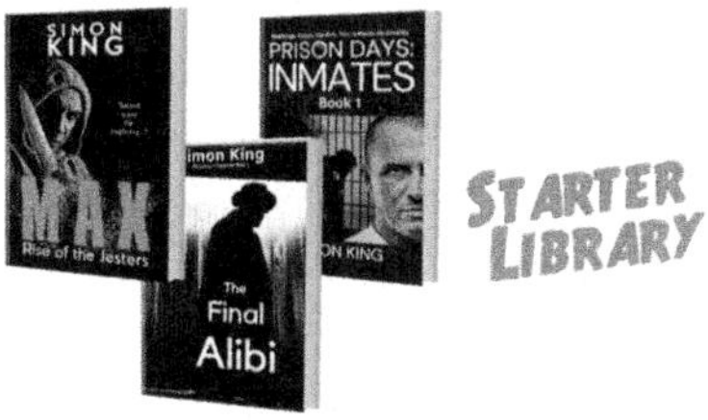
SIMON KING
MAX
Rise of the Jesters
PRISON DAYS: INMATES
Book 1
The Final Alibi
STARTER LIBRARY

# GLOSSARY AND UNIT DESCRIPTIONS

## Units

All the units in the prison are named after rivers and consist of management, step-down management, protection and mainstream.

Management Units- Units that are predominately single occupancy out of necessity or punishment and have 23-hour lock ins. Prisoners only receive a one hour run out from their cell.

Murray North and South are the Management Units.

Step Down Management- Units that are a step down from the 23-hour lock down. Prisoners are given extra run-outs throughout the day but limited to around 3 to 4 hours. Some prisoners can mix and have joint run-outs.

Goulburn East and West are the Step-Down Management Units.

Protection Units

Yarra North and South, Loddon North and South, Glenelg East and West

Main Stream Units

Thomson East and West, Tambo East and West, Campaspe, Avoca, Maribyrnong,

Other Areas
Kitchen, Laundry, Medical Wing

## Prison Terms

Air- Raiding- Yelling or abusing someone loudly in the middle of a unit.

Billet- A prisoner who is assigned a particular duty in the unit, on a daily basis, for a weekly pay packet. They hold the position until they are either transferred out, sacked or quit.

Bone Yard- A protection unit. Protection prisoners are also known as Boners.

Booted- To hide something in the anus.

Boss- What prisoners call an officer. It began early last century, is a reverse insult and means "Sorry Son of a Bitch."

Brew- A cup of Coffee or Tea.

Brasco- Toilet or brasco roll is toilet paper.

Bronze Up- To cover ones' self in faeces.

Bunk- A prisoner's bed.

Canteen- A prisoner's weekly shopping or shopping items.

Cellie- A cellmate.

Chook Pen- A fenced-in area attached to a unit for prisoners to walk around in. Approximately 15m by 15m depending on which unit. Management units have multiple chook pens as prisoners have individual run outs throughout the day.

Coee- A prisoner's co-accused.

Control:

Count correct:

Crook- How officers refer to inmates.

Dog- Someone who informs on another prisoner.

Greens or Greys- Prisoner's prison uniform.

Rock Spider- A paedophile.

Run Out:

Screw- How inmates refer to officers.

Shiv- home-made knife or blade.

Slash Up- To self-harm.

Stand overs:

Sup: Another term for supervisor

The T.O.'s- Tactical Officers, that are highly trained and armed with batons and capsicum spray.

Trap- A small latch in a cell door that can be lowered to allow access. It is normally either half way up or three quarters of the way up the cell door.

Codes

ALPHA- OFFICER NEEDS ASSISTANCE, officer emergency.

Bravo- Lock down of Unit.

Charlie- Lock down of prison.

Delta- Fire on premises.

Echo- A prisoner has escaped.

Foxtrot- A fight has broken out, Prisoner on Prisoner.

Mike- Medical emergency.

# BOOK 1

# INTRODUCTION

I still remember the first moment I stepped into a prison. It was a cold autumn evening and I was attending an information night. I had only registered my interest a couple of days prior and was surprised at the speed of the next step in the process, a process I wasn't even entirely sure I wanted to pursue. We were all screened, scanned, given a pat down and led through into a tiny room; what's known as an airlock.

Once there were a number of us, around a dozen or so, an officer showed us through a door and led us down a narrow walkway, high fences on either side, topped by razor wire. To say I wasn't intimidated would be a lie. I was shitting myself. We walked through another door into a large hall, which I would later find out to be the visitor's centre. There were around a hundred or so seats set up in the middle, of which I utilised one. No one spoke, and by the way everyone was sitting, I could tell it wasn't just me that was nervous. This was, after all, maximum security.

After waiting for about twenty minutes, a tall gentleman took the podium before us, holding a microphone. He began speaking, the usual welcome; "this is who I am, this is what I do" kind of thing. His next sentence however, nearly changed my mind.

"It takes a very special type of person to work in Corrections." My head was already full of a complete mixture of emotions, but that sentence sounded so cliched, that I almost walked out right there. I have always been aware of sales pitches. I have worked in a sales job myself in the distant past and understood the path to a sale; the steps one took to ensure a handshake at the end of the presentation. Buttering up the customer was a good beginning, and this felt like buttery. At that moment, I felt as if this was the kind of interview where everybody was offered a role.

But, for some reason, I stayed. Something made me sit in that chair and wait. And now, all these years later, if I was to conduct a presentation to new prospective recruits, I believe my opening sentence would be the same; that working in corrections takes a very special type of person. Because it really does. If you are the kind of person that's easily offended, then don't try and become an officer. If you are someone to run away when a fellow officer is being attacked, then don't become an officer. If the words Fuck, Shit, Cunt and Motherfucker offend you, then definitely don't become an officer. Because this world, this place behind the walls, is not what you imagine.

The first time I entered a unit, housing some fifty prisoners, my heart was in my throat. We could hear the prisoners long before we entered through the airlock, and let me tell you, it was loud. They were screaming so many profanities at us, that for some reason, it made us all wear these goofy grins. It felt weird. For me, it was a nervous grin, one I couldn't seem to stop. I remember feeling a lot of respect for the officers standing in the station towards the centre of the unit's common area, dealing with this shit on a daily basis. Hindsight is funny sometimes, because I have spent many nights since in that very same unit, manning it by myself, alone, with the only company for twelve long hours being the TV.

During our one and only guided tour, the officers took us to a second unit, one that left me shocked. What I had seen on TV and what I had imagined I would see, were nothing compared to what was now before me. I had always imagined that maximum security meant maximum protection as well. For the officers to at least be safely housed behind thick glass and steel bars, shielded from the danger.

There was no bullet proof glass. There were no cages or bars or even any form of separation from the prisoners. The unit we were standing in had two levels, each lined with cell doors numbering around maybe 40, running along the entire length of both sides. In the middle of the unit stood a raised platform with a step on one side that led into it. Around this raised platform was a circular desk with a counter top, maybe stomach height to me, with book shelves and a computer screen sitting on the desk level. Once the prisoners were released from their cells, all 60 of them, the 3 officers on duty would stand or sit in this tiny officer's station for the duration of their shift and perform their duties.

There was zero protection if anything was to go pear shaped. One of the officers taking us on this guided tour made an off-the-cuff remark that has stuck with me ever since. It is a remark that I have shared with new officers as well.

"Just remember one thing. They decide whether you go home," he'd said to me.

I left that information session numb. I had never experienced anything like it before. I had never been in trouble with the police, nor had anything to do with prison or anyone who had been to prison. I was literally fresh. Needless to say, I applied and after about three months, began my career as a Correctional Officer.

The experiences I have endured since, can only be described as unbelievable. Things that happen behind these walls, sometimes on a daily basis, never make it to the outside. It's as if the world behind the walls is on another planet. The rules somehow change, those that do exist. The rapes, stabbings, assaults, they all really do exist and are to be expected.

But it's the other things, the day-to-day experiences of prisoners just being prisoners and officers being officers that make you shake your head in complete amazement. I mean, the first time you are confronted by a prisoner who doesn't get their own way, and decides to "bronze up" by using faeces, that's something that makes you think "why?" To bronze up is a fancy term to describe a prisoner smearing their own shit all over themselves and their cell, but take my word for it, nothing will ever truly describe the experience of it. Or the first time you ask a prisoner to remove a shiv that they booted, as in, shoved up their rectum. It's those experiences that made me decide to write about them. To share them with you, so can try and make your own mind up.

I really do hope you find these entries interesting because it's not the sort of thing you hear about. My place of work is hidden, almost shielded from the outside world and I would love to share just how brave my fellow officers are to turn up to work each day and endure these experiences. To risk everything. They truly are, remarkable people.

The following pages contain the experiences that I have witnessed and read about in subsequent reports. While some days might come across as mundane, others will certainly make you sit up and take notice. And that's one the big attractions for correctional officers to the job. Every single day is different from all the rest. You never know what to expect. Some days might make for non-eventful reading, but to us, it just means everyone gets to go home safely and that's what matters the most.

I have tried my best to keep my own opinions to a minimum, so as not to influence how you read each incident. I think to experience this type of environment for yourself, you really need to see it with unbiased eyes. So here it is. Max, as I have seen it. I hope you enjoy the ride.

Now sit tight, hang on, and let me tell you about the day that was, in a maximum-security prison.

# FRIDAY, JUNE 1

IT WAS a relief shift for me today. I was working in Yarra North, which is classified as a Protection Unit. It houses fifty-five cells, some singles and some dual occupancy. Some of the prisoners that reside here include paedophiles, rapists, terrorists, informers and those needing protection because they are too scared to be housed in a mainstream unit. I am working with Sam and Ricki today, both permanently assigned here.

One of the things that always amazes me when I work in this particular unit is just how clean it is. Most other units are trash, literally. They smell. They are dirty. The fridges are filled with rotten left overs. Dirty washing is usually piled in the laundry area, bins are either close to or already overflowing, and it seems there is a permanent stench of sour sweat that hangs in the air like a bad toilet spray. But not in Yarra North. It is clean. It even smells clean, thanks to the efforts of a couple of long-termers. As an officer, it's definitely something you appreciate.

As I said, both of my fellow officers call this place home and because it's their normal place of work, makes the day that much easier. A fourth officer, Anthony, is the shipping officer today. He will be in and out of the unit most of the day, his main duty to ship protection prisoners around the prison to where they are needed. This includes the medical wing for appointments, the admissions area for transport to court and other jails, or to the official functions area the crooks call Centrelink, named after a Government department that handles welfare payments.

It's 7:10 am when I enter the unit. Unlock happens after morning muster is called correct by the Control room. After putting my belongings away, I wait for another officer so we can go door-to-door, or trap to trap, the small latch that opens in the middle of each cell door. Operational Standing Orders requires us to carry a ligature knife, in case we find what's known as a "Swinger", a prisoner that has hung himself through the night.

Unfortunately, suicide is a reality in this place, so you have to be prepared for it at all times. Sam Howell, a veteran of five years and a personal friend of mine, enters the unit five minutes later and after a few moments of pleasantries, we begin our muster. We count the entire bottom deck without incident, during which time our third officer arrives, Ricki Roberts, a fresh officer from the last intake. She has been in the unit since she finished her entry course and I've heard good things about her. Confident, which counts for a lot.

Sam and I continue to go trap to trap. All prisoners are friendly enough, some giving us a "good morning" as we peer in through the trap. It pays to return the pleasantries, regardless of their crime. The last thing we want is a shit bomb in the face because a crook took offence at you for not returning his good morning. And yes, shit bombs are very much a reality.

We continue up to the top deck and can already hear some sort of altercation behind door number one. We pause for a moment to make sure we have the right cell and can hear a muffled argument, so drop the trap. The first thing that hits me is the smell. Fresh, pure shit. "What's going on" I say, but I already know the issue. I can smell it.

An unspoken rule in prison is, if you share your cell, you don't shit during lock down. Watson, one of the two prisoners in 32, had broken the cardinal rule. He had only been in the unit for three days and I guess the rules hadn't been fully explained. The small cut to his right eye, told me that school was definitely in session.

"Pompinelli, get away from him. Come to the door and put your hands through the trap."

"Fuck Boss, can you smell that shit? I fucken told him not to. It fucken stinks in here," he yelled, glaring at his cellmate.

"Robert, are you okay?" I asked. He nodded his head but was clearly scared. "Sam, come to the trap and I'll get you out of there. Just put your hands through, man. Have to cuff you," I said, holding the bracelets up. He nodded, stepping towards the door. Cracking a cell before count correct wasn't allowed without a Supervisor present, and as the crooks had been fighting, I looked at my off-sider, who now called a code Foxtrot, Prisoner on Prisoner Fight.

"Code Foxtrot, Yarra North. Prisoners contained." Adding the "prisoners contained" part saves the mad dash of officers racing to the unit to render assistance, and is something fellow officers and supervisors appreciate. Pompinelli complies with my instruction and puts his hands through the trap.

Given the stink in the cell, fresh air would be his first priority. I cuff him and ask him to remain where he is. 30 seconds later, officers begin to come through the door, followed by the Duty Supervisor. I begin filling the Sup in and he motions for the cell door to be cracked. Pompinelli exits the cell and we walk him to the end of the top tier corridor. The Sup enters the cell and talks to Watson. He appears okay but the cut above his eye looks nasty, and we wait for the medical staff to arrive. When they do, they assess him and ask us to escort the prisoner to the medical wing.

We would find out later that Watson sustained a fractured eye socket, concussion and a fractured jaw. It wasn't just a one punch incident, it turns out. Pompinelli is moved to one of four management units, called Murray. He complies with all instructions and the move is complete within ten minutes. He is a long-termer, in for incest and rape, and to him, the move to Murray unit only means he gets to enjoy a single cell. He is already serving a fifteen-year sentence, so having an assault charge added, where the most he will probably receive is six months concurrently, isn't going to affect him too much. If anything, he has a win by the move to the new unit.

We continue our count once the Sup has left, and Control finally calls count correct at 8:05am, some 25 minutes late. Due to prison rules, a late unlock means a late lock up tonight. We proceed to unlock the unit, key in door style, and return to the officer's station.

Now, if you are picturing a cosy officer's station behind bullet proof glass, safely segregated from the unit population, then I have some grim news. The officer's stations in this prison are just circular desks on a raised platform with a gap on one side for access. If a prisoner wanted to enter the station, they could literally just walk in. There isn't even a little gate to close the station. You are susceptible to assault, shit bombs, spitting and hot watering. The second-floor tier is close enough that if a prisoner wanted to piss on an officer, he wouldn't have to strain too hard. For a maximum-security prison, it has zero protection for the officers.

The prisoners begin to exit their cells, voices now rising, a hive of activity around the toasters. Ten minutes later, the medical trolley arrives for morning medications. I put out the call over the unit intercom.

"Yarra North, first call for morning meds". A line begins to form out the front of the med window, the nurse preparing for the onslaught. One at a time, they front the little window with their I.D. cards. Some are polite to the nurse, some are not. Some demand minor pain relief on top of their normal meds, and more often than not, are granted their request. Each prisoner takes their medication, swallows it with a cup of water, then presents their open mouth to an officer for inspection. Diverting medication is a very common problem and officers need to be vigilant when performing this role. Stand-overs for medication are a daily occurrence in almost every unit. The pills can be traded for drugs, sexual favours or anything of value.

Today, the morning med run goes without a hitch. I sit at the computer and finish my report for the supervisor about the code Foxtrot from that morning. I also check my emails and note that we have two prisoners that are departing the prison for an alternative one. Transfers are very common and happen almost daily. There is also one internal transfer. The required prisoners are buzzed up and informed of their moves. All but one seems okay with it and walks back to their cell to pack their gear up. Only one grumbles and puts up a little resistance, but he too complies after a minute or so.

Keeping your cool and remaining calm are much better options than demanding, confronting and getting upset. It could mean the difference between a good outcome and an assault on a staff member. Officers only have their mouth and ears to rely on and they must learn quickly how to utilise them.

The morning passes without incident and before you know it, the announcement comes over the speakers that it's ten minutes until lunchtime muster. We wait another five minutes and then announce for the unit to stand by their cells for count. Prisoners make their way back to their cell doors and quietly wait.

It is in their best interest to remain quiet, as lunch is served immediately after Control calls the count correct. One officer grabs the unit muster sheet and begins to walk from cell to cell. The other two officers stand in the middle of the unit and begin counting to themselves. It is one of the things you do not want to get wrong. For one thing, if your numbers don't match the other two officers, then you have to recall the prisoners to their cells a second time. The other reason is, if count is called incorrect and your unit was the cause, the rest of the prison has a way of finding out. And they will certainly let you know about it. Plus, to make it really interesting, you have the added benefit of the report to write as well.

The unit is silent as we prepare ourselves to count the numbers. Ricki volunteers to take the muster-board around. Female officers are common and are a very good asset. They are prone to shutting down incidents quickly and firmly. We have quite a number at this prison, some young, some old, but all valued.

Ad Ricki begins her rounds, one prisoner makes a remark and his cellmate snickers as she passes them. I clear my throat, make eye contact with them and they look away, still grinning. Disrupting a muster can carry consequences. Penalties can hurt, such as a loss of TV for a night or two, or a week, depending on the severity. Ricki finishes her count, looks at us, and we give her the nod.

"Break off" she says sternly. We leave her be as she adds up her numbers. I show my piece of paper to Sam, and thankfully our numbers match. A minute or two later Ricki approaches me and quietly whispers, "fifty-four??" I nod in agreement. Control calls for muster numbers and we call ours in. Twenty minutes later count is called correct and the afternoon begins.

Shortly after 2:00pm there is a call over the radio "Code Mike, Tambo". Our fourth officer, who is sitting in one of the offices reading a newspaper, decides to attend and lend a hand. He rushes out the door. We find out later that it was a chest complaint and the crook was taken to the medical unit. The afternoon medical run enters the unit at 4.30pm and Ricki puts the call out.

"Yarra North, first call for afternoon medication." The prisoners begin to line up and I decide to stand in the cubicle and check mouths. It was going so well until an old crook, a small Italian with a fiery temper, gets to the window. He has forgotten his I.D. Card and when the nurse asks for it, begins yelling at her.

"You fucken know who I am, bitch. Just gimme my fucken pills!" He looks at me, hoping for some support. "Come on, Boss, she knows me. You can tell her." I see one of my off-siders begin to stand at the officer's station, ready to come to my aid if needed.

"You know the rules, Bruno. No I.D. card, no pills. You've been here long enough." He bangs on the window of the nurse's medical cubicle and she looks startled. Another crook, a big lad of about 6 foot 3 murmurs under his breath.

"Bruno, fuck off mate, you're holding up the line." A couple of other prisoners also begin to mutter, and Bruno begins to walk away.

"Fuck the lot of ya," he whispers as he walks back to his cell. There are two things that you never want to get in the way of when it comes to prisoners. Their pills and their meals. They don't want to be standing there any longer than they need to.

The rest of the medication round went without incident and we completed the five o'clock muster soon after. Once the count was called correct, I buzzed Bruno up to the officer's station. I couldn't let the verbal abuse of the nurse go and he would know that, too. He approached and I asked him how he was.

"Everything OK?" He shrugged and held his palms up, gesturing that he was so-so. "The nurse didn't deserve that Bruno. You know better. You also know the rules and abusing a nurse isn't on."

"I know Boss. I just forgot my card, and she has seen me every day for how long now? I just got fucken frustrated. It's my grand-kid's birthday today. I'll apologise when I see her next. I'm sorry, Boss."

"I understand you're sorry, but you know I can't let this go. I'll have a chat to the Sup when he's in and see what he wants to do. Just don't take it out on the nurse, mate. It's not her fault. She has rules she needs to follow as well."

"I understand, Boss. I'm sorry." He retreats to his cell and a couple of the other crooks mutter profanities as he walks past. It's a small thing and doesn't go much further. The Sup agrees that it can be handled in-house and Bruno loses his TV for a night. He surrenders it voluntarily and the situation is closed. It was a good result for everyone.

Just before dinner, we receive a phone call that a new transfer is waiting for us in the admissions building. Our fourth officer is currently out so I volunteer to go and get them. As I enter the building, there is a loud banging coming from one of the many cells. The echoes boom through the corridors, as a prisoner is kicking the shit out of the thick metallic door of his holding cell. I go and see the officer in charge and am told my prisoner is the one kicking the door. I open the trap window and see it's a returned regular, Jamieson. He sees me and begins grinning.

"Hi Boss" he smirks.

"Giving the guys here a hard time, Steven?" I ask

"Just letting them know I'm still here, Boss."

"I doubt they can forget with your communication skills." The last time Steven Jamieson was in Yarra North, he was caught providing the unit with substantial oral satisfaction in return for medication. He is a regular, often busted for drugs and small-time stuff. His favourite past time is trading sexual favours for drugs. I knew that having him back in the unit would not make things easier.

I prepare to take him back to the unit. In our prison, there is an area right outside the admissions building that every prisoner walks through when heading from one particular unit to another area. It's called the Quadrangle and contains a total of thirteen gates and doors and to take a protection prisoner through, this area requires clearance. Some of the gates lead into compounds while others into buildings. I radio the officer in charge of the area and he tells me to stand by. I wait. I see one of my mates walk past and tip him a wave. He waves back, sees my escorted prisoner and rolls his eyes, smiling. I fully understand his gesture.

"Yarra North, make your move," the voice says over the radio. I open the door and wave Steven through. As he enters the quadrangle, the heckling from two of the gates begins. They are mainstream compounds and the prisoners there despise protection crooks.

"Hurry the fuck up, you rat," one yells.

"Boneyard dog. Bring him in here Boss. We'll take care of him. Come on, Boss," the other joins in. Steven looks at them and batters his eyelids. He grins and grabs his crotch. I shudder at the thought of what would happen if they got hold of him. There wouldn't be much left. The unit houses some very large Pacific Islander prisoners and they are not known for their gentle dispositions.

I hurry Steven along and we enter the Yarra North compound. A couple of crooks are walking the perimeter path and start running over when they see my escort.

"Hey dude, you're back," one says, and by his smile I know what he is thinking. Steven replies with a hug for one, then the other, a third gets a fist bump.

"I'll come out after. Just need to get my shit sorted first. Wait here. Is Jerry still here?" he asks, Jerry being his previous cell mate.

"Nah, he got shifted to PFPP last month." PFPP is a prison specifically designed for protection prisoners, located some three hours from the city.

We make our way to the unit and enter through the airlock. Cheers immediately erupt as they see the new arrival. It's almost like a homecoming and I wonder to myself where the deterrence is with prison life. Ricki greets Steven and begins the induction interview. A bed pack is waiting for him, consisting of a blanket, a pillow, 2 sheets, plastic bowl, plate and cup. He also receives a TV.

He is assigned his cell, sharing with Anton, an illegal Spanish immigrant, who's finishing his sentence for drug trafficking before his deportation. It's not a pairing I would have suggested, but there was a bed shortage and cell choice was limited. Steven takes his items and heads for his cell on the upper tier. One crook takes his bag for him, his hope for a reward clearly on his face. Four other crooks follow and they all pile into the cell to greet their new arrival.

"Attention all stations. Ten minutes till lock up," the speakers bark across the prison. Prisoners hurriedly rush back and forth between cells, kitchen, hot water urn, microwave; desperate to tie off loose ends before their night-time lock down. There are hugs, fist bumps and shouts of "Catch ya tomorrow, bro!"

Ricki again takes control of the muster board and I lock the cells behind her, wishing each prisoner a good night. When I get to Steven and Anton's cell, I see Anton not looking very impressed. It's an issue I know will need to be addressed tomorrow. Ten minutes later, the Control Room confirms that count is correct and we head for the exit. Any day, that you can walk out of a prison under your own steam at the end of a shift, is classed as a win. Today was a good day.

# SUNDAY, JUNE 3

Called in for over time. If you make yourself available, then the reward is double pay for the day. I was offered a number of different placings but chose to return to Yarra North when offered that position. I wanted to see how Anton was and if staff had sorted out the sleeping arrangements from my previous shift in there. I was in a bit late due to being called at late notice.

Sam was already conducting the morning trap muster with another overtime officer who wasn't normally in this unit, but a unit officer just the same. A man named Pete. I didn't really know him as he was fairly new, and we shook hands when they completed count. Sam gave me a fist bump and rolled his eyes.

"You missed a doozy yesterday, man. Steven tried to rub Anton up during the night and Anton decked him. One of the adjoining cells buzzed Control and Steven got taken to hospital with a fractured jaw. No gobbies for him for a while," he chuckled.

"And Anton?" I asked.

"Taken to Murray. He isn't happy, though. One of the officers there said Anton has sworn to kill the stupid fag when he sees him. I don't think their friendship will ever really begin. I somehow doubt Anton will come back here."

It's common practice to flag prisoners on the system if and when they have issues with certain prisoners. It is a very in-depth system that keeps track of gang affiliation, drug debts or just plain hatred towards someone else. Once you're flagged, it pops up every time you transfer to the jail. Steven and Anton would now be flagged from each other. It's the same for different bikie gangs, drug dealers and those in danger from them for debts, or just simple differences. As prison officers, we have a duty of care to every prisoner, regardless of crime, race or sexual orientation. And a lot of the time, we have to protect them from each other. A short time later, count is called correct and we unlock all the cells.

Returning to the officer's station, I check my emails and the unit muster for any new names in the unit. All appeared clear. Nothing exciting in the emails other than a couple of hellos, as well as a couple of requests from officers wanting to swap shifts with someone. I check the dates and am able to offer a swap for the fourteenth of July. I wasn't working and didn't have much planned. I was hoping for the eighth off and so put forth my proposition. As I press send on the email, the intercom goes off next to my ear. I answer the call.

"Boss, I need help." I checked the muster and saw the cell was occupied by two prisoners, both in their very early twenties and both quite small in stature from memory.

"What's up, Jack?" I asked.

"Could you come to our cell, please? I don't feel safe coming out or talking over this thing."

"Be right there," I responded. This didn't sound good. I looked at Sam and he flipped me a thumbs up, as I stood to venture upstairs. It's good practice not to appear to make a beeline for a cell as it can be interpreted as someone wanting to lag and laggers were not too popular in prison.

Instead, I took the long way around. We were required to take a number of tier walks throughout the day anyway, so slowly walking around the unit wasn't seen as anything out of the ordinary. It's also quite common for prisoners to give each other a heads up when officers were out sniffing. Calls of "Ducks on the pond" were common.

I climbed the stairs and peered into a couple of cells, saying hello and making my presence known. When I reach cell 29, I peer in and repeat my greeting. The two occupants look quite sheepish, one sitting on a pillow, the other standing against the back wall.

"What's going on guys?" I ask, leaning against the doorframe. Maintaining awareness of your surroundings is important, given the environment we work in, so I try not to enter too far into the cell without back up.

"Dobson attacked us last night before lock down," one of them says, sheepishly looking at the ground. He is the younger of the two, sitting on the pillow, his voice sounding distant.

"What do you mean attacked? Did he hit you?" There didn't appear to be any facial injuries, but that didn't mean an attack didn't take place.

"He raped us. Both of us," the other one said, tears filling his eyes.

"Both of you? Like at the same time?" Unfortunately, rape was a reality in prison and often went unreported. But two rapes at the same time by a single perpetrator is not something you hear of every day.

"Yes. He held me by the throat while he raped Jack, and then he made him sit on the floor while he raped me. He held a shiv to my stomach whilst he did it." Tears began streaming down his face, the shame clearly visible in his eyes.

"Did you tell anyone last night before lock down?" I ask. I know that Shane Roberts was in the unit the previous day. He's a twenty-year veteran with a care factor of zero. He cares as much about crooks as he did about his appearance. A prisoner once asked if he was homeless due to his lack of personal hygiene. If Roberts conducted the cell lock-up's, there is no way he would have said anything to anyone, given the fact he was about to go home.

"We tried to tell Officer Roberts but he didn't want to listen. He said to talk to the day staff today," Jack said, clearly scared out of his brain. I was pissed. I knew what Roberts would have said.

Unfortunately, it's not what you know but who you know. How

that guy still had a job was beyond my comprehension, but when you've been around for twenty years, you tend to know people.

"I'll lock you guys in and get the Sup here. Do you need the doctor?"

"I'm bleeding from my arse," Jack replied, and Pete nodded in agreement.

"Okay, guys. Leave it with me. Just sit tight. I'll lock your cell door so no one can get in. Won't be long." I close the cell and lock it up. As I return to the officer's station, Dobson walks past me, wearing a wide cheshire grin.

"Morning, Boss," he quips.

"Morning, Jason," I reply. He continues past me, almost gloating. I take out my radio.

"Yarra North 1 to Sup 8."

"Send." The reply is immediate.

"Can you please call the unit?" I reply, and before I'm able to sit down, the phone rings. Supervisor Bruce Stephens is a really good person to have on your side. He is fair and will back up his team without questions, if need be. I fill him in on what's happened, minus the bit about Officer Roberts for the time being. He listens without interrupting, and when I'm done, suggests to have both boys moved to the medical wing for the time being. I agree. I speak to Sam and ask him to help me move Dobson to his cell. He obliges and together we approach Dobson. He understands before we even speak, his grin never faltering.

We follow him to his cell and lock him down without incident. I then unlock the two boys and escort them to the medical wing. They are shy and quiet, and when we walk through the quadrangle, the jeering from the mainstreamers fall on deaf ears. One of the boys is even limping slightly, clearly in pain.

We enter the medical unit and I escort them to a holding cell. A doctor sees them five minutes later and both are cleared of internal injuries. Just tearing and soreness, which will heal by itself in a few days. I don't know whether either of the boys has thought of it, but I wonder if Dobson has passed any diseases on.

For an officer, all prisoners are treated equally. We always assume they are infected with something, so always wear gloves and other protective gear as needed. We don't take chances. We know some do have diseases but not which ones, so we proceed as if they all have something contagious. Between the prison sex, rapes, needle sharing etc, spreading diseases is all too common.

Next, I move both prisoners to the admissions wing, where I can assist the Sup with interviewing them. Police will be called as well, as they will also need to conduct their own investigation. I lock the boys into separate cells and wait for the Supervisor.

I hang out with a couple of friends who work in the admissions area, catching up with the gossip of the day. I find out one of the officers working in industries had been walked off-site as they were caught smoking cigarettes. The scary part isn't the fact that they were caught smoking, but that they smuggled cigarettes into the prison. If they were able to smuggle cigarettes in, what else had they smuggled in? And did they share them with prisoners? It's an alarming thought. When things go pear-shaped, other officers were the ones you relied on to watch your back; to jump in and help and to protect you just like you would protect them. The dangers in this place are astronomical, so having a dirty officer just dampens the trust you have, and need, for your fellow workers. I have zero sympathy for the person. I hope they don't return.

The Supervisor comes into the room and beckons me over. We shake hands and I fill him in on what's happened. He listens intently then asks me to go grab the first prisoner, which I do. Jack sits at the desk, his eyes never meeting the Sup or mine.

"Tell me what happened," the Sup begins. Jack waits a long time before answering. I almost say something, but then he begins.

"Me and Pete were in our cell with Jason, playing cards. We were playing for bottles of Coke. I had been winning, and Jason was getting pissed. After I won the last hand, he threw the cards off the bed and grabbed me by the throat. He pulled a shiv out of his shorts and pointed it at Pete. He said he wanted to have some real fun and if either of us said anything, he would stick us with it. He said he knew where we lived and our family would cop it when he gets out. He then smacked me in the head with the shiv handle and told me to drop my pants." His voice was beginning to crack, quietly fading. "When he finished with me, he grabbed Pete and did the same to him. Pete was crying and I could see blood running down his leg."

"Did either of you tell the staff that were on duty?" the Sup asked.

"We tried, but the officer didn't want to do anything then. One said it was too late as everyone was going home and we should wait for the staff that came in the morning, which we did." I could see the questions in Bruce's eyes. I was guessing he was feeling the same frustration I was when hearing the bit about Robert's refusal of help. He had not only ignored a serious assault on two prisoners, but he also put the morning staff at risk. Anything could have happened when the unit was unlocked that morning. Jason could have repeated the act, assaulted them or worse, tried to shut them up for good. He put staff and prisoners at risk for no other reason than laziness.

"Okay, Jack. Thank you. The police will be contacted shortly and you will likely need to give them a statement." Bruce looked at me and I ushered Jack back to his holding cell. I returned with Pete and the story was the same. After a few minutes of questioning, I returned Pete to his holding cell and returned to Bruce. He looked at me, his eyes angry.

"Why the fuck would he ignore that? The first thing those boys will tell the police is that they told staff. We are going to look like fucking gooses when this gets out." I nodded, understanding perfectly that this would not be just a simple in-house matter. This could cost jobs. An external investigation at the very least. "Thank you, Kingy. Leave the boys here. I'll deal with things for now. Just go back to your unit for the time being. "

"And Dobson?" I asked. He would need to be separated, especially from the unit. If some of the guys caught wind of what happened, it could lead to this situation getting worse.

"Leave him locked down for now," he replied. I nodded and headed back to Yarra North. When I arrive back in the unit, there is a group of prisoners, maybe half a dozen, standing around the officer's station. Sam is talking to them but the crooks sound upset. It would seem that the secret wasn't so secret after all. The irony is that a unit filled with mostly sex offenders are upset at a sex offender for committing a sex offence. I walk over and ask them to quieten down.

"Is he gonna stay here, Boss?" one asks. "Because I can't guarantee his safety if he does." I swallow the urge to laugh. The one speaking is about seventy years old and precarious on his feet. A stiff breeze would send him airborne.

"It's Okay, Harry. Guys, he is locked down and the Sup is looking into it. Once he's finished, he'll decide the next step. For the time being, just stay away from Dobson's door and get on with your day." A couple of them turn and head for the chook pen, the outside courtyard where they can walk or sit or just take in the sunshine; another heads for the kitchen.

One stays, lowering his voice "I saw the boys try and tell the staff yesterday, but they didn't want to listen. I could see them from my joint."

"Okay, Harry. Please just wait for the Sup to do his thing." He gives in and returns to his cell. Sam gives me a look of disgust.

"Is it true? Did they ignore them last night?"

"It appears so, mate. Fucken idiots were in too much of a rush to get home," I replied, trying to sound calm. Inside I was fuming.

It's almost midday muster by the time Bruce phones. The police had been and taken statements. He was sending the Tactical Squad to come and escort Dobson to a management unit. I buzz Dobson on the intercom and tell him the good news. Good for us.

"Pack your stuff, Jason. You're headed to another unit." There is a muffled grunt and then a barrage of swearing spews out from the intercom speaker.

"Fuck that, Boss. I didn't do nothin. Those fags attacked me first and I didn't touch 'em. I'm not goin. Tell those mother fuckers that I'm not goin!"

"Your escort will be here in five minutes. I hope you'll be ready." He only had two choices and neither one to his benefit. They would either escort him walking, or escort him by carrying him. His choice.

He begins to say something else, but I break the connection before he has a chance to finish. He can take it up with the Tactical boys now.

Five minutes later, six rather large lads and two ladies enter the unit. The uniforms they wear speak volumes and are a good deterrent. The uniforms also convey a message. One very clear message. Don't fuck with us. They ask where he is and I point to the cell door containing Dobson. They climb the stairs and one slowly opens the trap. He speaks quietly and I can hear Dobson fire up. He isn't a stupid prisoner. He has done serious time and knows what the drill is. Fighting these guys would be useless. And when his hands come through the trap to be cuffed, I know that he has seen the light.

I make my way up and ensure his things are packed. They lead him down the stairs to a chorus of jeers and abuse from the rest of the unit. He grins again but doesn't retaliate. He is led out of the unit carrying his bag and the unit goes quiet once they have left. Sam yells to me that I have a phone call and I head down.

"Simon, it's Bruce. Can you arrange for the property of these two to be bagged and brought down to admissions please? They're both heading into town for a bit."

"Sure thing. Do it now." I don't ask questions. Sometimes it's best to just let things take their course. No doubt, they will be taken to another jail and be reinterviewed about the incident. The entire incident. I get Sam to help me pack their gear up and take the bags down to admissions. I know we will be hearing a lot more about this incident in the coming weeks. I return to the unit and the rest of the day is routine. A couple of medical codes are called throughout the prison but that's about all. I look forward to home time and quietly cheer when it finally arrives.

## MONDAY, JUNE 4

TODAY I WAS ROSTERED in the visitor's centre. It is used by both mainstream and protection prisoners but at alternating times, to avoid mixing. There is a total of six officers working in this area. Three officers work in the visits room and three officers are preparing prisoners for their visits. It is one of three main sources of contraband introduction, so vigilance is required both before and after a visit with in-depth strip searches.

The preparation of prisoners is normally conducted by male officers due to the stripping aspect of the area. It is also the area I prefer to work when here. Not for the stripping aspect, but more for the fact the role doesn't have a lot of contact with the public. I prefer to deal directly with the prisoners. The two other officers working with me are both normal visit centre officers and have over five years of experience. We shake hands, decide on our roles and wait for the first prisoners to arrive.

Our list shows that we have fourteen mainstream visits before 12:00pm, then eleven protections visitors between 1:00pm and 3:00pm and finally eight main stream visits between 4:00pm and 5.30pm. Thirty-one visits for the day is not too bad. It can get very busy in this area and it is not uncommon to process sixty to seventy prisoners in a shift.

Nine o'clock comes around and the first prisoners arrive. Three from Tambo East stroll into the room and we check their ID cards. They select the correct size overalls they will wear during their visit, which, once fitted, have the zipper cable-tied shut to reduce the ability to conceal anything. We take them into small side rooms and begin the stripping process.

The first crook I strip hands me his jumper, tracksuit pants and t-shirt, which I put aside to put in a locker. He takes off his watch as well. He hands me his shoes, which I search thoroughly, then his socks. He hands me his underwear, which I search and put on the bench. The prisoner then, upon instruction, opens his mouth and runs his fingers around his gum line. He lifts his tongue. He holds his hands up and spreads his fingers. He lifts his arms to have his armpits checked. He then separates his penis from his scrotum, and also lifts his scrotum. He then turns around and lifts each foot behind him to show me the bottom of each foot. He then bends and spreads his butt cheeks. Unfortunately, it is the perfect pocket to hide things. This process of stripping will be repeated with every prisoner that enters and leaves the visits area.

The first three are finished being processed and wait in the sitting room, ready for a front officer to take them through. There are two main reasons for flare-ups in this area. One is when time is up. It has been known for prisoners to not want to end visits and can get upset when officers let them know when it's time to wrap things up. But the most volatile flare up that can happen is when a contact visit is changed to a boxed visit at the last moment.

One reason a visit may be changed to a box visit is if the visitor scans positive for an illicit substance whilst making their way through the prison's reception area, or front door. If they scan positive and nothing is found during a strip search, then the visit becomes a boxed visit. If a visitor needs to use the bathroom facilities during a visit, then a visit can also be changed to a boxed one. People are born with built in "pockets" and unfortunately these pockets are not allowed to be searched as such, so if the visitor visits the bathroom, then the contact visit is revoked.

We process another eight mainstreamers during the next couple of hours and also have a couple of no shows. A code Mike is called at about 11.45am in a protection unit and it's a prisoner with chest pains. The morning quickly becomes afternoon with very little drama. Once lunchtime muster is called correct, we begin calling the protection prisoners up for their visits. The first one through the door is a grinning Steven Jamieson.

"Hi Boss," he says, sporting a black eye and a bruise on the right side of his face.

"How is the face?" I ask.

"It's okay. I'll be back to normal in no time," he says. Another officer takes Steven for his strip and I take over the book. Every unit and area within the jail has a book that is kept up to date by one officer. It keeps track of movements in and out of the area so any muster or emergency count that is conducted can be relied on for up to date information. It can be high pressure when there are a lot of moves but in this area, the book is a breeze when kept on top of.

"CODE ALPHA Thomson East! CODE ALPHA WEAPON!" The call pierces the air and everyone jumps. The other two officers are tied up with prisoners, so I race out the door and begin the run to Thomson East. It is amazing to see officers pour out of units and areas surrounding the quadrangle, with some manning gates to allow other officers a straight run through. You never know what will greet you when you run into a code Alpha, especially one involving a weapon. Your first priority is the safety of yourself and fellow officers. I see officers ahead of me enter the unit. There are officers in front and behind me and we reach the unit door together, the doors held open by more officers.

As we enter the unit, I see a group of prisoners congregated on the top tier, looking and laughing at a group of officers in the far corner of the unit. There appears to be a prisoner pinned on the floor, a broom lying nearby. To prevent a larger flare up, the best thing for spare officers to do is to lock the unit down. I head for the stairs.

"Lock down, guys" I yell. "Now!" I go to the nearest cell and usher a couple of prisoners inside and lock them in. Other officers begin to do the same. There are some protests but everyone eventually complies. Within a couple of minutes, all prisoners are locked in cells. They may not be in their own cells, but for the safety of officers, everyone is locked up.

The first responders have the prisoner detained on the floor and are questioning him, trying to ascertain what happened. He apparently began screaming about court then started hitting the officer's station with the broom. None of the officers were hurt and they called the code quite quickly. The code is stood down and the prisoner is escorted to Murray. I return to the visits area to continue with my duties there. I barely make it in the door when "Code Alpha Medical" comes across the radio. I turn and run towards the Medical wing, a short distance away. "Prisoner Contained," is followed and I breathe a sigh of relief.

The medical wing has a tendency for code Alphas due to both mainstream and protection prisoners being in such close proximity to each other. They are all locked away behind Perspex windows but can see each other clearly so a lot of burning goes on. It is very common for a main streamer to start banging on the Perspex to wind a protection prisoner up. This time, the overzealous crook is a protection prisoner giving it back to the mainstreamers. He is a large lad of twenty-five, named Vandenberg. The Tactical team are already escorting him next door to the admissions wing and their ample cells to cool off for a bit. He doesn't resist which is a smart move considering six Tactical Officers have hold of him. I see a mate, Shane, and he gives me a nod.

This time I make it back to Visits and continue processing prisoners. A couple of prisoners are just finishing their visits and coming back into the rear receiving area. I signal one to enter the strip room so I can check him. I unclip his overalls and notice a tear down one side of his leg.

"When did that happen?" I ask him. He looks, shrugs and mumbles something. I sense his defences go up and ready myself for anything. He takes his overalls off and I check them, tossing them into the dirty washing tub. He takes off his shoes and hands them to me. Whilst I check them, he quickly removes his socks and jocks, then does the dance, tongue, arms, fingers, pits, balls and turns, all in one motion. I know that he is trying to cover something, so beckon for him to wait.

"At my pace, yeah? Just wait." He glares at me, raising his arms in a "What" gesture. I finish with his shoes and ask for his socks and underwear, which he half throws at me. I make eye contact with him and he knows. The clothes all check out and I gesture for him to show me his mouth. He opens and rolls his tongue around. I signal for his hands and he tries to run away with the sequence once more, so once again I gesture for him to slow down.

"Come on Boss. Wanna get back to the unit," he mumbles. He lifts his scrotum and penis and that's when I see a flash of white. He tries to turn but I've spotted what he is trying to conceal. My insides are cringing at the thought of what I'm about to find.

"Turn around, man. Show me your dick." He turns and holds his penis up, pointing it at me. There, peering out from the eye of his penis, was the top of a syringe. A small one, but a syringe none the less. He had jammed it down his shaft, but unfortunately, size acted against him. His member just wasn't long enough. Size really does matter.

I do a double cringe and motion for the spotting officer to have a look. He does and his eyes nearly roll out of their sockets.

"Dude, seriously? How the fuck did you get that in there?" he asks, trying to hide the grin.

"Take it out and hand it to me please," I say, holding out my gloved hand. He groans, huffs and puffs a couple of times then sees my off-sider with his radio already in his hand, ready to call a code if need be.

"Fine. Fuck," he yells as he slowly withdraws the syringe from its "little" hide-away. I take the syringe and let him get dressed.

"Sup will be in touch, man," I say. We lock him in a holding cell and notify the Duty Supervisor. Once the evidence is bagged and tagged, we continue to process prisoners. The Duty Sup drops by some twenty minutes later and advises the crook that he will be charged. He is let out and returns to his unit.

For us, the last four prisoners are a no show so we have a relaxing last hour, talking shit and having a couple of laughs about penis size. A good couple of laughs. Down the eye of his dick, I think to myself, cringing all over again. As we head out to the exit after count is called correct, I bump into Bruce the Sup. I ask how things are going with the shit from the day before and he rolls his eyes.

"That dog will come to bite us soon enough, mate," he says. I know what he means and leave it behind for another day. I tell him about "Syringe Boy" and he laughs. It has been a good day.

## THURSDAY, JUNE 7

THERE ARE some days you wish you had just stayed in bed. Today was one of those days. I came in to the news that three officers had been hurt in an attack yesterday. All were taken to hospital by ambulance, and fortunately two had been released later in the day. The officers were working in Tambo East, when a large islander decided he wanted to bail out of the unit. He had words with the unit supervisor earlier in the day and didn't get his way.

Turns out he really wanted out of the unit and figured beating up three officers would be the best option. He was transferred out of the prison immediately, as is standard practice when assaulting an officer and has since been taken to another maximum-security prison nearby. The only good thing is that any assault on an officer also carries a mandatory increase in sentence. One of the assaulted officers had only just commenced his career at the prison and it also happened to be his very first shift in that unit, which he had been offered on a permanent basis.

I truly hope all three officers have a speedy recovery and return to work as soon as they feel able to. No one ever deserves to be assaulted, and everyone deserves to go home to their families at the end of a work day.

I was required to work in the admissions area of the prison today. It was my first time in there and very eye-opening. The admissions area is probably one of the busiest areas when in full swing. When it's quiet, it's the most boring. The other thing that you need to understand about the admissions unit is that you see a lot of naked men. If you have an issue with naked men, then don't ever put your hand up for that unit.

The shift starts quite early in the morning, and about forty prisoners need to be processed and made ready for pick up so they can attend court. Nearly half the population in this prison is on remand, therefore still need to attend court. And if forty prisoners go out, then most of the forty, if not all, will return. That means stripping them on the way out, and then on the way back in. That's eighty naked men. On top of that, there are transfers from and to other prisons. Thirty to forty going out and thirty to forty coming back in. There's another sixty to eighty naked men. And generally, there are only two or three people stripping. If you are not a regular that knows what's going on, then there's a very good chance they will use you to conduct the strip searches.

I swear, I saw over a hundred different penises today. And, yes, they really do come in all shapes and sizes. My day consisted of stripping, then breakfast, morning muster then more stripping, a small break for a cup of tea then more stripping. Lunchtime muster, which someone got wrong, a recount followed by more stripping. Small gaps in between buses arriving, filled with more stripping. Afternoon muster, which was all correct, followed by, you guessed it, stripping.

I began conducting strip searches five minutes after starting my shift and did my last strip search as the guys were walking out telling me to get my bag. I do not care if I never see another naked man again. And the first thing I did when I got home was to give my wife a massive, long embrace and then took a long shower to cleanse myself of the memories. It didn't work.

Today was definitely not a good day.

# MONDAY, JUNE 11

TODAY I WORKED in Tambo West. Normally, I'm not too fussed with the people I work with, but unfortunately sometimes the direction of your day can very much be decided for you by the officers you work with. While most will make the day run smoothly, add fun and interesting conversation, there are a few that will ensure you need to carry a fire extinguisher in your back pocket for all the little spot fires they leave in their wake. Tony Malone is the latter. If common sense was sunshine then this guy lives on the dark side of the moon. I have been to more code Alphas because of this bloke, than the next two officers combined. And today was no different.

The morning began quite calm. Three officers sitting in the station, talking shit about weekend football and stuff. Myself, Tony and Bob. Bob had been at the prison for going on six years, so knew the processes. The morning rush had passed, meds had been and gone and the methadones had been to receive their doses. Our next stop would be lunchtime muster, a couple of cell searches, followed by the regular afternoon duties.

I stood to begin the intercom checks for the day, when Tony interjected. "I'll do it," he said. I wasn't too fussed. It saved me from having to go cell to cell pressing buttons and stuff. "All yours, mate. Thanks," was my reply. He almost made it out of the officer's station when he turned and took out a large black garbage bag. Inside, I deflated. Bob and I exchanged a look that needed no words.

Bob was running the book so he would be acknowledging the intercoms as they came through and marking off each cell as they completed it. It was Tony's job to go from cell to cell and press each button. Whilst in each cell, it is also a requirement to check that the security and integrity of it is perfect. No cracked windows, no holes in the walls, flushing toilet, things like that. You generally spend about two minutes per room. Any contraband you find is confiscated and any serious contraband such as drugs is reported. And confiscated, of course.

What Tony was about to do, was stir the pot. None of the three officers today were regular staff in this unit. So, prisoners will try and use that to their advantage and try and get one over us. Sugar rations, coffee rations, single cell allocation, stuff like that. But we will not change their world in a day, so what ends up happening with the wrong attitude? You create shit. And we could see it unfolding before us.

Tony entered the first cell and a few seconds later the console buzzed. Bob answered it and we waited for Tony to exit. Three minutes, four minutes, nothing. I looked over to the cell and saw the prisoner standing just outside the cell looking in. Arms folded, angry expression. He looks at me and indicates to his cell. My expression is one of "well he is doing what he needs to do". Then Tony exited the cell, bag swinging, and made his way to the second cell. The first crook went into his cell and the swearing that instantly flowed from his door, told the story. A couple of other crooks now stand in the middle of the unit, looking in through the door. The bag looks a bit fatter when he exits the second cell and by the time he exits the fourth, makes his way back to the officer's station to change bags. He places the first under the desk and with a couple of fresh ones, heads for the fifth cell.

The murmurs I hear from the peanut gallery are not positive. Most notable, the comment stating "Me thinks someone's looking for

a hot watering today." I just hope they wait for me to s
There is one thing that an officer told me on my first d
something that I have never forgotten. And it's quite simple. ..
oners decide if you go home at the end of your shift. When there are seventy prisoners and three unarmed officers, the numbers are greatly in their favour.

A number of prisoners are now standing just outside the door of the cell Tony is in. It wasn't looking good. Bob and I were both on our feet, Bob with his hand on the radio. Just then the unit sup walks in and senses the situation.

"Everything okay, guys?" he asks

"Uhm, I'm just gonna say that Tony is going cell to cell," Bob says, pointing at the door. The sup groans and makes his way over. He looks at the prisoners and they break away a little. As he pops his head in, I hear him say

"All good there, Tone?" I don't hear the response, but judging by what the Sup says next, it's clear he isn't happy. "You're a blow in today, mate. Probably not a good idea to wind these boys up any more than you have to."

Tony comes out of the cell and a couple of prisoners begin clapping. "What a hero! Super-screw!" they yell. His face is the colour of rich tomatoes as he returns to the station. He sits on a chair, shaking his head.

"Just doing my bloody job," he says.

"Yeah, but there is a way to do things mate. Anyway, all good, I'll continue the intercoms." I head over to the last inspected cell and proceed to complete the checks. I find minor contraband but really nothing major. I just hope the crooks will let the morning slide and we get through the rest of the day without incident.

Lunchtime muster came and it went okay, apart from the mumbled remarks directed at Tony. I could tell they weren't letting go, and judging by Tony's mood, neither was he. Count was called correct and the prisoners had lunch. I brought up the cell-searching page and we were automatically allocated two random cells to search.

Bob and I said we would conduct them and Tony would man the station.

We made our way to the first cell and called the prisoner over.

"Anything in your cell that shouldn't be in there?" Bob started. The prisoner shook his head. "Okay, jump in and we'll do a quick strip search first then." The three of us entered the cell and conducted the strip. It was all clear and the crook left the cell. I closed the door behind him and began searching. It's not like in the movies where everything is tossed in the middle of the cell. You show a little respect and put things back. You still perform a thorough search but without the theatrics.

We didn't find anything and proceed to the second cell and repeat the process. Once the prisoner leaves, I again close the door and we begin searching. Bob speaks as he begins rifling through the crook's belongings.

"You know, I was in here with him yesterday."

"No, I didn't. How did that go?" I ask.

"He is just so fucking abrasive with them. And there's no reason for it. A crook asked him to see if it would be alright to wash his clothes for court as it's in a couple of days and he said they only do it on the weekend. The crook says "but I've got court in 2 days, can't you just ask? I kinda need it." You know what he says to him?"

"Tell me," I say.

"He says 'how is that my problem?' The kid was polite, not rude and he says that to him. You know one day he is gonna..." and that's when we hear the thud, followed by a bellow of cheering. I jump at the door and see crooks lined up on the top tier. I look at the officer's station and see Tony frozen in his seat. A shit bomb has hit him on the right shoulder, bounced into his head and disintegrated into the wall of the station. Shit is dripping off the walls and there is a big splatter on the side of his head. I grab my radio and call a code Alpha. Control responds.

"Back to your cells," I yell, and then repeat it louder to get them moving. Tony gets up and walks to the toilet immediately behind the station. Crooks begin to walk to their cells, clapping and cheering, happy with their achievement. I begin to lock the unit down as staff begin storming into the unit. The prisoners begin to move a bit quicker, not wanting to get caught up in the real shit storm about to start.

The Sup enters and once enough staff are in the unit, calls Control to stand the code down. He knocks on the toilet door and Tony opens it. He is topless and wiping the side of his head with paper. I continue to lock cells, aided by several other staff members. We find out later, that the bomber was a new crook named Delaney. He's on remand and has only been in the unit for two days. There is a very good chance that he was coaxed into it by a couple of the heavies in the unit. He was in for unpaid parking fines. Now he can add an assault charge to his list. Stupid move.

He's immediately taken to Murray North and placed in solitary confinement. The police will be called and he will be charged. Tony is taken to the medical unit and assessed and subsequently sent home. He will be undergoing a number of screening tests over the next few months to ensure he is disease free, but in the meantime, he can't even kiss his wife. I hope he is okay and it all checks out clear.

We end up with a replacement officer for the rest of the afternoon and it runs smoothly without incidents. I go home that night reminding myself that they decide if you go home. We work in a place where trouble is around every corner. Why go searching for it as well? Attitude is everything.

# TUESDAY, JUNE 12

TODAY I WORKED in the medical unit with another officer called Pam. She has been in the prison for a number of years and is assigned to this unit. It is a very quiet place to work compared to some of the other units. The medical area has two sections, separated by a long corridor. One side is filled with prisoners coming and going, both protection and mainstream, all kept separated by thin Perspex and walls. It is loud, busy and unpleasant.

At the other end of the corridor is the hospital wing. It is the complete opposite, filled mostly with elderly prisoners well above fifty-five, who just sit around chatting during their run out. Each prisoner is allocated a run out time, usually in conjunction with other prisoners of their classification, being mainstream or protection.

There's a chook pen for them to walk around and grab sunrays, as well as a main sitting area with a television. For the most part, it's outside on a nice day and inside in front of the TV on a shitty one. There are also several cells dedicated to prisoners that are on watch; as in suicide watch. They are assigned different categories based on their level of seriousness.

Having a prisoner on watch means they are limited to what possessions they can have in their cell, what they get their meals served on and even what they wear; the most serious of which having access to nothing more than a canvas gown. They are required to be visited at intervals of fifteen, thirty and sixty minutes. All of these observation cells have cameras in them so they can also be monitored.

On this beautiful Tuesday, we only had one prisoner on watch and he was being calm and reasonable. We checked him every sixty minutes and he was due to be taken off watch later in the day. I don't mind working in this unit and often accept overtime shifts in here. The staff that work in here are also quite pleasant and knowledgeable making the shift enjoyable. No real war stories came out of today. One prisoner was a little disgruntled about not receiving the right dose of medication, but he was compliant with everything asked of him.

Some days are just smooth sailing. Today was one of those days.

# FRIDAY, JUNE 15

TODAY I STARTED a run of 3 night-shifts. Officers are either allocated a unit to man for the entire shift, or a couple of units to search and manage for the night. If prisoners need after-hours attention, then officers responsible for that unit would be called to assist. I'm assigned to Goulburn East, which is a step-down management unit. It is manned twenty-four hours a day, with prisoners generally locked down twenty-three hours a day.

I have worked in here before and don't mind being in a nice warm unit on a cold night. I'm asked by a couple of other officers if I want to swap with them, but my Cheshire grin answers their question. Being assigned a unit is almost a gift on cold nights.

I head straight to the unit so to ensure enough time for a proper hand-over from day staff. I could have difficult prisoners or prisoners on watch so I want to ensure I get the full run down. I am greeted by the three day-officers, Luke, Darcy and Rob, Rob being a good friend of mine who was on my training course when we first started in the prison. We shake hands and he pointed to a cell on the top tier.

"Enjoy that one tonight, Brother," he snorts with a hearty laugh. The other two also chuckle and I check the name on the muster;

Cooper Shelley. My heart sank, right down to my toes. I looked at Rob and pretended to swing the muster board at him.

"Seriously? Why the fuck is he back here?" I ask.

"Been back a few days, and yes, he hasn't changed," Darcy replied, her smile still teasing me.

What can I say about Cooper Shelley? Serial pest. Serial masturbator. Serial everything. He begins tugging his dick from the moment he wakes up to the moment he falls asleep. I'm surprised he hasn't ripped the thing off.

Rob and Luke grab the muster board and begin their final count, opening every trap, including Cooper's. Judging by the chuckle from the officers, he is still beating ferociously. They finish their count and wait for "correct" to be called. We catch up on some brief gossip. Tony returned to work today and has been placed on light duties in reception. That basically meant he was on a "no prisoner contact" roster for the time being.

Count is called correct shortly after and the three of them head out of the unit, one last chuckle as they exit. Within seconds, the console beeps. Manned units have a console that accepts calls from the cell intercoms throughout the night. Instead of bugging Control room staff like unmanned units, they get to annoy staff allocated to their unit all night long. Sometimes it can get pretty painful.

I look at the console and see cell 44 flashing on the display; it's Cooper's. I push the answer button and begin my night shift.

"Yes Cooper?" There is no answer, but I can hear heavy breathing. "Yes Cooper?" I repeat, louder. He still doesn't respond and I can hear his shower running. Good times in Cell 44.

I cancel the call and begin checking my emails. When I finish scanning all 242 new emails, I put my dinner in the microwave. From the staff room, I hear the buzzer again. It's Cell 48 this time: Luke Jones.

"Yes, Luke?"

"Boss, I didn't get my meds." I check the movement book and see that Jones had been out at court for the day and only returned a half hour before lock up. He would have been out of the prison at afternoon medication time.

"No worries, Luke. Leave it with me. I'll see what I can do."

"Thanks Boss." I cancel the call and return to the microwave. I'm half way there when the intercom buzzes again. I do an about-turn and look at the console. Cell 44.

"Yes Cooper?" No answer. "Yes Cooper?" louder. Still no answer, I cancel the call again and retrieve my dinner. I take it back to the station and phone the night supervisor, Clare Davies. Claire is a lovely lady with some fifteen years' experience in the prison. She has a lot of respect from the staff for her hands-on approach and always backs officers when needed.

I inform her of the meds for Luke and she says she will organise some night staff to escort him to the medical wing and I hear the call over the radio a couple of minutes later. I buzz Luke and ask him to be ready. Five minutes later, two staff enter the unit, cuff Luke through the trap and take him for his medication. I turn on the TV and begin to eat my dinner.

The buzzer goes off yet again and I groan again as I press the button to answer Cell 44.

"How can I help you, Cooper?" I say.

"Boss." he says quietly from the shower.

"Yes?"

"I may need a mop," he replies.

"You know I can't give you a mop right now. You'll have to wait till the morning," I inform him.

"Okay then."

I go back to eating my dinner and ten minutes later, the officers return with Luke. They put him away and I return him in the movement book. We have a quick chat, tell a joke, and they go back to their duties. I quietly sit back and watch TV, some reality show about people looking for a rental property, followed by a show about people looking for a home in another country. It's weird what you get into sometimes. Who would have thought that a show about searching for a home could be so enthralling?

I'm just about to find out if they choose house one or house three, when I hear a trickling off to my right. I peer over in that direction and see a thin stream of water leaking from the top tier onto the carpet below. The cell where the water leak appears to be coming from? Cell 44. Cooper.

"Fuck!" I say to myself. I buzz him on the intercom. "Cooper, what are you doing, man?" I hear him chuckle a little.

"I may need a mop, Boss," he answers.

"Turn the water off, mate." No reply. "Cooper, turn the water off." Now one of the crooks opposite the unit sees the water and alerts the rest of the unit. He laughs loudly, then yells

"Boys, Cooper is flooding up. Welcome back, Coop". Others join in, egging him on. I quickly grab a big garbage bin and put it under the water stream. It will fill quite quickly, and I'll need to do something fast if I want to prevent a flood. I phone the night sup but get no answer. I call her on my radio, asking for her phone location. She calls me a couple of minutes later.

"What's Up, Kingy?"

"Cooper is flooding his cell, Ma'am. It's running off the top tier," I inform her.

"He was doing it last night as well. He normally stops after a few minutes. Grab the laundry tub and put that under the stream. That should catch most of it." I acknowledge her reply and hang up the phone. I find the laundry tub and exchange it with the bin which is already half full. I return to the station and let things be.

Just as she had predicted, the water decreased in volume after about ten minutes. Then, twenty minutes later, it stopped completely. I return to my TV and am able to watch a few hours of uninterrupted reality TV. At around 5:00am I buzz two prisoners that have court. I inform them that staff will be picking them up shortly to take them to Admissions. One acknowledges me and begins to get ready. The second one refuses.

"I don't have court today, Boss."

"You're on the list, Brodie. I hear you but when you're on the list, they have to get you ready."

"I'm not going, Boss. I don't care," he snarled back at me, clearly wanting to return to his nap.

"I'm just telling you mate. If you refuse then I will have to get you a firm escort. You don't want that, do you?"

"Whatever," Not good. I phone the night sup and inform her of the situation. She says she'll just organise the Tactical boys to come along and assist. They have an uncanny ability to convince prisoners to comply. And sure enough, when they drop the trap and speak to Brodie, he happily obliges and makes his way out of the unit, even giving me a good morning salute on his way past the station. The worst part though, is when he returns to the unit an hour later because he was cancelled off the bus. His smirk when he returns tells me exactly what's on his mind. "What the fuck do you know, screw." Thirty minutes later, I'm exiting the prison and heading to my car. It was an okay night, but I knew I had two to go. And tonight, I would be back in Goulburn East to do it all again.

## SATURDAY, JUNE 16

I RETURN for my second night shift. I can't say I'm looking forward to it but am also a little curious as to what the night will bring. It is how war stories are born after all. The same staff are in the unit when I arrive and they tell me that it has been a pretty cruisy sort of day. A couple of small codes throughout the prison but that's about all. I point up to Cooper's cell and they both shake their heads.

"He's been pretty quiet," Rob says, without any sign of sarcasm.

They begin their final muster of the day whilst I put my supplies in the fridge; spaghetti bolognaise with chorizo. I made it myself. Ten minutes later Control calls count correct and I'm left alone in the unit once more.

I begin my night by checking my emails and get through those relatively quickly. Next, I set the TV up and check out the guide for anything worthwhile. From the look of things, I'll be able to catch up on some more renters hunting for a home as I settle in for a quiet night.

At around 9.30pm the console buzzes. Its Cell 33, a prisoner named Mark Russell. He is in prison for producing child pornography and fairly new in the unit. I know that he's been getting burnt quite a bit from the other prisoners.

"Yes, Mark?"

"Boss, I'm having chest pains." he says.

"Okay Mark, but I'm not a doctor, I'll have to call a code."

"Thank you, Boss," he said as I grab my radio and call a code Mike. The Control room announces it to all radios and I go to the trap and look inside. He is sitting on the bed watching TV. When he sees me, he begins rubbing his chest and groaning. I leave the trap open and wait for the Sup and staff.

It is a quite common ploy to fake chest pains when wanting to bail from a unit. The prisoner may have debts or is being stood over for medication or possessions, or might simply be the receiver of a lot of abuse from other prisoners. Unfortunately, you cannot prejudge and must make the call to have them checked out. The ramifications for not calling a code are astronomical. In any case, calling a code and writing a two-minute report is not the end of the world when you have twelve long hours of nothing anyway.

A couple of minutes later, staff begins to arrive. The night Sup, Clare, enters and I fill her in. She listens then heads over to the cell and cracks the door. They talk for a couple of minutes, then when the medical team arrive, she asks them in. They enter the cell and begin their assessment.

Suddenly, there is yelling from the cell across the unit.

"Look who's trying to bail, lads!" I hear movement in several other cells and half a dozen prisoners begin barking and howling.

"Don't leave us, Dog. Stay and play with us ya fucken fiddler," someone else yells out. Pretty soon it's like the whole unit is joining in. One of the other officers just smiles at me. The sound is so loud, I don't hear what she says when she does speak. She shakes her head and gives up.

The medical team ask for a stretcher and within a couple of minutes, Mark is being wheeled out of the unit to the chorus of howls and abuse. Once they leave, it doesn't take long for the unit to go quiet again. I resume my position in front of the TV again after writing Mark out in the book.

Not two minutes later I hear a familiar noise. I look across and it would seem the commotion had awoken Cooper. There is a stream of water leaking onto the carpet. I quickly wheel the laundry tub under the waterfall and hope he doesn't take too long to quit. I call the Sup just to give her a heads up in case it goes pear shaped and her advice is the same as the previous night.

I watch a bit more TV, monitoring the trickle of water, and after about fifteen minutes see it subsiding. I check the tub and see it's less than half full. I breathe a sigh of relief and leave the tub where it is, in case he fires up again.

The phone rings a couple of hours later and I check the time to see that it's already a little after midnight. I answer and it's the duty sup.

"Kingy, Russell is coming back to you. He's been checked and given the all clear. He may buzz you up again as I'm guessing he wants to go to one of the management units. He's not getting moved."

"Thanks, Clare." I go to the cell and crack the door, ready for his return. Ten minutes later, he's led in, cuffed and not looking happy. They place him in his cell and I lock the door. He reaches through, and the cuffs are removed. He doesn't speak as I close the trap and then thank the officers. A minute later I'm alone again.

The rest of the night is quiet and there is virtually no activity. Apart from the occasional cough and fart, the unit remains silent. No one buzzes and the phone stays quiet. That's the perfect ending to an okay night. And as I drive home, I remind myself that there is one to go. Fingers crossed.

## SUNDAY, JUNE 17

It's my last nightshift for a while and I'm keen to get it over and done with. The eyeballs tend to struggle a bit after three nights and I really want to get back to normal. I enter the prison and see a couple of familiar faces heading down the path towards me. Sam is on his way out and gives me a fist bump as we pass.

"Have a good night, Bro. Cooper has been a pain in the arse today. Hope he doesn't give you too much stick."

"Wonderful. Last night anyway. Fingers crossed. Have a good one mate." We part ways and I head for the unit. I can hear the burning as I enter the compound, some forty or so metres from the unit door. I groan, my heart sinking slightly. As I enter through the airlock, my ears begin ringing from the yelling. It would seem Mark Russell is copping a pasting.

The staff are standing in the office, trying to stay out of the noise. I join them and they just laugh. When they finally get themselves under control, one of them says

"Yup. You're in for a treat, Champ. Cooper is practically ripping his knob off; Russel is copping a burning of epic proportions, and you have two on watch, both SI's."

"Two SI's?" I sigh. That means a written observation log every fifteen minutes for two prisoners. I would have a busy night. But on the bright side, I won't fall asleep.

The unit doesn't let up as the two officers begin their final muster. Russell is quiet in his cell and either very good at ignoring the uproar aimed at him, or passed out. I buzz him to make sure he is okay, and he says he is. As long as he is alive on my watch, that's all that matters.

Control calls count incorrect a few minutes later and the officers repeat their muster. They go trap to trap and reconfirm their numbers. They call in the same number and await count correct which is called about five minutes later. The unit has quietened considerably by the time I'm left alone.

The occasional howl and insult are thrown towards Russell but not as bad as before. I start by checking my emails again. No love from anyone so I turn the computer off and warm my dinner. The microwave buzzes as the unit erupts again. I wonder whether there isn't anything good on TV that would occupy these guy's attention for a couple of hours. But after another ten minutes they settle down once again.

By 9 o'clock, I've eaten my dinner, completed the latest round of checks and am settling in for some TV when, again, that familiar trickle starts.

"Fucken idiot," I mutter under my breath. I wheel the tub under the water flow and sit back in the station. Less than five minutes later I notice that instead of diminishing, the waterfall is increasing; actually beginning to full-on rage. I phone the sup as the tub begins to overflow.

"He is flooding up, Ma'am, and the tub is already overflowing."

"Is there a bin or something? I'm sure he'll stop again soon."

"Okay, I'll have a look. I'll keep you posted, Clare." I hang up and locate a bin which I exchange with the tub. The water is now a small window pane wide as it's rushing off the top tier. The bin is half full within a matter of minutes and I call the Sup again.

Meanwhile, the unit has once again jumped onboard and are

egging Cooper on. Cheers and howls of laughter echo around the unit as I try and get Cooper to talk to me over the intercom. He doesn't answer and after a couple of minutes, I cancel the call. I am powerless to stop the water and have run out of containers.

When the Sup and a couple of night officers do show, the carpet is under a couple of inches of water.

"I've got the key for the utilities door. Should be able to switch the water off," Clare yells, trying to raise her voice over the cheering. I nod and follow her up the stairs. The entire top tier is flooded and you can see the water bubbling out from under the door of Cell 44.

We reach the utility door and open it. There are a number of switches but no water valve. We check the door on the other side but no luck. Next, we try the door at the end of the tier but still no cigar. Clare calls for the maintenance crew to be contacted and we wait for their response. The phone eventually rings and she heads down stairs to answer it. When she returns, she points at the ceiling.

"It's up in there." She makes her way to the far corner, stairs leading up into the attic. One officer remains at the cell door whilst we go and search for the valve.

After several minutes, we finally locate what appears to be the cut-off valve. We turn it off and call out to the officer at the cell for confirmation. They call back to say the water has been shut off.

"Fuck him. We'll leave it off till the morning. Can sort it out then." I agree and head down stairs. The floor will also be fixed in the morning. I check in on Cooper and see him standing in a now water-less shower, madly masturbating. I close the trap and shake my head. As I reach the officer's station, the intercom buzzes. It's Cooper. Clare looks at me as I answer the call.

"Yes Cooper? I ask.

"I think I need a mop, Boss," he says. Several prisoners laugh at this and begin to cheer again. Clare shakes her head as she heads out of the unit. I'm left alone again and after fifteen minutes or so, the rest of the unit goes quiet. I do my welfare checks and write them in the book.

A couple of hours pass before the intercom goes again. It's Cell 33.

"Yes Mark?" I say.

"Boss, I have chest pains." I groan.

"Mark, same as last night, mate. I have to call a code. Sit tight." I grab my radio and make the call. The staff, some looking like they just woke from a fourteen-hour power nap, slowly roll into the unit a short time later, followed by Clare. She points at Cell 44 and I point at Cell 33. She nods and goes to the trap, opening it and peering inside. There's a sudden gush of water followed by a painful scream. Clare pushes herself away from the door and drops to the ground. The unit erupts with howls and screams of laughter as Clare clutches her face.

The bastard hot-watered her. One officer lunges at the trap and slams it shut as I grab my radio and call a code Alpha, adding "staff down", which is sure to hurry the medical staff up. They come running in a few seconds later, wheeling their trolley, the unit still vocal and enjoying the show. They rush to Clare and try and calm her. Another officer managed to get a cloth with cold water and hand it to her. She grabs it and holds it on her face.

We find out later that the glasses Clare wears, saved her eyes from the initial contact. They may have even saved her eyes completely. The stretcher arrives a minute or two later and we all help Clare on to it. She is groaning in pain and what I can see of her face, it's quite raw. The second and third sups run into the unit and see her.

"Who did it?" one asks.

"Mark Russell," I say, pointing at the cell.

"Cunt. Absolute Cunt. Just because we wouldn't move him," he barks, the veins in his forehead bulging.

"Well he's moving now, isn't he?" the other sup pipes in. Standard rule is that once you assault an officer, you are transferred out of the prison immediately. I wouldn't be surprised if the bus was already on the way.

"Leave the fucker in the cell and wait," the first sup says. His name is Matthew and has been a sup for a number of years. The other sup, Norman, only made supervisor last month. They both now occupy the officer's station, one on the phone, the other on the computer, organising a bus trip out of here for Russell. The Special State Extraction Team arrive an hour later and quietly speak with both Supervisors. Clare had already been taken to the hospital by ambulance, so hopefully was receiving the treatment she needed to lessen the pain.

"Let's grab him, boys," the senior extraction officer said to his lads. Norman followed them to the cell and opened the trap.

"What's happened?" the senior asks. I don't hear the response, but hear the senior continue. "Well, I don't think that would be my first choice of action. Anyway, we are here to take you to another location. Come and put your hands through the trap so we can cuff you." There is a loud reply from within the cell but no hands. "I suggest you put your hands through, Mark. Otherwise you will not like your second choice." Still no hands.

"I'm not playing with you, Mark." He steps away from the door and turns to an off-sider. "Okay, let him have it." The second officer takes out a can of capsicum spray, looks through the trap, then releases a five second squirt. He closes the trap and stands back.

There is a whimper, a screech, then a howl of pain from within the cell. Maybe two minutes pass before there is a very persistent tap on the door. Somewhere behind me, on the lower tier, a crook begins to chuckle.

"Guess he got the message," the senior says to no one in particular. He opens the trap, standing to one side to avoid the spray leak, and two shaking hands appear through the trap, accompanied by loud, uncomfortable groans. Mark is cuffed, and an asp baton is fed through the cuffs to prevent him from pulling his hands back inside.

The cell door is cracked and Mark is grabbed by three officers, who pull him to one side. The baton is removed, Mark is placed against a wall and the cell door is resealed to prevent capsicum spray leaking into the unit, all within the space of a couple of seconds like poetry in motion.

"Thank you, Gents," the senior shouts out as they exit the unit. Within a few minutes I am alone once more. I type my report and email it to the Duty Supervisor. The rest of the night is quiet and the crooks are silent.

I end my shift as the day staff enter the unit and I give them a full run down of the night. They are shocked and saddened to hear about Clare and commit to making a call to the hospital later to see how she is. Twenty minutes later, I am driving home through morning peak hour, listening to some classic eighty's tracks.

Last night was not a good night.

# WEDNESDAY, JUNE 20

Called in for overtime today. I enter the prison for a new day and immediately ask about Clare from a staff member at Reception. They tell me that she was released from hospital Monday afternoon and is in very good spirits. She will be returning in a couple of weeks. Great news to hear there is no permanent injury.

I head to my unit for the day; Glenelg East which is a medium sized protection unit housing some 54 prisoners in 38 cells. It's a mix of single and dual occupancy cells. It also has a very high percentage of prisoners over the age of fifty-five, giving it its nickname of the Retirement Village. It's generally a pretty easy day in Glenelg East, as the prisoners aren't as volatile as some of the younger ones and they still know the meaning of words like respect and manners. As long as you keep your own opinions to yourself and don't try and judge them verbally, you generally have a lovely day.

I do want to point something out here. And it's not my personal opinion, which I try for the best part, to keep out of my writing. Prison Officers are not there to judge. They are not there to punish either. The prison system as a whole is designed as a rehabilitation system, meaning the locking up of a prisoner is their punishment.

The punishment isn't things that happen in the prison. The punishment is the removal of their right to freedom and the removal of certain privileges. They aren't handed big sledge hammers and a pile of rocks. For the most part, they are given a room with a shower and hot water, a toilet, a bed, some bedding and a TV. They have a communal table tennis set up, a gym, a treadmill, an exercise bike, boxing equipment, pool table and a big screen TV. That is their punishment.

I enter Glenelg East and find my other two off-siders already in the unit. Sam Howell and Thelma Wallace. Sam you know from my June 1st shift. Thelma is as old as the hills and just as aggressive. She is like a pit-bull and doesn't put up with shit. She is known as "Repo Lady" amongst the prisoners (and maybe a few officers as well), for her endless confiscations of televisions. She is not afraid to go toe to toe with prisoners with her 5-foot-1 stature, and even though she may need to look up to most, she yells that little bit louder to make sure they can hear her words.

She is currently standing in the officer's station, reading the muster sheet, and when I enter the station, her smile widens when she sees me.

"Simon, hey. Long-time no see."

"Hi Thelma. Good to see you, love." I give her a brief hug, and reach out to Sam for a handshake. Our shipping officer arrives and he completes our team of four. It's Sashi, one of the most well-known officers in the jail. He has a tenacity for crude and totally inappropriate jokes at inappropriate times, but he knows how to put a smile on your face.

After a couple of minutes of general chit chat, Thelma and Sam head out to complete morning muster, Thelma carrying the muster board and Sam, the ligature knife. I open my email and check the daily movement sheet, taking note of the moves to and from the unit. It looks like we have one prisoner leaving to another prison and two new prisoners arriving from another unit. I check the unit muster and allocate the two new prisoners their new rooms, both into dual cells. Suddenly there is a call over the radio.

"Code Mike, Glenelg East." I look over and it's Thelma calling the response. Her and Sam are on the top tier at the other end of the unit. I hurry up the stairs and over to where they are standing, the trap lowered on the cell door. As I reach them, staff are already entering the unit, a supervisor, Jason Rigby with three other officers.

As the Supervisor nears us, Thelma relays the issue.

"He isn't responding, Sir." The Sup peers in and tries to wake the prisoner up. I don't hear a response from where I'm standing and when the Sup cracks the cell door, I gather there was none. The Sup, Thelma and one other officer enter the cell and I hear the sup yelling.

"Stanley! Stanley!" I see the Sup feel for a pulse. Something bumps into my elbow, and it's the medical team. We make room for them and they enter the cell and begin feeling for a pulse. They beckon to two officers, who lift the prisoner off the bed and bring him out onto the tier. They remove his shirt and one of them begins CPR. The other is on the radio calling for an ambulance to be summoned immediately. She then grabs a respiratory mask and begins giving breaths.

After about a minute, one of the nurses reaches for a portable defibrillator and begins hooking up the wires. A few seconds later she shouts "CLEAR!" and I see the prisoner briefly jerk. She checks the instrument then feels for a pulse. She nods and says something to the Sup. He turns and calls someone on the mobile. I see him nod to the nurse as she yells clear a second time.

"Come on, Stanley mate!" I hear a prisoner yell from a few cells down. Another one echoes the first one from the other end of the unit.

The nurses continue working on the prisoner for about five minutes before a second team of medical staff arrive. Their trolley looks to be a bit more technical than the first, and they immediately replace the wires with their own. When one shouts clear a few seconds later and the prisoner jerks, I actually see one of the nurse's sigh with relief. It appears they have restarted his heart.

They begin to wheel him out and take him to the medical unit.

Unfortunately, ambulances take time to admit into a prison and it's another ten minutes or so before Stanley is taken on board.

Once the staff have left, we continue with our morning muster, and then begin to write our reports while waiting for count to be called correct. When it is finally called nearly two hours late, a couple of crooks cheer. I unlock the top tier, while Thelma unlocks the bottom.

The crooks immediately exit their cells and head for the officer's station. A couple approach me and a couple, Thelma. All are asking about Stanley, concerned about their prison brother. The other two officers give exactly the same answer that I do. There is no current information, and they knew as much as we did. If I found out something throughout the day, then I would let them know.

Most of the time, you wouldn't hear the end of it with crooks hovering, eavesdropping and repeatedly asking for answers. Glenelg East just had a different type of crook. The kind that still had respect, and so they let it be.

The morning, or what was left of it, ran very smooth. Thelma and I went to Stanley's cell and packed his belongings into bags, which Sashi would take to the property department to be organised and if he didn't return, would be picked up by his family.

Sashi escorted our exiting prisoner to the admissions building and half hour later, returned with our incoming ones, both of which are older prisoners. One is fifty-eight, Roger Norman, who has been in the system for three weeks for his first offence. The other is Brian Unsworth, seventy-four, a serial killer who has been jailed since the late 80's. Brian will never see the outside world again and has become somewhat of a model prisoner. He often volunteers around the prison as a mentor to other protection prisoners, offering advice on how prisoners can deal with their sentence.

Prisoners don't always cope with the length of the prison terms and need guidance. Help can sometimes come from the most unlikely of people. Brian is one of those people that resigned himself to the fact that his life was over, on the outside at least, so he only had two choices. He once shared his first couple of weeks in prison with me, when I worked in Yarra North for a couple of years.

"Mr. King, I could have either topped myself or turned things the fuck around and make a go of it. I chose the latter. I've never been one to give up," he said, smiling, his eyes distant. And he has been in prison for thirty years, this year, twenty-six of which were spent in this very prison.

As Brian approached the officer's station and saw me, he tipped his head a little in a hello gesture.

"Morning Mr King," he added.

"Good morning, Brian. Your bedding is over there, just sign here, Cell 42. Roger will be in 44. Morning Roger." Roger doesn't make eye contact, but signs his name on the sheet of paper on the bench in front of him. Both are carrying a single duffle bag of their possessions.

They go over and get their bedding, a couple of prisoners now making their way over to offer assistance. Both are welcomed into the unit as they head up to the top tier. They drop their belongings off then return to the main area of the unit, Brian introducing Roger to the rest of the boys. Roger is looking mighty uncomfortable but manages to shake a few hands.

In this unit, there isn't a lot of judgement from other prisoners. They know who they are, where they are and why they are here. Their offences are very similar and everyone just wants to do the time they are sentenced to. There are four Lifers in the unit already, including a resident magician, James Cagney, a man convicted of killing his entire family. Brian made 5.

The unit starts to get busy as more prisoners become aware of new arrivals. They slowly make their way to the growing crowd and the greetings and laughter increase. Five minutes later, Control calls midday muster time and the congregation return to their cells.

Count is completed without a hitch and once Control calls it correct, Sashi takes a couple of prisoners for their medical appointments. When he returns half hour later, he volunteers to help me with the daily random cell search. I check the computer and the lucky winner is Cell 20, Gordon Luck, aged forty-eight and in on a short six-month stretch. We call Gordon over; give him the good news and he leads us to his cell. Sashi enters the cell after Gordon and I follow, closing the cell door behind me. Sashi beckons to Gordon to stand still and commences the strip search, talking in his deep Indian accent.

"Okay, my friend, let's begin. Is there anything in this cell, or on you, that you shouldn't have?" Gordon shakes his head. Sashi motions to each article to come off and inspects it when handed to him. When the underwear comes off and he is inspecting it, he signals for Gordon to raise his arms and open his mouth. I fight hard to resist the laugh when Sashi next speaks.

"Oh dear. My friend, God was not smiling the day he gave you that penis." I bit my lip, Gordon looking embarrassed but managed a small laugh. We finish the strip and Gordon exits the cell.

"Seriously, dude," I snap, "God didn't smile? That crook is an ex Catholic priest. You want to get us reported?" He smiles, and then beams his toothy grin at me.

"Relax, man, he fiddled some boys. He knows all about little dicks. Fuck him." Sashi says. I don't share his sentiment or his professionalism, but the man was born for humour, whether inappropriate or not. The search is fruitless and the cell is given the all clear.

The afternoon goes by quite quickly. There are a couple of code Mikes but that's about all. One prisoner began air raiding in the middle of the unit about someone stealing his milk, but we dealt with it quickly before it caused a major event. Funnily enough, stealing, even in units filled with thieves, is frowned upon and can have dire consequences. Broken fingers, bashings or even getting stabbed by a home-made shiv. Lock up count comes quickly and we finish up our duties for the day.

As we begin our lock up, James Cagney asks me if there is any news on Stanley. I say there isn't but they should know something by the morning. He nods and heads for his cell. We lock the cells, make our final checks and call in our count. Five minutes later it is called correct and we head towards the exit.

As I walk through reception on my way out of the prison, I find out that Stanley, the prisoner from that morning, had passed away this afternoon at the hospital. He was a convicted paedophile, sentenced to eight years jail, with six left to serve. It was his very first conviction in almost eighty years of life. He was seventy-eight.

# THURSDAY, JUNE 21

I'M ROSTERED in Glenelg East and am glad to see both Thelma and Sam on again today. Our fourth officer is Chris Upton, a lovely fellow with about four years under his belt. He is big, he is loud and when he laughs, you can hear him two units away. I've always enjoyed working with Chris and like Sashi, he loves a good joke; still some inappropriate, but some you would pay for.

With the usual morning greetings complete, Thelma mentions Stanley. I acknowledge her and we don't really spend more than a passing comment on the subject. As an officer, I don't really have feelings either way. I can't speak for everyone, but I don't get involved too much in the personal lives of prisoners.

For me, it's a job and so I try and stay out of things for exactly that reason; because I don't want to be emotionally involved. The other reason is that you open yourself to a lot of conflict of interest. To befriend a prisoner beyond the basic pleasantries means you are open to coercion and pressure to bring in narcotics and contraband. Officers have lost their jobs in the past, or even ended up in prison themselves, for trafficking goods into the jail.

Some officers have been offered substantial financial reward for doing so and probably realised too late, that once you agree, they own you forever. Some say everyone has a price. In here, there is no amount of money that would convince me to bring in illegal goods. None. A hundred plus grand a year job with security and benefits is not worth risking for the sake of a quick buck. Not even a few thousand. And that's not even taking into consideration the moral issues. For me personally, when I have been propositioned, which I have, my answer has and always will be, a very firm no. And I like to believe that the majority of officers that I work with, feel the same.

Time passes and, I check the emails and see that there are no movements to or from the unit today apart from the usual medical, court, visits and education moves. Even though Chris is the shipping officer today, I offer to help him out and do some moves for him. It's a beautiful sunny day and I wouldn't mind getting out and about a bit.

Thelma and I begin to conduct our unit count. Thelma marks the names off as I open each trap and call out the name. I'm greeted a good number of times and return the greetings cheerily. All cells check out fine and we call in our count once we return to the station. Ten minutes later, count is called correct and the day begins.

I decide to escort the first prisoners of the day, while Chris helps with the morning medication. Two have to go to the medical wing; one for the dentist and the other for a psych appointment. I call them to the officer's station, check to make sure they have their ID's and head out. As we approach the gate, I call the Quadrangle to authorise our move through it.

"Glenelg East, make your move." I unlock the gate and we head toward the medical wing. The usual chorus of abuse and insults comes flying through the fence from the opposite fence line as if the mainstream boys have been lying in wait. The two prisoners I am escorting show very little interest and make a beeline for their destination.

As we leave one chorus of abuse behind, we enter another. The medical wing's holding cells are filled with prisoners, both protection and mainstream. I usher my prisoners into one of the cells and lock them in, the yells echoing through the corridors. I mouth the names to the officer sitting at the station and she gives me a thumbs up. I return to the unit as the crooks will take time to process. The officer in charge will contact the unit when they have finished and one of us will go and retrieve them. In the meantime, there will be other moves to complete as well as unit duties to perform.

I re-enter the unit and Thelma asks if I can help Chris do a couple of cell searches. I happily oblige and we head to the first one, Cell 11. A long-termer called Russ Stanton occupies it. He has been in the unit for a couple of years and doesn't object to our search. I conduct the strip search and nothing is found. Russ exits the cell and Chris and I go to work, checking food containers, bedding and under his bunk. We flush the toilet; check the kettle, radio and TV. Chris checks the clothing, piece-by-piece while I look through his books, magazines and toiletries. It all seems to check out, until I pick up a tube of toothpaste.

As I pick it up, I notice that it's a little too heavy. It's squishy but when I try and bend it, I find that it won't. There is something concealed in it. I call out to Chris, and as he comes over, I undo the top of the tube. I squeeze the tube out and find a long mini screwdriver hidden in the toothpaste. I put it aside, Chris giving me a thumbs up and we continue our search.

Although we are thorough, nothing else is found. I put the screwdriver in my pocket and we head to our next cell, number 36. This cell is occupied by our kitchen worker, Jesse Thompson. Jesse is a convicted drug user, dealer and isn't afraid to lag on anyone if it means he doesn't have to face the music. He's in protection as he has accumulated so many drug debts, that he's wanted in almost every unit within the prison. On top of that, he gave information on a couple of prisoners, hence his permanent residence in Glenelg East. He's responsible for reheating meals when they arrive in the meal trolleys, then serving them out at the designated meal times.

When we motion for him to join us in his cell, we see his demeanour change immediately. He becomes animated, shaking his head and remains in the kitchen. We call him again, waving him over. Another prisoner, in the kitchen with him, says something to him and Jesse begins walking toward us.

"Just a quick cell search, Jesse," Chris says to him, and we follow him into the cell. Once inside, Chris is standing in front of me and continues. "Anything in here or on you that you shouldn't have, Jesse?"

"No, Boss," he says, low and abrupt. He strips and nothing is found. We let him leave once he is dressed and close the door behind him.

"Clearly something in here," Chris says.

"Think so, buddy. Wasn't happy, was he?" I reply, already scanning the cell. I begin at the front, including bathroom and clothing while Chris takes the back of the cell including bed, desk and food items. I flush the toilet, then begin searching the clothing, one item at a time. I search the socks individually but find nothing. I search the toiletries, the toothpaste in particular, shampoo bottles, but again nothing. Chris finishes searching his area and locates nothing. We look at each other.

"There is something here, mate," I murmur as I scan the cell again.

"I know, but where the fuck's he hiding it?" Chris asks, also looking around. I recheck the small shower curtain, squeezing it from top to bottom, but nothing. I then peel it off, tearing its Velcro attachment from the wall, where it connects to its anchor point. Nothing. Then I hear Chris almost cheer.

"I'll be fucked. Look at this." He had been sorting through a cup of pens and pencils. He was bending over the desk with a pencil held out in front of him. It was the kind that had an eraser attached to the top of it. He had removed the eraser and its small metallic attachment, to find the pencil had been almost completely hollowed out. Inside was a fine white powder. There were four other pencils of the same variety in the cup and each one contained the same white powder.

"Sneaky Fucker," Chris exclaimed, almost jumping for joy.

"Nice one, mate. Nice one," I answered, clapping him on the back.

We took all the pencils, scooped the powder into a small plastic bag we carry, and exit the cell. Jesse was eagle eyed as we came out and began pacing in and out of the kitchen when he saw Chris carrying something.

As we neared the officer's station, a prisoner began yelling from the kitchen area, his voice tense.

"Jesse, don't be a fucken dickhead, man!" Gasps and something crashing to the floor echoed around the unit.

"Jesse!" another yelled. Then "Oh fuck". Chris and I made our way towards the kitchen, when Jesse came out, holding his arm up, blood gushing in a fine arc across the floor from a deep slash to his wrist. He had slashed up and was still holding the blade. He slashed again, another slice opening his arm from wrist to elbow. Blood began pouring out and pooling on the floor beneath him.

"That wasn't my shit, Boss. They're gonna fucken kill me for losin their shit. May as well kill me now." I heard Thelma call a code Alpha with a weapon as Chris and I approached Jesse, waving other crooks away. I could hear Sam and Thelma begin to lock the unit down, ushering prisoners into cells, any cells, and out of the way.

In situations like this, the less prisoners that are roaming the unit, the better. Prisoners love to rubberneck. They are also known to get involved so locking them away lessens the risk of a spark up. They don't necessarily have to go into their own cell. Any cell will do.

"Jesse, drop the blade mate. You don't want to do this," Chris says to him, keeping his distance. I stand behind a chair, ready to raise it if he comes at me. There are very few things more dangerous in a prison than a prisoner with a blade. The area is clear of other crooks when the T.O.'s arrive, bursting through the door. One comes up behind me and taps me on the shoulder.

"Step back, Simon," he whispers to me. I back off, Chris following, never turning our back. Four T. O.'s now begin to negotiate with Jesse, blood still freely flowing, covering the floor. His white T-Shirt looks like a horror movie, completely drenched. Two of the T. O.'s have their spray out and are holding it in front of them, the other two, their batons drawn. They won't negotiate for long. And it turns out they don't need to.

Half a minute or so later, Jesse's arm drops, his legs begin to unbuckle, and he hits the floor, unconscious. He has either lost consciousness from blood loss or from exhaustion, but either way it's made the situation a lot easier. The officers slowly approach, spray still at the ready, when one kicks the blade away. Another drops and holds one arm while another grabs the other. They handcuff him and motion for the medical team to approach. They approach with their trolley and begin working on him.

Turns out he lost a lot of blood which caused him to lose consciousness. The cuts were quite deep, a couple severing arteries in his arm and wrist. He is eventually stretchered to the hospital wing, then subsequently by ambulance to hospital, although is returned later in the day, his arm stitched and heavily bandaged.

We speak to the Duty Sup and show him our find. He nods his head in appreciation and asks us to complete our reports as soon as possible. He also asks us to leave the unit locked down for the time being, although to return crooks to their own cells, one at a time.

A couple of minutes later, our normal compliment of four officers are left alone in the unit. Chris and I begin our reports and a half hour later, I assist Sam and Thelma return crooks to their own cells. I am happy with our find. Crooks don't always know what the substance is when they consume it, and it can seriously compromise the safety of officers and other prisoners. A drug-affected prisoner can be extremely dangerous, and as experience has proven in the past, they can cause serious damage and injuries.

Once the prisoners are all returned to their cells, Chris and I return to Jesse's cell and begin itemising and bagging his belongings, as is standard procedure. It prevents theft and also frees up his cell, which he won't be returning to for a while. He will be taken to a management unit where he will be on suicide watch as well as in protection until it is ascertained whether he is in danger or not, based on his claims.

Sam is called to the medical wing for the two prisoners that I escorted down earlier, whom he escorts back to the unit. Lunchtime muster comes and goes and the unit remains in lock-down. Our floor cleaner is let out and begins cleaning the blood up, while Thelma helps the nurse go trap to trap with lunchtime medications. The prisoners have special training on cleaning blood spills and it gives them an extra kick in their weekly pay.

It takes him around an hour to finish cleaning up and once done, we contact the sup to get an update. He asks us to leave the unit in lock-down for the rest of the day. We happily oblige, making our afternoon a little easier.

There is a code Mike called in the middle of the afternoon but that's about all. We escort the nurse around for afternoon medications, then let the second kitchen billet out for evening meal prep. He asks if his cellie can help and we agree. The meals are handed through the trap and once finished; the billets return to their own cells. It's not long until evening muster, and once count is called correct, its home time.

Just like that, our shift has come to an end.

## MONDAY, JUNE 25

I RETURN to Glenelg East again and find Thelma in the unit already. She beckons to me as I enter the unit, putting her hand to my ear.

"The Unit Sup wants you to call him. And good morning, Love," she says.

"Morning, Love. Jason?" I ask. She nods. I phone him and rather than having a conversation, he tells me he will see me shortly. Curious, I hang up the phone.

"He is on his way," I say to Thelma just as Kon Giopoulos nears the officer's station. Kon is our third and has been in the prison for about ten years. He is one of those Greek men that love being Greek. He is in his early forties and has a giant belly with a laugh to match. He is one of those officers that everyone knows and everyone talks about with a smile, just a really likeable guy. I haven't seen Kon in a while and enthusiastically shake hands with him.

"Good to see you, my friend," I say, still shaking his hand. "How have you been?"

"Very good, buddy, very good. Been back to Greece for a month. Now I'm back to this shit hole," he replies, giving Thelma a hug. He puts his bag down and turns his head, seeing the fourth officer coming in. It's Barb Toohey, a tall lady of thirty with about a year in the prison. She doesn't look too happy and as she nears us, shakes her head.

"Was supposed to be working in Visits but they shifted me here, bastards."

"Never mind, Love," Thelma responds, "you'll play with us today. We'll look after ya." Barb smiles, sees Kon and gives him a peck on the cheek.

"Welcome back, stranger. How was it?" she asks.

"Amazing. Such a beautiful time. Sue and the kids loved it," he says, smiling. Barb gives me a brief hug, then heads to the office with her bag. Jason, the Sup, enters a short time later, waves at everyone, then beckons me to the office.

"Shut the door, Simon," he says as he sits behind the desk. "Would you mind working in here permanently for a while?" he asks. "I need someone in here that's a little more switched on."

"Is that a compliment, Sir?" I ask, more curious.

"I need someone in here that I know is trustworthy. Management have a suspicion that contraband is coming in via this unit. They don't know how and they don't where. Just keep your eyes and ears open. Anything suspicious. Okay?" I nod, we shake hands and I leave the office. As I enter the officer's station, Thelma gives me the eye and asks if everything is OK. I nod and check my emails.

Kon is out taking a couple of crooks for their medical appointments and Barb is finishing up with the morning medication. When I get through my emails, I take a tier walk and pop my head into a couple of cells. I am greeted in a couple by the occupants and stop for a chat with Gordon Luck, to see how he is doing and ask him if he has any concerns. He says he is all good and looking forward to a visit with his daughter today. I nod and continue my rounds, then return to the station.

Kon returns a few minutes later and I ask him about his holiday. He tells me about the amazing places he visited and how great it was to catch up with family. His face lights up when he mentions seeing his Mum again. His wife and two children, his daughter Jane, who is twelve, and his son Nick, nine, and very energetic, had an incredible time. They were especially excited to meet their extended family and were hoping to visit again during the summer holidays. He sounded so happy and looked totally refreshed.

"And how long did it take to get back in the swing of things?" I laugh. He nods and smiles.

"About five minutes after I walked through the gate." I know exactly what he means.

Barb enters the station and offers us cuppas. Both Kon and I ask for a coffee and Barb goes to make them. Thelma joins us and we continue our chitchat. A few minutes later Barb brings the cuppas, as well as a packet of chocolate chip cookies. We all take one and silently drink our coffees.

"Medical to Glenelg East" comes over the radio.

"Glenelg East receiving." I reply into my radio.

"Two to pick up in medical." comes the reply and Barb stands and nods, heading for the door.

"On our way." The three of us finish our coffees and Thelma checks the random cell searches.

"Ready to see some dick, Kon?" I ask, grinning. He laughs and stands.

"Not something I missed but let's go." I follow him and we complete the searches with little fanfare. The crooks are obliging and within 20 minutes we finish.

As we head back to the officer's station, the call comes over the radio to prepare for lunchtime count. Thelma announces muster over the unit P.A. System and we conduct muster. Half-hour later, Control announces count correct and we commence our afternoon run.

About an hour later, the phone rings. It's the visits centre asking for Gordon Luck. I call Gordon up and Kon offers to walk him there. Barb says she will but Kon insists. He heads for the door, giving us a salute. Thelma looks at the door and says

"I really like that man." I agree with her as I fill in the movement book.

Not two minutes later a frantic call comes across the radio. It doesn't sound like an officer as the person is speaking freely and not in radio lingo.

"I need help. There is an officer that's fallen down!" My ears prick and Thelma takes out her radio. Before she has a chance to speak, Control answer the call.

"This is Control. Where are you?"

"I'm in Glenelg East yard. The officer is turning blue!" the voice answers, sounding frantic. I am up and out of the station as soon as he mentions the unit name. I burst out the door and run down the path.

In the distance I see Kon lying face up on the ground with 3 prisoners standing over him. They don't appear to be attacking him, but rather trying to help him. All three are pushing seventy and one is tapping Kon in the face, trying to wake him. I raise my radio and yell

"Code Alpha, Glenelg East, officer down, Code Alpha!" I reach Kon and see that his lips are blue. I feel for a pulse in his wrist, then on the side of his neck. I feel nothing. I immediately begin CPR, not easy on a man easily tipping the scales at around 140kg and that weight on a frame only about 170cm tall. There is a lot of insulation to get through.

I frantically push down on his chest, anxiously looking around for help. Barb comes running up; she must have been a split second behind me and begins mouth to mouth. She is crying, tears spilling down her cheeks. I find out later that I'm also crying. I frantically continue pressing his chest, counting to try and keep time with Barb. I have no idea how long we were there for before staff began arriving. It felt like at least five or six minutes but I was later told it was within a minute.

I see the medical team running up the path, their trolley in front. I only stop when they push me aside, leaving me sitting on the ground with my arms sore and my own heart thumping hard as I desperately try to catch my breath.

Two of the nurses begin CPR while a third takes a defibrillator out of the trolley. I have flashbacks to Stanley and my stomach begins to heave. I fight to control it and when I feel confident of hanging on to my lunch, I stand and go and hold Barb. She clings to me, holding me tightly. I hear the nurse shout clear and hear that familiar zap. I don't want to look. I don't want to see that convulsion that I saw so recently.

She yells clear a second time, followed by the snap of electricity. In the distance, I hear an ambulance siren. It is still a long way off, but I know that officers will be manning every gate between here and there to ensure it arrives in the fastest possible time. There is a collective sigh of relief as the defibrillator begins to beep with a regular rhythm. The nurse checks his wrist and nods.

Colour slowly returns to Kon's lips and face and his eyes begin to flutter. He tries to speak, mumbling something, but the nurses quieten him. He already has a bung in one hand and one nurse is injecting something into it. He rests his head again as comments come from the officers standing around, telling him to stay strong, and you'll be fine.

Five minutes later, two paramedics and a stretcher come rushing up the path. They reach Kon and begin their duties, taking information from the nurses. Barb asks the Sup, Jason, if she can accompany Kon in the ambulance and the paramedics shake their head.

"Not with a critical patient," one says. Jason whispers something in her ear, and motions to one of the other officers. I don't need to hear to understand that he is asking Barb to be driven to the hospital in one of the prison vans.

Six officers help to lift Kon onto the stretcher and a few minutes later, the ambulance exits the prison, full lights and sirens wailing. I cannot describe the feelings to you. All I know is that I sat down on the grass and cried. I cried freely and without shame. My body felt absolutely exhausted and I was told later that my body would have been inundated with adrenaline. I sat in that yard for God knows how long.

Eventually Jason came and asked me if I was okay. I nodded but wasn't so sure. He said that I should go home for the rest of the day and take it easy. Also, I should go and see my doctor the next day. I just felt cold all over. I remember shaking and Thelma giving me a hug. She too, had tears in her eyes and I just held her. Again, for how long, I cannot tell you. Eventually, I pulled myself together and drove home. I phoned the hospital and was told that Kon was in intensive care and they couldn't elaborate much more. I didn't sleep much that night, but I do remember holding my wife, tight.

It was not a good day.

## TUESDAY, JUNE 26

GIVEN the day off and went and saw my doctor. When I phoned Barb, she told me that Kon was still in intensive care but stabilising. The doctors said that he was showing some very positive signs at this stage. When I call in to work, Jason tells me to take the rest of the week off. He said they can run the prison just fine without me for a few days. I laugh, thank him and hang up. I stay home and relax.

## WEDNESDAY, JUNE 27

I PHONE Barb and she tells me that Kon is being taken out of intensive care and to a ward in the coronary care unit. He is making positive progress. She tells me that they are allowing visitors the next day and I tell her I will definitely go and see him.

## THURSDAY, JUNE 28

BARB TEXTS me a photo of Kon. He is sitting up in a hospital bed, giving a very toothy grin and a thumbs up. I grin, relieved at seeing my old friend smiling. My wife and I go and visit Kon and his family in the hospital later in the day.

He looks very relaxed, apart from the wires and tubes hanging off him. His wife, Maria, looks tired, almost exhausted, and her eyes are bloodshot from crying. I hug her and whisper in her ear.

"It will be okay, Maria." She squeezes me tighter, acknowledging me. Kon shakes my hand, and I kiss him on the top of his head.

"They tell me you pounded on my chest pretty hard, Buddy."

"Maybe a little harder than needed. But it felt good to give you a couple. Time to cut down on the Baklava?" He smiles.

"Everything but the Baklava" he snorts and laughs.

THANK you for reading this book. May I ask you a small favour? Reviews are so important for new authors and also help other readers decide whether the book suits them. Would you mind leaving one here? It would really mean the world to me.

# AUTHOR'S NOTE

I would like to thank you for allowing me to share with you some genuine experiences that occurred in our prison this month. Whilst this has been written, there have already been 4 staff assaults, a rape, 2 deaths and a drunk officer on duty, all in the first week of July. If you enjoyed reading this book, please share it with your friends. You can also purchase the next edition, or read it for FREE on Kindle Unlimited, right now.

My website is a good source of information on my other releases, including an off-shoot from the Prison Days series. Inmates, Books 1 through 5 are now available and offer a quick glimpse into some of the personal stories of specific prisoners housed in this prison. Thank you for your continued support.

Simon King

Join my Facebook Page

I have tried to recreate events, locales and conversations from my memories of them. In order to maintain their anonymity in some instances I have changed the names of individuals and places, I may have changed some identifying characteristics and details such as physical properties, occupations and places of residence.

# BOOK 2

# INTRODUCTION

It was such an amazing experience for me to release the first volume in this series. I was nervous, almost as nervous as that late Autumn day when I first stepped behind the walls. Almost. Although it may have sounded like a crazy month to you, June was a pretty average sort of month.

Apart from what happened to my good friend Kon, the rest of the experiences you read about, are pretty much how most work days play out here.

This month, however, was not. Things happened that I would have never expected, even for this place. I am still shocked from a couple of the incidents and angry from a couple of others. I don't want to spoil the ride for you. So, let's not delay any longer. Put on your seat belt, keep your arms and legs inside the moving vehicle at all times, and enjoy the ride that was July, in a maximum-security prison.

# SUNDAY, JULY 1

CALLED IN FOR OVERTIME TODAY. Was given a choice between Visits Centre and Murray North. Murray, being a management unit, means prisoners are on 23-hour lock down and given an hour out in one of six chook pens. I know it can be quite challenging working in there but I decide to take it, anyway. I haven't spent much time in there and am keen for a bit more experience.

I ARRIVE at the unit a little after 7, around thirty minutes before my scheduled shift. Two officers are already in the unit, one the night officer, the other a 6 o'clock start. I greet both, shake hands then take my bag out the back and put my lunch in the fridge. When I come back out, the night officer gives me a brief rundown of the previous night. There is one prisoner on suicide watch although only on S3 (hourly observations) and I recognise the name immediately, Jesse Thompson.

"Ah, Jesse Thompson," I say, pointing at the name. The night officer, John Simons, nods.

"Came back from hospital yesterday afternoon. He's been pretty quiet," he says, pointing at one of the monitors. Jesse is lying on his bed and appears to be sleeping. The other officer, a man named Russel Rawsley, looks at the monitor.

"Were you there when he sliced himself up?"

"Yeah, I was there. I did the cell search that sent him over the edge," I reply. Russel shakes his head.

"What a clown." Just then the door opens and two more officers enter. The full complement of officers in Murray North is six officers by day and one by night. A supervisor is also present for most of the day. Janine Riley and Jacob Davidson wave as they walk to the back. Another officer, Paul Jackson and the Supervisor, Julia Billings, enter a few minutes later. I'm asked if I want to run the book today and I agree, a little apprehensively. The book can be quite daunting in any unit, let alone a unit where I've had little experience. It involves manning the console for prisoner communications, answering phone calls and organising the running of specific events such as visits, medications and run outs. The Sup gives me a clap on the back and says

"You'll be fine, mate. Don't be shy." I smile and sit at the console. Russel and Janine grab the muster folder and make their way to the cells to begin morning count. The night officer bids us farewell and heads out, one last wave as he walks out of sight. I watch Russel and Janine as they make their way around the cells, dropping each trap and peering in. The Sup stands next to me and asks if I have heard anything about Kon. I shake my head.

"I know he is still in the coronary care unit, but not sure when he'll be let out. Probably not for a while."

"Code Black, Murray North!" suddenly comes over the radio.

"What? Where?" I hear the Sup say. I look around and then up to the top tier.

"Ma'am, we need to open the cell," Janine shouts from the cell door. "He's not answering us. He's lying on the floor." The Sup walks to the stairs and I follow as Control announces the code to the prison. The Sup peers in.

"Chris. CHRIS!" She knocks on the cell door, then bangs with her fist. Nothing. She unlocks the door and the prisoner is lying on the floor, face down, his head near the door. Prisoners are known to converse with fellow prisoners by shouting under their doors, sometimes for hours depending on the topic of conversation. Lying that way could cause positional asphyxia, if left for too long in the wrong circumstances. The worst part though? There were three slices of toast lying on the prisoner's back. The night officer is supposed to provide toast to prisoners, as they have no cooking facilities in their cell, and conduct a welfare check at the same time, ensuring they receive a response from the prisoner, to ensure they are OK. The Sup bends down and shakes the prisoner without a response and feels for a pulse.

"No pulse," she says. She beckons for two officers to come in and then has them lift the prisoner out on to the walkway. They begin CPR immediately. I remember the unit being eerily quiet, the other prisoners not making so much as a peep. The prisoner is blue, almost purple and his eyes are partly open. The Sup leans down again and feels for a pulse, but shakes her head. The officers continue CPR until the medical team rush in shortly after and immediately take over. They begin to hook up their defib machine and one nurse asks the Sup to arrange an ambulance.

"Already on the way," she responds. The nurse nods and they continue to apply the machine. They zap the prisoner, again and again but there is no response. A doctor enters the unit and also attempts to work on the prisoner. The minutes seem to drag as the doctor and nurses desperately try to save him, hitting him again and again and again. Finally, the ambulance officers arrive and assist the nurses. They continue working for a long time, almost an hour, before they declare the prisoner deceased. He is covered in a sheet and left where he is as police are called in. He was 28 years old and a father of two.

When the police arrive, they conduct an investigation, talking to staff and taking photos, before the body is allowed to be removed. It takes another couple of hours for everything to be returned to normal and the prison is finally unlocked. In situations such as this the entire prison remains in lock down. We begin to conduct prisoner's run outs, escorting them one at a time to a designated chook pen. The mood is very solemn in the unit as we escort each prisoner out and begin our trap to trap duties.

It is nearly lunchtime count by the time everything is caught up with. The unit noise is almost back to normal, prisoners shouting to each other under the doors, the occasional burn of some "boneyard dog" somebody has an issue with. The medical trolley enters the unit and lunchtime medications are dished out trap to trap. It takes around ten minutes and as the trolley exits the unit, count is called and Paul and Jacob go trap to trap and conduct muster. When they finish, they show me the numbers and I call it in to control. Count is called correct 10 minutes later and we start the afternoon session.

Shortly after count is called correct, the phone rings and there are visitors on the way for a prisoner. I organise for him to be brought out of his cell and into the visits box, a small cubicle we have in the unit, divided in half by a bench and thick glass. There is a small grill beneath the glass through which the people communicate with each other. The phone rings again and we have a new prisoner that needs to be picked up from the admissions building which I allocate to another 2 officers. Because every single move and escort takes 2 officers, the staff numbers can reduce quite quickly if a few things happen so I wait with some moves to ensure we don't end up short. I'd rather take my time escorting prisoners than end up with too few officers in case something kicks off.

Once the visit is finished, two officers, Russel and Jacob, head down to pick up the new arrival. Two other officers, Janine and Paul prepare the cell he will be going into. They prepare a bed pack, a TV (yes, solitary these days entitles them to a TV, and when I say "entitles" that's exactly what I mean. These prisoners know their entitlements and rather than ask for them, they demand them), and food utensils. They can bring food, reading material, drawing material, clothing and a kettle with them. Nearly all the comforts of home.

THEY RETURN a short time later accompanying their prisoner, Ryan Blake. He is checked in, interviewed and taken to his cell. As he has been here before, more than once, Ryan knows the procedure and as such makes the process a lot simpler, not needing us to run through the finer details with him. He is upbeat and chirpy as he is lead away, greeted by friends who are shouting at him from under their doors as he walks to his cell.

"Blakeeeeeyy!" one yells.

"Hey crazy cunt! Watcha doin back in this joint?" another shouts. He looks in the direction, smiling, giving them a thumbs up.

"Jacks got me doin a burg," he yells back. There are several laughs from behind the doors.

"Allegations, Brother, allegations," one finishes as he enters his cell, his cuffed hands put through the trap and a bolt lowered to hold his hands in place. The door is closed and his handcuffs are removed through the trap, the bolt lifted again and the trap resealed. It never ceases to amaze me just how happy they are to come here. It only takes a few minutes before the chatter restarts, the crew welcoming their new tenant to the building.

THERE ISN'T much to report for the rest of the day. Run outs happened without incident, the afternoon medical run was completed without too much fanfare and dinner was dished out to the prisoners, the meals rewarmed and served up door to door by the staff. The night staff member came in just before lock down muster and we did a brief handover before heading out of the prison to end our day.

# MONDAY, JULY 2

WORKED in the Visits centre today. Received news that the officer from the previous morning's event had been suspended, pending an investigation. Not good. I head straight to the Visits Centre and am placed in the back again. There are 3 female officers already manning the front, so me and a couple of guys are only too happy to man the back and stare at penises again for the day. It's a good opportunity to compare, I guess.

THE TWO OFFICERS working with me today are both new from the recent intake and as such, quite fresh. I will have to guide them and try and show them the ropes a bit. It can be quite confronting to have to conduct endless strip searches when still new but it does get easier with time. Raj and Roger are both keen to learn and I'm also happy to teach. Our shift starts after count is called correct and we await our first couple of customers. The list isn't too bad today, with protection first and last and main stream in the middle. The first lot of prisoners only number 14, so we should be able to get through them relatively easy with our inexperienced team.

. . .

I MANAGE the book and enter all the prisoners coming and going into the building. I also allocate lockers and which strip room to enter. My two offsiders take a strip room each. The first four crooks show up within a few minutes and I conduct a couple of the strips for the new officers to follow, highlighting which parts to focus on. Once they are all processed, I speak to both Officers and highlight the importance of being extra vigilant when they return from the visits. This is one of the main areas of contraband introduction when involving visitors and we really are the last line of defence if anything does get through. They nod and acknowledge the instructions. As we wait for the next group to arrive, I share the syringe story with them from my previous time in here and the laughing lasts until the next group enter the door (see June Edition). 3 more prisoners enter with their escort officer and I enter them in the book, directing two to their respective strips. The third, a prisoner called Cooper Taylor, stands quietly awaiting his turn. I ask him if he is excited about his visit and he tells me that he can't wait to see his partner and little girl. She is 1 next week and I see the sadness in his eyes when he tells me he won't see her for her birthday. I tell him that she is probably a very good reason to try and stay out of prison and he nods as Raj beckons him over.

THE PRISONERS CONTINUE to come in sporadically over the next hour. I call the two officers over and remind them of the importance of being really thorough with the strips once they start coming back out. I highlight the fact that they can hide things in their mouths, butts and eye of their penises, between their toes; anywhere really. Eventually, the first ones start exiting, take two straight in and conduct their strips. I can see they are taking their time, which is good. The last group of prisoners come in for their visits and we have a bit of a cross over. A couple start arcing up but we quickly settle them down and continue to process the groups. As each prisoner is finished with their exiting strip, I contact their units for their escorts, who enter soon after.

. . .

The day is running pretty smoothly and it feels like a well-oiled machine for three blow ins who don't normally work in here. I see Cooper coming back out, a smile missing from his face. He is looking quite stern; not angry, just serious. Roger calls him over and conducts the strip. I spot for him and don't notice anything out of the ordinary. I ask him how his visit went and he said it went great, loved seeing his baby girl, a smile appearing but quickly fading again. I call for his escort back to Yarra North and they are there within a few minutes. I decide to give the unit a call and just give the officers a heads up that even though his visit went well, he seemed nervous about something. Maybe nothing, but it doesn't hurt to give a heads up. They thank me and hang up.

We process each prisoner as they come back out from their visit and pretty soon it's another waiting game for main stream. It doesn't take long and before we know it, we have a room full of ins and a few outs, all waiting to be processed. A couple of them try to burn the new officers but we quickly process them and move them on. It's a game to them and they know exactly how to play it. Especially when they've finished what they came for and it's 5 minutes before count. The speed with which they're processed can be the difference between making it back to the unit for lunch or remaining here for the muster. So, they manipulate the system by "playing the game". Make an officer uncomfortable and he will process you next to get you out of there. Unless of course it's an officer with some experience behind him who will go the opposite and make them last in line instead. Like I said, it's a game.

Lunchtime muster is called a short time later and thankfully we managed to process all the prisoners who had finished. We walk around the building to count our numbers, including the front, and give our tally to the desk staff. They call it in and five minutes later it's called correct, signalling the afternoon session. Ten minutes or so pass and more prisoners enter for their visits while others have completed theirs. The game starts again for the second half.

THE AFTERNOON RUNS JUST as the morning did and we are processing them in a steady stream. Main streamers are soon finished and gone and protection are ready to begin their afternoon run. Things are flowing just like we were hoping. It's around 4 o'clock when there is a code called on the radio.

"Code Mike Yarra North," is the call. I check the sheet and there are no prisoners due from that unit for visits as they all pretty much had the morning stretch. We continue to process the ones we have and then wait for the code to be stood down. A minute or so later a second call comes across the radio and it is the sort of call that brings shudders. Not because of what it is, but because you can actually hear the panic and anguish in the officer's voice.

"Yarra North! I need urgent medical help in Yarra North!!" As we still have a number of prisoners waiting to be stripped and a couple now coming out, none of us are able to go and assist the unit. Another minute passes and we hear radio chatter pick up about an ambulance being on its way, gates to be manned and ready for them and staff readying themselves to go on the escort to the hospital. We see a number of officers running past our door and it doesn't look good. No new prisoners will be escorted to the visits area while the code is in progress so all we can do is wait once we have finished processing everyone. I see one of my mates come walking past the door and I crack it to ask him what's happening.

"Crook just died in Yarra North. OD," he says. I close the door.

"Fuck, two in two days," I think to myself. Another twenty minutes pass and a Sup comes in through the door. It's Bruce and he has a very serious look on his face. I ask him if everything is OK and he shakes his head.

"Think he swallowed a balloon." He doesn't need to tell me who the prisoner is. I had a suspicion which, in time, is proven correct; Cooper Taylor. I shake my head but am not surprised. Unfortunately, this is prison and he could have swallowed that balloon for any number of reasons, from being threatened or forced to money or favours. I know there is one child that isn't going to care why. She just lost her Dad.

THE PRISON IS LOCKED down for the rest of the day. Ambulance and Police officers remain in the prison for a couple more hours and we have already gone home by the time everything is cleared. I find out from a friend later in the evening what happened as far as they could tell. Cooper's visitor had been strip-searched when she came into the prison but nothing was found. They suspect she hid the balloon in her vagina. Video footage rules out the balloon being in the nappy as neither mum nor dad ever reach into it throughout the visit. Taking an infant, or any visitor for that matter, to the bathroom, instantly converts the visit to a boxed one, meaning no contact and that didn't happen. They do see mum reach into her own pocket quite deep and shuffle her hand around, suspecting she had ripped a hole in her pocket so she could reach in and pull it out. There was a packet of chips on the table between them and she had simply pulled the balloon out, reached for a chip, leaving the balloon in the packet and then Cooper went in for a handful, including the balloon, and simply put the lot in his mouth and swallowed, together with a swig from the orange juice they had.

I was told that as the officers were conducting CPR on him, Cooper began leaking thick reddish-brown fluid from his mouth and nose. The term he used was "He looked like a frozen coke machine." I felt sick. But more so, I felt sad. Not for Cooper. Prisoners make their own choices and I have no sympathy, especially when drugs are involved. But I do feel sad for his daughter.

# TUESDAY, JULY 3

AM ROSTERED in Visits again today and find a familiar smile as I enter the unit. Clare's smiling face greets me and I welcome her back after her hot watering incident the previous month (see June Edition).

"Welcome back stranger. How you feeling?" I ask her.

"Good. Glad to be back," she responds.

"You our sup today?". She nods at this and I am happy to see her back again. I am working with the same crew as yesterday and that is a good thing. They did well and I was glad to be with officers that were as keen as them.

I CHECK the list and see it will be quite a busy day. It is an entire day of main stream and that means prisoners will be coming and going without escorts all day. Raj and Roger enter a few minutes later, we shake hands and they put their bags away. They are keen to discuss the death from the previous day and I fill them in on what I know. I also reassure them that there is nothing they could have done. We aren't allowed to perform internal searches, with prisoners or visitors. As sad as it is, what happened was of the prisoner's own doing. We leave it at that and just as the two put gloves on, the door buzzes and four prisoners enter, signalling the beginning of another day of strips.

TWO PRISONERS TAKE seats and two are taken into separate strip rooms as Raj and Roger begin the first round. I can hear one of the prisoner's arc up, annoyed at how slow the process is taking and Raj calms him down. I go and stand just behind Raj, making myself visible. Sometimes just having another officer present is enough to stop a situation from escalating. It works on this occasion and once finished, he heads inside. Sometimes complaining over an extra thirty seconds is not worth risking your visit over.

THE DOOR BUZZES and another five prisoners are let in while Raj and Roger finish the first group. One of the new ones is a prisoner called Tully Johnson. He is renowned for baiting officers and at 6 foot 6, can be quite intimidating. His favourite target? New officers. He sits, already grinning as he checks out the two newbies working with me. He looks at me and waves.

"Hi Boss," he says, grinning widely.

"Hello Tully," I respond. Roger beckons him over and his grin broadens as he stands and enters the strip room. I can hear him begin almost immediately, his voice loud and obnoxious. I stand just behind Roger but Tully knows our tricks and doesn't let go. He is currently discussing the prettiness of Roger's man bun; asking him if he's had it long and what his boyfriend thought of it. I'm not surprised when Roger begins going faster. I ensure he still performs all the right checks and we move him on, the other prisoners laughing as he walks past. We finish the rest of the group after a few minutes and enjoy a small break, the place empty.

WE EXPECT ANOTHER 22, staggered between now and lunchtime, some three hours away. A code Mike is called for one of the far units and we can breathe easy as no prisoner movements occur during a code. I walk in the front and see how the visits are going.

THREE FEMALE OFFICERS are manning the front and wave at me as I walk into the station. Julie, Rachel and Emily are all experienced officers, the least having 4 years. They have several monitors in front of them from cameras scattered around the large room. A children's section is off to one side and there are a couple playing there now. I see one of the cameras is trained on Tully, who is being visited by a blonde lady, wearing tight jeans and a tight t-shirt with a jacket that is hanging open around her. I leave the ladies to it and head back to the strip area. The code is stood down a few minutes later and the buzzer goes off a few minutes after that. Another three prisoners enter as two from the front also return. We begin processing each and sending them on their merry way.

WE ARE ABOUT to send the last of them out when I hear yelling from the front followed by a code alpha in visits. Raj ushers the last prisoner out as Roger and I bolt to the front, the yelling now louder. As we reach the Visit's Hall, we see Emily and Rachel standing near Tully, that wide Cheshire grin beaming. He is holding something and it looks like he spilled something down the front of his shirt. His girlfriend is also standing and has the same thing over her face. As we get closer, we see the issue and it's pretty straight forward. What he is holding is his dick. What he has spilled is semen; across his girlfriend's face and on his t shirt. He begins putting his dick back in his pants as other prisoners begin howling and cheering. A mum has gone over to her children in the play area and is shielding them. Tactical Officers burst in and begin escorting Tully out of the area, that Cheshire grin never wavering. His girlfriend is also grinning' as she is wiping semen from her face hungrily licking it from her fingers and giggling.

. . .

The scene is quickly brought under control and within a few minutes the visits area is back to normal. The dozen or so prisoners still seeing their visitors have calmed again and within an hour, all the prisoners have been rotated out, new ones taking their places.

Lunchtime muster comes and goes without incident and we continue to process prisoners throughout the afternoon. Around 2 o'clock a Code Alpha is called for one of the back units. We have half a dozen prisoners currently being processed and are unable to attend, although we see quite a few officers go rushing past our door. The call was from a female officer and her panic was clearly conveyed through her voice. A few minutes pass and a second call is put out, requesting all available officers. It lets the prison know that it's more serious than just a simple confrontation. We only have a couple of prisoners left and Raj runs out the door to assist. Roger and I continue with our duties, finishing the last two together. When the prisoners are through to the hall, we follow and see the girls talking. We head over and they tell us that three officers have been assaulted in Tambo West, one quite bad. Jeff Stebbins was knocked out cold and another had a broken jaw. The female officer had managed to call a code but was also attacked; we didn't know how bad yet. This was definitely not a good start to the month and we still had almost 4 weeks to go. I was about to ask Roger if he wanted to run down, when another call came across the air, a code Charlie. Roger looked at me puzzled and I mouthed "Lock Down" to him. The entire prison was about to be locked down. That would mean resources were stretched to breaking point and if something extra kicked off now, they would struggle to respond.

"Sorry everyone, we have to lock down the prison. Visits, unfortunately, are cancelled for the time being," Emily calls out and we hear a group sigh reverberate around the centre, some swearing and one prisoner beginning to argue. But Emily holds her own and shuts any argument down.

"You heard the code, guys. We have to lock down." I'm thankful that the current prisoners in the centre don't include trouble makers. It appears that most of them are fairly new and the only two long termers are both in their sixties and mostly beyond confrontation. We shuffle all the prisoners to the back and begin to process them, most clearly not happy. But unfortunately, our hands were tied and they seemed to understand. A couple of officers had been allocated to help us return the crooks back to their respective units and the visits centre is cleared out by the time we return from our first drop off.

THE CODE STAYS in place for the rest of the day and the prison remains in lock down. All up, there were four officers hurt, three requiring medical attention, five prisoners hurt with four needing medical attention. The unit also had OC spray deployed and would need to be decontaminated. A number of staff were overcome by the effects and also took the rest of the day off. There were several ambulances deployed to ferry the injured to hospital and extra officers deployed to assist with all the moves. The five prisoners who attacked staff were all quickly isolated and removed from the prison entirely, being immediately transported to another nearby maximum-security facility.

BOTH ROGER and I are redeployed to help with afternoon moves, medical rounds and meals. We each escort a medical trolley to a unit and conduct medical rounds trap to trap. It's a long process but just how it is during a lock down.

MY LEGS ARE WELL and truly aware of the walking they do for the final few hours and I am glad once the final muster is finished.

. . .

Today was not a good day.

## SATURDAY, JULY 7

CALLED IN FOR OVERTIME. Worked as a General Duties Officer and thus, had several duties throughout the day. The prison has returned to normal after the drama from previous days. I check my emails as soon as I get in and read up about all those injured, confirming all are doing well. All have left hospital except for one and he is doing OK and in very good spirits. I run into Supervisor Bruce Stephens while walking to my first duty and he whispers that Shane Roberts had been suspended pending an investigation into the rapes of the two boys the previous month (see June Edition). I shake my head. Why would anyone want to throw away a twenty-year career for the sake of plain bad attitude and laziness? We shake hands and part ways, him to his unit, me to the medical wing to escort a medical trolley to a unit for morning medications once count is called correct.

I ESCORT the nurse and her trolley to Tambo East and as we enter the unit there is silence. A couple of crooks are milling around the toasters and one is on the exercise bike in the far corner. A few are sitting around a couple of tables eating breakfast but other than a couple whispering to each other, the unit is quiet. The nurse wheels the trolley into her dispensing room and I give the officers in the station the thumbs up to call the prisoners down for morning medication. They comply and within a couple of minutes there is a neat line outside the door. It feels eerie to have no noise and it's a little unsettling. It almost feels like something is in the air but I try not to let it bug me too much. Each prisoner comes in, shows their ID card and then, after downing their pills, present their open mouth to me for inspection. One prisoner has forgotten his ID card but rather than firing up, simply walks back to his cell and gets it, returning a short time later. He goes through the motions of getting his meds and all prisoners are finished shortly after. I look at the officers in the station and hold my hands up in a "what's going on" gesture and they shrug their shoulders in a "Don't know" reply. I wave bye to them and the nurse and I head next door to Tambo West.

"Chalk and cheese" are the only way I can describe the transition from one unit to the next and the units are practically next door to each other. We can hear the shouting even before we open the doors and the nurse looks at me, grinning.

"Wow," is all I can manage. She enters her dispensing room and I enter the unit to find two prisoners yelling at each other on the top tier from within each of their cell doors. It appears that one had been offered a single cell on the bottom tier and the other believed he was more entitled to it. Single cells are a valued commodity. You could sleep in peace, shit in peace, masturbate in peace without constantly having to hide or keep quiet or hold your shit in for 10 hours because you simply didn't need to go during unlock.

When a prisoner transfers into a unit, their name is added to the bottom of the "single cell" list and once your name reaches the top, you are offered the next available single cell when a prisoner transfers out. Sometimes, the wait can be months and so, things can get quite heated when someone believes they are entitled to one more than someone else. In this case, prisoner Wiebeck believed he had a claim to cell 11 over prisoner Earnshaw. One officer, Tom Barkley, was standing next to Earnshaw, red-faced, flustered and unsure of what to do. Another officer, Mike Renshaw, was yelling for Wiebeck to shut the hell up and come down to the station before he called a code. The third officer, Amy Smith, waved at me and called for morning medications.

Renshaw ended up going up to the top tier and locked Wiebeck down until he calmed down. Wiebeck followed all instruction so as not to cop a disciplinary charge and quietened down once the cell door was locked. Earnshaw wanted to continue and was told to let it go and move his shit to the new cell.

Meanwhile, a couple of the prisoners decided they wanted different doses to what the doctor had prescribed and were voicing their dismay at the nurse for not doing as they said. Funny that. They will try though. The nurse held her own and put them back in their place, telling them to make another appointment with the doctor. They gave up and complied with her requests, taking their meds and presenting to me. Another prisoner, Fraser, took his pills, turned to me and quickly walked off, but I had seen the flash of red capsule, calling him back to show me his mouth a second time. He did and the capsule was gone. Again, funny that.

When we finish our allocation of units, I escort the nurse back to the medical wing and bid her farewell. I next have gate duty in the quadrangle for an hour. There are a number of gates that have adjoining building and corridors, all needing access to protection and main streamers alike. As they couldn't mix, we had to act as traffic lights, halting some gates while releasing others. Main streamers loved hanging out at their gates while protection prisoners filed past, giving them everything they had. It would be scary to think of what could happen if we allowed them in. Or if someone screwed up and mixed them.

I MAN THE gates for an hour, monitoring my radio for movement requests and allocating gates to open and close as needed, each one opened by hand with a key. Two other officers help and open gates as I allocate them. We take it in turns with who opens and closes gates and who monitors the radio and in a very short time, the hour is up. It's all fun and games.

ONCE I FINISH THE GATES, I have a spare hour before lunchtime count and I go to Visits and see if they need a hand. The Duty Sup will radio if he needs me, his daily work sheet highlighting when officers are available. I enter the unit just as a code mike is called in Tambo West. As I am on general duties and in between jobs, I head over to see if I can lend a hand. As I enter the unit, I see officers standing at a cell door on the bottom tier, cell 11. I begin to help another officer lock down prisoners. Code mikes are normally just medical and don't require units to be locked down, but another officer asks me to help and I comply. I find out after that shortly after the nurse and I had left the unit, Earnshaw had moved all his belongings down to his new cell and Wiebeck was compliant and was allowed out of his cell. The officers had seen Wiebeck shake Earnshaw's hand then proceed to jump on the exercise bike for an hour. Without making it obvious, Wiebeck had jumped off the bike at some point and entered Earnshaw's new cell. He was quite a bit bigger than Earnshaw and probably scared the smaller prisoner into submission. He had simply snapped the interior lock in place, grabbed the smaller prisoner, then forced him onto the bed, raping him repeatedly for around thirty minutes. The Tactical boys already had Wiebeck and were walking him out of his cell and down the stairs. Earnshaw was lying face down on his bed, blood on his buttocks and the bed linen. A nurse was inspecting his butt and the duty sup was on the phone, probably calling an ambulance.

A STRETCHER IS WHEELED into the unit and Earnshaw hobbles onto it, face down. A couple of prisoners start hooting, obviously more on Team Wiebeck than Team Earnshaw, but one look from an officer and they call it off. The stretcher is wheeled out a short time later and eventually Earnshaw is taken to hospital. He returned later that night and was taken back to his cell.

LUNCHTIME COUNT IS CALLED SHORTLY after and I stay in the unit to help out with muster and subsequent lunch through traps. The cell is a crime scene and Intel staff inspect it before anything else. The unit is eventually unlocked and it goes back to normal quite quickly. I leave to meet the nurse and commence afternoon meds.

WE HEAD to Campaspe unit first and as we enter the unit, I see one officer on the top tier, doing a security walk. Another officer is sitting in the station and the third is in the office. The station officer sees me and beckons me over. I don't know them. I walk over and introduce myself, finding out he is from the new course, Frank Turner. He asks me to go and see the officer in the office as she doesn't seem to be quite right.

I WALK to the office and walk in, the smell of alcohol quite strong. The officer is sitting at the desk and smiles when she sees me. It's Thelma. Hey eyes are bloodshot and she is eating a bowl of grapes.

"Everything OK, Thelma?" I ask her.

"All good mate," she replies, but her voice is garbled, her eyes opening and closing in a tired, worn out parody.

"Grape?" she offers, holding up the bowl. I oblige and take one, popping it in my mouth. I sit and am about to ask her if she needs help, when the taste of vodka fills my mouth. Its strong and bitter taste instantly overtaking my mouth. I spit the grape out in my hand and am about to ask her something when the duty sup enters. He takes one look and asks me to escort Thelma back to his office. She tries to grab her grapes but he takes them first. She gives him a disgusted look but follows me out of the office and out of the unit. A couple of prisoners start laughing as we walk past and mutter something unintelligible. Thelma is half staggering as she hangs on to my arm. We don't speak and I take her to the duty sup's office and sit with her. Eventually we get a call from the duty sup to say Thelma's husband is waiting out the front of the prison and she is escorted out.

It turns out, Thelma had been injecting vodka into her grapes and was smuggling them in through the front in her lunch box. No one had ever checked them and she had been able to sneak them in for God knows how long. She is suspended pending an investigation. Thelma's special grapes will probably turn into an urban legend eventually. Hopefully she doesn't lose her job completely. Although I don't like her chances for keeping it.

Another officer had finished my afternoon medical run and I complete my afternoon by returning to Campaspe where they are now an officer short. The other two are busy chatting when I come back in and both begin questioning me when I enter the station. Having an officer drunk on duty is not an everyday occurrence and before long, the phone begins to ring with inquisitive questions. We spend the afternoon answering a multitude of questions over the phone and have multiple visitors drop in.

It's just as well that the afternoon goes by incident free and the prisoners leave us to our own devices. It ended up being a strange day considering all that happened and as I drive home that night, I think about what would make an officer feel so depressed that they would consider smuggling alcohol into a prison to then get pissed on the job, not only endangering yourself but the officers around you.

## SUNDAY, JULY 8

Today I was rostered in Reception. It is located at the front of the prison and is outside the walls hence no prisoner contact. There are six officers working in the front area and one x-ray officer who sits behind a partition and scans all bags and personal items through an x-ray machine. The security measures that are in place to ensure there's no contraband smuggled in to the prison include random pat downs, random strip searches, a metal detector called a wand waved over each person, contraband detection dogs, x-ray machine and random drug swabs. I am assigned to the x-ray machine and being a Saturday know that the day will be a massive one. It is one of the biggest visitor days and most sessions in the visits centre are booked out solid. I begin my shift at 7am, just in time to check the bulk of the day staff coming on for their shift and it's a nonstop process for a solid hour.

Once count is correct, we beckon visitors to come in and we begin processing each one. There are Mums, Dads, sons, daughters, friends and whole families. Some are friendly while some are not so friendly.

Others can be downright painful. Especially like one Mum who we weren't processing quick enough.

"Can you hurry up? Here to see my fuckin son," she barks at the crew.

"Please don't swear at me. You won't miss out." Samantha responds to the lady calmly and you just know she gets more wound up. She waves at her to come forward and the detection dog gives her a once over. Samantha then takes a swab of her purse, running the detector tab along all sides, as well as her hands. Another officer, James, gives the lady a pat down and asks her to turn her pockets inside out, which she does, frowning and mumbling under her breath. Samantha comes back a couple of minutes later and informs the lady that her swab returned a positive reading for Cocaine and her visit would be switched to a boxed visit. She begins to holler and complain, her voice becoming louder and louder, but she knows it's no use. If she causes too much of a scene then her visit will be cancelled altogether and she gives in, again mumbling under her breath. She is led through to a holding room with another group and eventually escorted to the visits area.

THE DAY IS long and doesn't let up. I run the x-ray machine for the bulk of the day, only taking a break for lunch and a short stint running the wand for an hour. There really isn't much to say about today. It's just a busy day of processing visitors without any flare ups or incidents. We hear a couple of code mikes in the prison but they are normal run of the mill codes with nothing really to report. One was a bit bizarre where a prisoner was doing push ups with his feet up on a chair. He apparently was trying to impress his mates and was clapping his hands in between each push up and ended up falling down flat on his face, two teeth snapped on the concrete floor and cutting his lip quite badly.

. . .

Other than that, it was a run of the mill day and I'd rather not bore you with filling each page with meaningless words that won't hold your interest.

# WEDNESDAY, JULY 11

Today I was called in for overtime and chose Visits again. I enjoy working in here, especially if I'm out the back. It's like a little hidden world, away from the outside. It's just a place to do your processes and go home. Raj is with me again and I greet him as I walk in. Russel Rawsley is there as well and we shake hands.

"You are going to love today, Mr. King, Sir," Raj says to me, beaming a moon smile at me.

"Why?" I ask. He holds a sheet of paper out to me. My smile grows as I inspect it. All the visits for that day fill less than half the page. 14 in total.

"What?" I say, but my smile remains intact. Vanessa Green walks in from the front.

"Morning Gents. How do you like the list for the day?"

"Is this for real?" I ask her and she nods. I fist pump the air.

"Now that is the sort of OT I like." I add.

"That list and OT? Lucky fuck," Russel says disgusted but he is joking, slapping me on the back as he walks passed me.

"Why so small?" I ask of Vanessa and she shrugs her shoulders. I don't complain and put my bag away. We have 6 prisoners between now and lunch and then 8 for the afternoon, the last booked in for

4.30. I find out later that the visits booking system malfunctioned and all visits were scrubbed, only able to be re-booked the day before. There wasn't enough time to fill the schedule so we have been given a gift and no-one complains.

THE FIRST COUPLE of prisoners enter soon after and Raj and I process them while Russel mans the book. I strip my prisoner, inspect his clothing, check him and allow him to redress himself. He heads inside almost skipping. Raj finished his as another two prisoners enter. I repeat the process and within five minutes we are two thirds through our morning work load. I follow the prisoner through the door and go and sit in the officer's station in the visit's hall, greeting the officers there. Vanessa is monitoring the screens and judging by the quietness of the room, doubt whether she needs to focus too hard. There are only four prisoners and only one has more than one visitor.

WE TALK shit for an hour or so, even giving the prisoners a little extra time. The others ask me about Thelma and I tell them what I know. It's a sad story and we don't dwell on it too long. After giving the prisoners and extra twenty or so minutes we take them back and reprocess them back in. They all check out clean and as we send them out, our last two for the morning come in. They are processed and in to their visitors in a few minutes. Lunchtime muster occurs during their visit and again we give them extra time. Once their time is up, we usher them back to the strip rooms and they are all jovial, happy to have been given extra time. They are finished and leave the building as we wait for the afternoon rush to come.

THE AFTERNOON IS EVEN BETTER than the morning. The prisoners come in dribs and drabs and we process each as they arrive. It's almost one at a time for most of the afternoon and only once do we have two at once. Once the last is processed and out the door, we sit around again and talk shit for a while. We all know that some days in here can be trying, busy and quite confronting when crooks or visitors get pissed off, but today is definitely not one of those days.

I DRIVE HOME LATER that evening whistling, happy to have a fatter pay check and happy that the day went so well.

TODAY WAS A GOOD DAY.

# THURSDAY, JULY 12

TODAY I WAS ROSTERED in Admissions. I know just what to expect as I make my way there, knowing I will be staring at penises again all day. It's a funny place to work with some of the humour thrown around certainly not fit for human consumption. If the things said inside prison were spoken out in the real world, you could bet that people would find themselves out on their ear in no time. For some reason, things are just accepted in prison though.

I GO and see the officer that has the day's run sheet and see that the day is pretty average. There are around 20 courts for the morning and then around the same transferring out of the prison after muster. The afternoon has around a dozen or so prisoners transferring in to the prison. Compared to some days, it can be seen as a fairly easy day. This week was starting to look like a cruise in the park, although nowhere near as easy as the week between Christmas and New Year when the transfers and courts come to an almost stand still.

WE BEGIN PROCESSING courts almost immediately, stripping each one and placing them into a holding cell. It's a little after 6 and everyone is still sleepy, so no one is really thinking about firing up. The process doesn't take too long and before the sun is even rising, we are helping to load the prisoners on to their respective buses. Once all the prisoners are all loaded, we have breakfast.

COUNT IS CALLED and as we are empty, it's just a simple waiting game for us until it's called correct. Once it is, we wait for our transfers to make their way up to admissions and we begin the task of processing them out. They bring all their property from their cell up with them and we have the rest of their property stored in a tub. Once they are up here, it's just a simple process of marking off a checklist to ensure they still have everything they took to their cell or deleting what they have disposed of. It's also the perfect time to see just who has been helping themselves to other people's property via stand-overs or theft. There are usually a couple per day and today is no different. One crook in particular has four different pairs of runners, 3 Nike and 1 Asics, yet there are only a single pair of prison issue runners on his property sheet. After quite a bit of arguing back and forth, he finally gives in and surrenders 3 pairs, being allowed to keep 1. Of course, he chooses the most expensive looking Nikes.

ALL THE TRANSFERS are eventually processed and sitting in their cells waiting for their buses, again, each heading in a different direction. They start to get restless around 11 o'clock and begin banging on their cell doors. Some of the officers do the rounds, letting them know that the buses shouldn't be too far away, but we don't know how long they will be and pretty soon the building is echoing to the sounds of cell door bashing. The clanging reverberates through the corridors makes conversation difficult. Fortunately for us, it's not our first day and we know how to sweet talk them, bribing them into silence. Lunch. We simply start to hand out sandwiches to the prisoners and pretty soon admissions is sweetly quiet, like a day care centre during afternoon nap.

SHORTLY AFTER, the buses begin rolling in and we load each as they show up. Within half an hour, we are empty again, all transfers now out for their road trips. Lunchtime muster is called shortly after and again we pull the lucky straw, being empty of prisoners. It is called incorrect some 20 minutes later and we wait as the prison conducts a recount. It is finally called correct 45 minutes late. Immediately upon correct, buses begin to roll in with some of our afternoon transfers. There are 4 from one jail and 2 from another. There is also a third bus with a couple of court returns. Once the paperwork is all checked out, we begin taking them off the buses and putting them into individual cells until they can be properly inducted. The court returns are taken around to the strip rooms and processed back into the jail. I take one and another officer takes another. I begin the stripping process, then hear the officer next to me begin his. He is fairly new but has never worked in admissions before. He has a spotter just like me but he is being allowed to run it his way.

"OK, let's strip down to your birthday suit and hand me your clothing," he begins. The prisoner must have been having a bad day because he begins heckling the officer instead.

"Want me to strip, you homo fuck? Like this?" he says as he strips his pants and jumper, tossing each item to the officer who in turn passes it behind him to his spotter for inspection. "Like what you see, faggoty freak?". The officer doesn't speak, but continues with the strip. The prisoner is naked now and grabs his dick, twirling it around in a circle.

"Could you stop masturbating and let me conduct this strip search?" he finally says and the prisoner starts yelling more abuse.

"I bet you'd love me to masturbate for you. Love what you see?" he says and the officer fires back just as fast.

"I'm sorry, I don't have my glasses on, I can't see it." He then beckons for the prisoner to present his fingers, hands, open mouth, arm pits, penis, butt and feet for inspection and completes the process. When the prisoners are gone, I pat him on the back and congratulate him for keeping his cool. He did well under the circumstances and he thanks me for the compliment.

All of a sudden there is a commotion coming from one of the main cells where there are four prisoners held. One of the officers lowers the trap and peers inside, immediately withdrawing, holding his nose.

"Boss, he shit himself," comes through the trap and upon looking inside, I see three prisoners holding their noses, almost climbing the wall. I crack the door and wave them out, placing them in the adjoining cell. The stench is unbelievably strong, the fourth prisoner deciding he wanted to let rip in his pants. He simply sat on the bench watching as the others filed out, not embarrassed in the least. I close the door again and am glad not to be a regular. They would need to take him out, have him wash and change and then interview him. Another bus arrives and it is more courts. We take them off and into the building, filing past shit pants, and take them to the strip rooms. They are all processed and returned to their units within a few minutes. Shit pants is escorted through to a holding cell with a shower and given a new set of clothes, the soiled ones bagged in a haz-mat bag. Once he is finished, he is also processed and soon in his new unit.

The rest of the day is a similar process and no events worth mentioning.

Today was a good day.

# FRIDAY, JULY 13

TODAY I WAS ROSTERED as a Urinalysis Officer. In laymen terms, I was going to be conducting piss tests all day. But today was Friday the 13th and of course nothing was going to be as simple as that. There were two teams of piss testers and each team consisted off three officers. One who would be manning the booth and contacting units to send prisoners up, the other two actually conducting the tests. My offsider? Tony Malone (see June Edition). I literally groaned inside when I saw him. All I could ask myself was who had I pissed off to deserve this. But I knew there was nothing I could do, so I shook hands with him and the other officer and we checked our list. We had 30 names on it and planned our strategy for the day. Who we would start with, which units and where we would end? Once we had finished, Tony and I entered the test room and the third officer went into the booth and began contacting units. We ensured we had all the equipment in good supply and ensured we wouldn't run out of anything.

THE FIRST PRISONER arrives and we take him into the test room. Our first job is to strip him and ensure he doesn't have anything on him to adulterate the sample. Or possess a clean sample which to substitute for his own. Prisoners have many varied and ingenious ways with which to mess with the urinalysis process. The most common is to cut the finger off a rubber glove and have a clean prisoner piss into it. They then tie it off and somehow hide it on their person, the methods of which are numerous. It takes a very alert officer to pick up a fake sample. But it does happen quite frequently so we remain vigilant. I start the stripping process and Tony takes care of bagging the sample once we have it.

THE ROOM IS SET up in such a way that the officers have a perfect view of the prisoner no matter which way he turns. There is a toilet in the far corner and a convex mirror hanging on the wall above. When the prisoner turns to urinate, we can still keep an eye on what they are doing. The prisoner strips for me and I inspect every piece of clothing he has. I then inspect him from a distance, paying particular attention to his anus, underside of his penis and foreskin, common hiding places. They all check out and he gets dressed again. He grabs a jar and urinates into it. Once he finishes, Tony seals and labels the jar then seals and labels a sample bag. The prisoner signs each process and once completed is allowed to return to his unit. When we let him out, there are already 3 prisoners waiting in holding cells. We ask each if they are ready to piss and one of them is. We lead him into the room and repeat the process, paying particular attention to his underwear and pockets of his track-pants. They all check out and he takes a jar and immediately begins to urinate.

WE REPEAT the process once he is finished and when he leaves the test room, we are down to 28 to finish. We do our rounds of the holding cells and another one is happy to have a go. We lead him into the room and he seems a little too keen to begin. My senses are instantly peaked when he is smiling and laughing about having to do a piss test. But his strip checks out fine and he produces as asked. Nothing out of the ordinary. We finish bagging and tagging his sample and lead him out of the room. As he passes the holding cells "All good, Boys" to the prisoners in the cells and walks out. Now I know something is up. I ask Tony if his sample was warm and he nods.

"Think he got one by us?" he asks.

"I know he got one by us." I reply. "Just don't know how." I add. We knock on a couple more cells and another prisoner is given the go ahead to produce. I switch positions with Tony this time to try and see a different point of view. The prisoner again is all smiles and complies with Tony's requests. I can sense something is odd but am unsure of what. He takes a jar and turns toward the toilet, shielding himself from our eyes. We can see the mirror but can't quite make out his hands and penis. I can see that he is fiddling a bit and sneak over while he is concentrating and looking down. I peer around his body and cringe. Sticking out of the end of his dick are three straws, each with a tiny eraser you find at the end of pencils, jammed into the end.

"I'll take those," I say and the prisoner just about jumps into the toilet bowl, completely unaware that I was there. He was trying to unplug the straws and hadn't heard me. He pulls all three straws out and tries to throw them in the toilet but I grab his arm and Tony grabs the straws. We are gloved up, by the way. He surrenders and gives up, the smile finally leaving his face.

"How the hell did you jam them down there?" I ask but he isn't talking. We lead him back to a holding cell and inform him he will be waiting for the Sup.

"Nice job," I say to Tony and he smiles back. We bag the straws, each one cut down to around 4 inches and it looks like they are melted closed at one end. Together, the 3 straws held just enough urine for the sample to be sufficient. As we bag the evidence, I wonder how many more of the prisoners had hidden samples shoved down their piss holes. I cringe again.

WE ASK the cells again and another prisoner volunteers. He is morbidly obese and is out of breath after walking the 20 or so steps from the holding cell to the piss room. I can see as soon as he turns to piss that he isn't hiding any straws in his penis. For one, it is almost completely hidden and only about an inch visible. The other reason? He cannot reach it. He struggles to reach it with one hand while trying to twist as hard as he can but it is almost near impossible. He exhales loudly and manages to just grip the head, grunting and groaning while trying to keep a hold of it. He farts loudly from the straining, apologises, then tries again to grab it after it slides out of his reach as he breathes. I ask him if he will able to piss and he says he will manage, just to give him some time. We oblige and wait. He takes another 5 or so minutes to finally manage to hold the jar and piss enough urine into it to be accepted. He washes the jar then hands it to me and I label and bag it, him signing each step. We escort him to the door and another one is done.

We continue to process urine tests for the morning with little fanfare. All the prisoners except one are able to produce on demand. The one that cannot produce, Stan Sutcliff, has three hours to produce and remains in the cell during muster. We ask him again once muster is correct and he refuses. He has an hour left and is happy to wait. We continue to process the ones called up and we get through another 8. Stan has just 5 minutes left when we ask him a final time and he is happy to give it another go. We walk him into the room and do the strip. Once done he turns to the toilet with his pants around his ankles, desperately trying to piss. He stands there for a good two minutes, his face getting redder and redder.

"I'm trying, Boss." he cries, the strain visible on his face.

"Last chance, Stan. You've had 3 hours man," I say and he gives an almighty groan as his teeth clench, his face grimaces and he turns purple. He farts, jerks forward and a turd comes shooting out of his arse, hitting the floor sideways. The officer in the booth begins to bellow and Tony starts gagging. Stan begins to apologise profusely, bends and scoops it up in his bare hands. I throw him some toilet paper and squeeze my nose shut. He wipes the floor and deposits the turd into the toilet, flushing it away. The only thought that comes to my mind is that I don't get paid enough for this.

THE REST of the day is nothing compared to finding straws jammed down the eye of a dick, fat guys who can't reach their dicks and being fired upon with turd projectiles. The Sup drops by a couple of hours later and notifies the crook that he will be charged with interfering with a urinalysis test and returned to his unit. We end the day by completing 27 of the 30 assigned and are happy when the day is over. It really is a shitty day and I whistle as I drive out of the place.

# TUESDAY, JULY 17

TODAY I WAS ROSTERED in Campaspe. Not a very exciting shift and more frustration than anything else. For one, being a main stream unit, you are stuck in the officer's station for pretty much the entire shift.

It begins to get really monotonous after an hour or so and by lunchtime you are ready to put on a white jacket. Backwards. I am rostered with Vanessa Green and Russel Rawsley and am grateful that I have someone to chat to at least.

We begin with morning muster and it's called correct a short time later. I begin to unlock the cells as Vanessa begins to get things ready for the moves around the prison. Being a main stream unit, prisoners don't need to be escorted but are allowed to move around themselves as long as they are in possession of their ID card. The ID card has a bar code and some of the gates have readers on them making their move less of a hassle. They can get to far more places alone. That makes it easier on officers, but unfortunately it also means we don't get to leave the unit for escorts. For me personally, I prefer protection so you can at least leave the unit occasionally to go and escort a crook.

The day turns out to be nothing more than a simple run-of-the mill shift, which makes it very good for us, but not so much for you.

## WEDNESDAY, JULY 18

Today I was rostered in Admissions again. As I walked into the unit, Raj met me and I learn that he has been offered a permanent gig in here. I congratulate him and put my things away. He tells me that the list for today is quite decent and when I see it, know what he means. There are 32 courts, 28 outgoing transfers and 24 incoming transfers. I put on some gloves and join the crew already processing the courts. Raj is stripping so I offer to spot for him. He is becoming a lot more confident, even able to tell some jokes along the way. As we finish stripping each prisoner, I point them towards the next officer that walks them to their allocated cell to wait for their ride. It becomes almost a production line with some officers standing at the counter handing out clothes, others stripping and spotting, some walking crooks to their cells and others out loading buses as they show up. A couple of prisoners fire up slightly at not being allowed to take books on the bus but rules are rules and they are stowed in their property box.

It takes a good hour and a half to process all the courts, but all eventually leave on their bus, leaving admissions nice and quiet as morning count is called. A short time later there is a recount called and we quickly do a walk around to ensure we truly are empty. We are empty and breathe a sigh of relief. The fault is elsewhere. The problem with a late morning count and unlock is that the prisoners require 12 hours of unlock per day. A late unlock means a late lock up and the longer it takes, the longer the units remain unlocked. This doesn't affect us here though, as we have set times to work and no lock ups to worry about. A few minutes later count is called correct and we await the arrival of our outgoing transfers.

ITS 10 MINUTES later and the first of the transfers begin to roll in. Some with a little property and some with a lot. It's funny how prison works. A beefy guy shows up and he carries 2 or 3 bags of property. A small and wiry guy turns up and he carries half a bag. It's when a small guy turns up wheeling a tub full of bags that you begin to question the norm. You know that it's either that he is a really friendly kind of guy, or he has the ability to provide either sexual favours or drug related favours. And you can normally tell which. I try not to get involved in that side though as I am here to strip, and strip is what I do. Raj and I swap roles and it's my turn to live some nakedness. I begin to strip them then Raj walks them to their cells. The process repeats many times over, one prisoner leading to the next and so on. It becomes a repeating highlights reel of naked dicks and butts as I strip one then another and another. Nothing found, nothing said, nothing noted. Just one after the other. Half way through, Raj and I again swap and he takes the helm.

IT GOES on like that for the better part of the morning until we finally process the last one. Once I close the cell, I sit and take a break with the rest of the crew, enjoying my first cup of coffee since the last one at home. It's 11.30 and the crooks are already banging up, asking where the buses are. Again, we shut them up with food, the sandwiches fulfilling their double duties. Lunchtime count is called shortly after and we do the rounds in pairs, Raj and I teaming up, him dropping traps and me writing the numbers. Once we have finished, I take the number, 28, to the person on the book and they call it in to control once they have confirmed the number with a couple of other teams. We talk shit as we await count correct. 10 minutes later count is called incorrect and we repeat the process, changing team members. I pair up with Gary Dales, a regular in here. Raj teams up with an officer from the last course, Jude Trevally. I drop the traps and Gary takes the numbers down. Once we complete our second circuit, he confirms the number as 28. Again, that sigh of relief. The book calls it in shortly after and we sit around once more, talking shit again. 10 minutes later and count is called incorrect once more.

When a count is called incorrect a second time, units are required to swap with nearby units to ensure they aren't making the same mistake. We all head outside and swap with Tambo West, and their staff go and conduct the admissions count. Gary and I decide to stay as a team and do the rounds. When finished we ensure everyone has the same number, 51, and I call it in to control. We patiently wait in silence and let out a unified groan as count is called incorrect again.

"For fuck sake," Gary said, frustrated.

"How hard is it to count heads," I said. We repeat the process a second time then call in the same number, 51. Count has now been going for over 45 minutes and I could just imagine the line of buses sitting outside the jail. We sit around some more, literally twiddling our thumbs and when count is called incorrect again, almost throw our radios at the wall. With 4 counts now incorrect, we return to our respective units and conduct an ID in hand muster. Every prisoner is identified individually with the muster and their ID. We head back into admissions and are told that the count is one under. That means someone is missing and could mean an escape of some sort. With these many recounts, managers and higher are all involved as an escape could mean severe repercussions. We conduct our recount and given the complexity, it takes a good 40 minutes to finish. It is now close to two hours late. Some of the crooks voice their frustration as we conduct the count and we tell them there is nothing we can do. They have to grin and bear it just like us.

JUST AS WE are about to count the last cell, I hear a string of profanity from the far end of admissions.

"What the fuck are you doing in here? Who put you in there?" We all walk over and see a small Asian prisoner, maybe 25 years old. He is pointing at his mouth and shaking his head. He doesn't speak English. He had been locked in a small toilet, situated in one of the far corners of the admissions area. The prisoner looked around and pointed at Jude Trevally. The person who unlocked him is a manager, Shane Thompson.

"Did you put him in there?" Shane asks of Jude. Jude is the shade of scarlet and looking very nervous.

"He needed to go to the toilet and all the cells were full." he said defensively.

"So, you shove him into a staff toilet for one, then leave him in there and forget about him completely. Is that right?" Shane said, clearly pissed off. "THIS COUNT HAS BEEN GOING FOR OVER 2 FUCKING HOURS!" he yells. Jude just looks at the floor and remains quiet. Shane takes his radio and calls it in to control. A second later count is called correct. People disperse and head off to other areas, leaving Jude to himself. A golden rule when new is ASK. If you are unsure of what to do then ask someone. Jude will no doubt receive a written warning for this little fuck up, but at least he will learn from it.

THE BUSES BEGIN ROLLING UP ALMOST IMMEDIATELY and all the drivers begin questioning the delay. There is a lot of chatter, laughter, whispers and pointing as the story is relayed. Jude takes it on the chin and even joins in some of the banter. After all, it was a simple fuck up and it has been corrected. Given that it was the middle of the day, it didn't interrupt everyone's day too much. If it had of been at the end of the shift at lock up, then that would have been a disaster.

THE PRISONERS ARE all loaded an hour or so later and a number of court returns are processed along the way. There are still a few courts to return and they will keep us busy throughout the afternoon. The good thing is, that day's midday muster is the only excitement to report to you. The rest of the day went smooth and involved nothing more than more stripping, more processing and more counts. Nothing that you haven't heard before and nothing that you will miss out on not reading about.

TODAY WAS AN INTERESTING DAY.

## THURSDAY, JULY 19

TODAY I WAS ROSTERED in Loddon North, a protection unit and mostly filled with prisoners who have been in the system for a long time. Not a lot of changes occur in there and the unit tends to run quite smoothly because of it. Incoming transfers have been known to upset the apple cart at times and not having them means things remain the same. The prisoners in the unit are mostly rated as sex predators, mostly charged with sex crimes involving rape, incest and paedophilia. I find it easiest to work in these units when I don't know the charges for individual prisoners. There are of course the high-profile ones that everyone recognises and those you deal with as they come up but for the most part, I don't know them and I don't know what they are in for specifically.

I AM JOINED in the unit by two other officers, Rob Delaney, an officer from my intake course and Rachel Ward. They are both normal officers in this unit and it will make the day that much easier. We meet and greet and have a quick catch up before morning count is called which Rachel and I undertake. I grab the muster and Rachel opens the traps. We start on the bottom tier and tick off the names, then head upstairs. We are about half way through when Rachel opens a trap to cell 32. The name on the door reads Smith and it doesn't mean anything to me. Rachel tells me one, as in one prisoner and is about to close it again when I hear a soft voice come through.

"Scuse me, Miss.?" She stops and peers back in. It is quite dark in the cell and she can make out the prisoner standing towards the back of the cell.

"What's up, Greg?" she asks.

"Can you please take this?" he says and steps forward, placing something on the trap. Rachel peers at it, then takes a step back. I look at it and at first am unsure of what it is. At first, I thought it was a sausage, maybe left over from the previous night's dinner. Then my stomach turns as I come to shocking realisation what it is. It turns out to be his dick. Rachel has already got her radio to her mouth and calls an urgent code mike. I turn the lights on and see the prisoner with a large patch of blood on his pants. The penis doesn't have a clean cut and by the serrations visible, can only imagine the horror that he must have felt when removing it. He is ghostly pale and sits on his bed.

"Medical are on the way, mate." I say through the trap and we wait for the nurses to show up. We keep Greg talking and when the Sup comes in, we get the OK to crack the cell.

HE HAD USED a plastic knife to hack his penis off. The nurses begin working on him, stopping the flow of blood and the whole time he kept talking to himself.

"I don't want it anymore. I don't want it anymore." He clearly had mental issues and needed more than just medical help. The nurses do an amazing job and not only calm him down but stop the blood and get him talking about something else. A stretcher turns up and the prisoner is lifted onto it and taken out of the unit. His cell his locked and we continue with our count, now minus 1. Once we finish our count and call it in, Rachel and I begin writing our report for the

Sup regarding the morning amputation. Count is called correct and Rob heads out of the station to unlock the unit. There is a rush of feet toward the toasters and a number of prisoners turn toward us, anxious to find out what happened. Most can hear and see quite well from their cells so already know most of it anyway, but for those that don't are quickly filled in by their fellow roommates.

THE MORNING medical trolley arrives and this is one of the units where practically every single prisoner has medication. They all begin to line up and I go to supervise the operation. The one thing that always gets me in these types of units is the politeness from the prisoners. 99% of them are so well mannered that you actually appreciate working in here. That is until you remind yourself of what they are in for. The manners are probably due to the fact that if they were ever exposed to a mainstream prisoner, they would suffer some pretty severe retribution. We are the only thing standing between them and that pain.

THE NURSE BEGINS to dispense the medication and I begin to check the open mouths as they are presented to me. No one argues, no one attempts to divert and no one jumps the queue. Before I know it, everyone is dosed and back to their regular activities. A fourth officer comes into the unit and it's Raj. I greet him and he tells me he is working OT today. His first OT shift since he started and I congratulate him, a little jealous. It's always better to be working for double pay. He is here to escort a prisoner to medical and Rachel calls him up. Raj takes him and I have a read of my emails. It doesn't take me long and turn the computer off. Rob begins telling me about his upcoming holiday to Greece. I am jealous for the second time that day, a destination I have always wanted to visit. I tell him how much I love Greek history and he agrees with me. He has all the main places already on his itinerary, especially Santorini, Mykonos and Athens. I am happy for him and he shares his excitement as it is his first ever overseas holiday. Rachel agrees and also shares her passion for overseas travel. I have never been for an overseas holiday myself and understand how excited he must be.

LUNCHTIME MUSTER GOES off without a hitch, count called correct shortly after. There is a code Foxtrot called in one of the machine shops and a code mike called shortly after. That's normally how Foxtrots go. First, they have some sort of fisty-cuffs then one needs the doctor. Most of them are over before anyone can react anyway. Punch here, punch there, punch back and boom, finished. They sort it out quickly and efficiently. The afternoon med trolley arrives soon after and I again head down to give them a hand and again it all runs smoothly. Lots of thank yous, pleases and have a great day are exchanged, but no fuck yous, jam 'em nor I wants. Everyone is handed their meds, everyone swallows them and everyone returns to their activities. Now why can't every unit be like this.

THE AFTERNOON IS FAIRLY QUIET. I start to think that maybe, apart from that morning's events, we might have a perfect day. That is until we get a phone call from admissions. There is a new prisoner ready for pick up and Raj is already there ready to get him when we are ready. He was a late add on and not on the original daily list. Rachel scans the muster and allocates him to a cell on the top tier. With 3 free cells in the unit, no one is required to share. It's a good thing and keeps everyone happy. We call Raj on the radio and confirm his move. He acknowledges and begins the transfer.

THE PRISONER'S name is Gus Van Fankel. He and Raj enter the unit and judging by his body language, he was going to be trouble. He marches straight up to the desk and fronts Rachel.

"I need a single cell," he demands instantly. Rachel just stands there, staring at him. They have a bit of a stare of and he repeats himself.

"I need a single-"

"I heard you. You don't run this unit, I do. I conduct the interview," she says calmly. His face grows red and he looks a little flustered.

"Sorry, Miss. I need a single cell. I've been here before," he repeats a third time, but Rachel holds her own.

"And again, I heard you. I will conduct the induction interview and you will find out all the information you need," she says, still calm.

"But I'm just saying, I-"

"And I need you to shut your mouth," she says, cutting him off and he closes his lips, clearly not happy. He is a small wiry looking man of about 50, with round, thin wired glasses on the end of his nose and a very diminished head of hair. Rachel then proceeds to conduct the interview, telling him all about the unit rules, policies, some day to day requirements and finally his cell allocation.

"I need a cell on the bottom tier," he snaps at her, cutting her off. She takes a step back and just looks at him. Then at me and back at him.

"I have given you your cell allocation. I suggest you go to it."

"I need a bottom tier cell. I have bad knees and can't climb stairs," he starts but Rachel has switched off, closing his file and sitting at the computer.

"I suggest you go, mate," I say. A cardinal rule with officers is to always back your colleague. Whether you agree or not, always back them. Van Fankel looks at her a final time, then picks his bag up and heads for his cell. Rachel turns to me and gives me that WTF look. I know exactly what she's thinking.

I DECIDE to have a wander around the unit and begin taking a walk. I stick my head in to a couple of cells and do some welfare checks, ensuring all is OK. I then head upstairs and do the same. As I pass Van Fankel's cell, he sticks his head out.

"Excuse me, Boss?" I turn to him.

"Yes?"

"I really need a cell on the bottom tier," he says.

"Do you have a certificate?" I ask and he shakes his head.

"Never needed one before."

"Unfortunately, there are no cells available on the bottom and if you need one then you need a certificate. If you had one then you may be moved to a unit with one available." I inform him but he doesn't like my answer.

"But I have really bad-"

"You don't like listening, do you?" I ask him.

"Fine. I'll go on a hunger strike then," he says folding his arms.

"You do that. But unless you make an appointment to see the doctor, then there is nothing anyone can do," I say and continue my walk. He slams the cell door closed and the bang reverberates around the unit. I look at the station and Rachel looks at me and rolls her eyes. Rob just shakes his head. I finish my walk and head back to the station, taking a seat and accepting the coffee Rob hands me.

"What a fuckwit," he adds. I agree with him and sip. We spend the rest of the afternoon relaxing, not much activity happening until the afternoon medication trolley turns up. Everyone lines up except our new arrival, his door staying closed. Rob heads to the line and conducts mouth inspections, everyone presenting as per the previous rounds and it's all over quite quickly.

AFTERNOON MUSTER IS CALLED SOON after and everyone stands by their doors. Rachel buzzes Van Fankel on the intercom but all she can hear is a muffled grunt. She asks him again to stand by his open door and the response is more aggravated, still muffled grunting. I take the muster sheet and begin walking cell to cell. When I reach Van Fankel's closed door, I tap it but it doesn't open. I take out my key and override his internal lock. I open the door and see him standing in the middle of his cell, arms by his side, just looking at me.

"You coming out?" I ask him and he grunts.

"Is that a yes?" and he grunts louder. He takes a step towards me and when I see the issue, I nearly drop the muster sheet. I cannot stop the smile that lands on my face, a small chuckle escaping as I try and speak.

"Would you...like me to-" but I can't continue, the laugh getting caught in my throat. Rob and Rachel are looking up from below and cannot see what I can see. I wave them up, hanging on to the hand rail. Rob reaches the cell first and immediately turns back when he sees. Rachel doesn't.

"I suppose you think that's gonna help you in some way," she says, pissed off. He grunts again, more aggravated. She pulls out her radio and for the second time that day, calls a code mike. Gus Van Fankel has sewn his lips shut.

NOW AT LEAST we knew why he couldn't answer us over the intercom. He had done a pretty good job and the stitches looked neat and in line, almost OCD level. The unit becomes a buzz as he exits his cell and hangs on to rail, other prisoners cackling, hooting and cheering. Gus's face remains stony, his demeanour never changing. The Sup, Clare, enters the unit and one look tells her all she needs to know. The medical team arrive and OK the Tac boys to escort the prisoner to the medical unit under his own steam and he walks out with his escort, giving Rachel one final glare.

WE FINISH count and it is called correct almost as soon as we call it in, control obviously waiting for us. The evening goes smoothly and uneventful. We receive a phone call from Clare ab out an hour later to say that Gus was coming back. The doctor refused his request for a medical and apparently, he tried to say he felt in danger as Rachel and I had bullied him on his arrival. Clare refused his request and said he would be returning to his allocated cell. He entered the unit a short time later and didn't peep a word. He didn't even look in our direction.

FINAL LOCK UP came and went and we all walked out together, still laughing, almost in stitches about..the stitches.

## MONDAY, JULY 23

TODAY I WAS sick and have taken a couple of days off. It's a cold and the headache is what gifts me with a medical certificate for two days. The mental image of a penis sitting on the trap is also still playing on my mind and I try hard to block it out. I'm not sure what would prompt someone to slice off their own appendage, but with a plastic knife??

## TUESDAY, JULY 24

TODAY IS my second sick day. I still feel pretty shitty and decide not to put myself down for overtime.

## FRIDAY, JULY 27

TODAY I WAS ROSTERED BACK in Loddon North. I am more than a little excited to see how Gus ended up. He seemed so intent on trying to manipulate the system, I'm more than interested to see if he succeeded. As I enter the unit, I see Rachel already at the officer's station and she gives me a thumbs up as she sees me. I point up to Gus's cell, she looks up over her shoulder and makes a growling face. She points at a cell in the bottom corner and I realise he must have gotten his way, somehow.

"How?" I ask as soon as I am in the station.

"Tony Malone," she says.

"What? How? He isn't normally in here?"

"He was in here with 2 blow ins and didn't bother running it past the Sup first. That guy really pisses me off," she replies and I can see it written all over her face. Looks like Gus managed to get his own way while no one was looking. It happens quite a bit unfortunately, especially when no regular staff are working in the unit. Crooks take advantage and you can't really blame them. It is their job after all.

. . .

OUR THIRD OFFICER comes in shortly after, Jacob Davidson.

"Hi Jacob." I say as he approaches and we shake hands. He is a good officer and always happy to help. He shakes Rachel's hand and goes to put his bag away.

"How has the unit been?" I ask.

"Pretty good. Quiet as usual," she says and I know what she means. I hope that is the case today as I feel a headache coming on.

WE START to conduct trap to trap muster, me with the sheet and Rachel dropping traps. We get to cell 8 and she peers in, the name on the door is Van Fankel. I can feel the expression on his face through the trap and Rachel doesn't say a word. We continue our count and once finished, I call in the number once called for by Control. It's called correct a few minutes later and I do the rounds unlocking the cells. The prisoners all begin to exit their cells and most head for the toasters, a couple to the phones and one to the laundry. The morning medication trolley arrives and Rachel heads off to assist them, while I check my emails. Nothing noteworthy except one. It's from one of the administration staff. They are writing to me to ask whether I would accept a permanent role in Loddon North. I am instantly torn. I love the unit, the simplicity of it. It's known as one of the retirement units amongst the other officers and know it's a good place to hang my hat. But the other side of my heart is telling me not to. And the reason being what you are reading right now. I know that if I was to work in a unit, I would not have nearly enough material to be able to fill a month worth of excitement for you to read. Especially in a unit as quiet as Loddon North. Admissions maybe, even Visits would be OK but not here. I think about it for a few minutes then write my response, a very polite no thank you. Unless of course you guys think I should. I've even opened an email address if you would like me to work in a unit full time. It's listed at the end of the book.

ANYWAY, I typed my response and pressed send without a second thought. As I close the email, there is a frantic call of a code Alpha in visits. I look at the clock and wonder if they would even have any prisoners up there yet. Turns out they did have one, a billet, in for the morning clean before the visitors show. Turns out he had helped himself to some of the staff's lunches and snacks and when confronted had taken a swing at the officer, Vanessa Green. She sustained a broken tooth and cut lip and he was in a world of pain about two seconds later when 3 large Tactical boys took him to ground. He is taken to Admissions and transported out of the prison about half an hour later. The process following an assault on an officer is always swift and final and always with the removal of the prisoner.

SUBSEQUENT PHONE CALLS to Visits inform us that Vanessa is fine, just shaken and off to see her dentist. She will most likely have a couple of days off for that punch and so she should.

JACOB, Rachel and I are sitting in the station drinking coffee when we hear a commotion coming from the far corner of the unit on the top tier. Two prisoners appear to be having some sort of disagreement and they are in each other's face. No punches are being thrown but a lot of finger pointing and that can be a good indication that things are about to get physical. We all get up and Jacob and I head over to see what the problem is. Rachel remains in the station as one officer is required to man the station permanently. We head upstairs and try and calm the boys down. They seemed to be arguing over the mop and bucket.

"It's fucken my turn. I been waiting," one cried.

"I got it first, mate. Shoulda been quicker ya dickhead." he yells back.

"Guys, guys, guys." Jacob yells at them. "It's a mop and bucket. Geez."

"But boss, I been wai-". But he is cut off.

. . .

THERE IS a scream of pain from the other side of the unit. We look just in time to see Van Fankel drop a bucket and run back to his cell. Rachel is screaming from the officer's station, pulling her jumper off. The bastard had thrown a bucket of hot water on her. He used the altercation to his advantage and wasted no time in using his freshly boiled kettle while we were here and she was there alone. I call a code Alpha and request urgent medical help for an officer. I run to close Gus in the cell and Jacob runs to Rachel. He grabs a blanket and holds it over her as she begins ripping some of her clothing off. People don't realise that when someone is hit with hot water, the hot water can get soaked into clothing and continue burning. She lays down on the floor crying, her pain clearly audible. The doors burst open and a flood of officers come running in, including the nurses. They run to the station and begin treating Rachel, officers helping move her on to a stretcher. The Sup heads for the cell holding Gus and cracks the trap, whispering something I don't hear. I know what the next step is for Gus and Tactical boys are already gearing up to enter the cell.

"He is just sitting there, boys." the Sup says to them and they peer in. They crack the cell and head in, three squeezing into the small room. We hear a cry of pain as they handcuff him and drag him out. The same stony look is on his face and no sign of remorse. They drag him out of the unit, his eyes never leaving the floor. I don't know whether that was his intention, or whether he just wanted to hurt Rachel. Sometimes prisoners are known to assault staff as a way of bailing out of a unit when there is no other way out. I decide I don't care what his intention was; I'm just glad he is gone. Whatever his sentence was, he can now add an "assaulting an officer" charge, which can carry up to ten additional years. I know that with our justice system, he will never get ten years, but I hope he gets the maximum possible anyway.

. . .

Rachel is wheeled out of the unit a short time later, her face covered in some sort of gauze. I gently touch her shoulder as she wheels past me and she looks at me, her eyes doing the talking for her. The Sup stands the code down and Jacob and I begin to write our reports. We finish almost at the same time and just sit there in silence for a bit. The unit has taken on that all too familiar silence and we wait for another officer to replace Rachel who would be on her way to hospital now. Raj walks in a short time later and we fill him in on what's happened. He looks shocked and voices his anger.

That was how the morning came to a close for us. It's truly sad to see officers, both male and female, assaulted, spat on, have shit and piss thrown on them, be abused and just be spoken to like shit, just because they work as a correctional officer. Unfortunately, prisoners believe they have a right to treat staff as they do. But every case of assault is passed on to police and fully investigated. In most cases, prisoners are charged and time added to their sentence.

The afternoon was the exact opposite to the morning. Everything ran smooth and efficiently. The med runs all went without the slightest hiccup and musters were done in almost complete silence. When we lock the prisoners in their cells during the final lock down, a couple of them ask about Rachel and ask us to pass on their well wishes. They are as shocked as we are and know that these sorts of units always run smoother when regular staff man them. Having one of the regular staff off injured only means a blow in comes to replace them and that can upset the apple cart.

Jacob and I walk out together when count is called correct. He says he'll give the hospital a call and check on Rachel and will let me know. I thank him. And I thank him for his help today. And as I walk through the outside gate and into the car park, I remember one important thought that was told to me by an officer long ago.

ANY DAY that you get to walk out of a maximum-security prison at the end of the shift, is a good day.

TODAY WAS DEFINITELY NOT a good day.

# AUTHOR'S NOTE

I WOULD LIKE to thank you for allowing me to share with you some genuine experiences that occurred in our prison this month. Like last month, the events that happened have shaped some officer's lives, some prisoner's lives and ultimately shown just how volatile and crazy things can get. The descriptions do no justice compared to actually being involved in these incidents and I highly recommend trying out for a role within a correctional facility if you find these books interesting.

PRISON DAYS AUGUST Edition is already available for Pre-Order.

THANK you for your continued support.

Simon King

# BOOK 3

# INTRODUCTION

Thank you for joining me for yet another ride into the weird and crazy world of life behind the bars of a maximum-security prison. If this is your first foray into this series, I strongly suggest you give the previous 2 outings a try, otherwise, I humbly thank you for sticking with me for this third book.

I don't know what makes this job, over all the others I've had previously, so unbelievable that it warrants writing a story about. The sad fact is that, if you switch on any television these days, you are confronted with an avalanche of disgusting and shocking crimes. It's a sad reality of our community. What I find so shocking is just how accepted the crimes you read about here really are.

But let's not bore you with lengthy introductions. You paid for a ride and a ride is what you shall receive. So, hang on to your hats and let's go and find us some genuine drama from behind the walls.

## WEDNESDAY, AUGUST 1

It's the first day of the month and I was hoping for a good start. I'm rostered in Glenelg West, a protection unit, but unlike most protection units, Glenelg West prisoners are all on 23-hour lockdown. It is a unit filled with high-profile prisoners as well as those deemed at above-normal risk. Most of the prisoners in the unit are considered compliant and easy to deal with, making the day flow with ease. But Glenelg West is also home to Toby Manning. What can I say about Toby Manning? If I had to describe him in a single word, that word would have be 'painful'. Painful in every sense of the word.

Born with a mid-range brain disability, Toby has been in and out of jail for over 15 years. He is aged in his late 20's and shouldn't be in prison. Where he should be housed, is a disabled facility with trained professionals that know how to deal with him. Instead, the state has chosen to throw him in prison to keep him under control. He isn't what you'd call a regular crook. He just tends to breach his parole conditions and then make bomb threats and assault people. And by assault, I mean throw piss or shit on them. He is, as I said, painful.

I enter the unit and find one of my offsiders already sitting at the computer. Vicky Temple has been an officer for 8 years and is a very easy-going lady. She has an obsession with Golf and unfortunately for me, a game I know nothing about. She waves as I enter the officer's station.

"Morning, Vick," I said, putting my bag in one of the cupboards.

"Hey, how are you?" she asks. We exchange pleasantries for a bit and a few minutes later, a third officer joins us. His name is William Laudon and he has been in the prison for about 5 years, and much to my dismay, also a golfing nut. I groan at the lack of stimulating conversation the day has in store for me.

When Control announce they are ready for morning musters, Vicky and I head around the unit, going trap to trap to add up numbers and provide a welfare check. The process takes around ten minutes and Vicky calls the tally in to control when we finish. We wait for count to be called correct and when control announce a recount, we all groan in unison.

"Fuck sake," Will grumbles as he and Vicky take the muster sheet and head for round 2. "How bloody hard is it to count heads?" I understand his frustration and watch as they retrace our previous route. When they are finished for a second time and we confirm the same count, I call the number in and am relieved when count is called correct a few moments later. Someone else will take the rap for calling in the wrong number.

I begin to unlock the bottom tier cells as Will heads upstairs to do the same. A few minutes later, the unit is a hive of activity with 72 prisoners out on the floor. Some head for the toasters, others to the washing machine.

I hear the unit door close behind me and turn to see the medical trolley set up. Glenelg West, like any protection unit, has an extremely high percentage of prisoners on medication and before I have a chance to announce medications, a long line is already forming in front of the dispensary. I grin as I make the announcement over the intercom and watch as even more prisoners shuffle into line. As I watch the line wait patiently, I begin to count; more for my own curiosity. I'm surprised to count 68 of them waiting in line; all but 4 have pills, paid for by the good people of this state.

Once the meds have been dispensed, several prisoners make a beeline for us and I already know their question before they ask.

"Can we go to the gym, Boss?" The gymnasium, because of its popularity, has time slots allocated to each unit, so as to provide everyone with the same opportunity to use it. Wednesday a.m. is Glenelg West and almost two dozen prisoners begin to congregate around the officer's station, waiting for one of us to escort them. A fourth officer enters and volunteers to take the crooks, freeing us up to continue with our morning duties. Remarkably, the unit noise diminishes substantially once the gym crew are gone.

"Fuck off, Cunt!" a voice suddenly yells from the laundry area and I turn to see two prisoners pushing each other back and forth.

"Guys!" I yell at them and they separate immediately. Fighting over a washing machine is one thing, but getting busted over it is totally not worth it.

"Have it then, Prick," the other crook yells and throws his laundry bag on the floor in disgust and retreats. Most times, crooks have a tendency to bark a lot, but when it comes time to bite, most will back down. With camera footage available to be reviewed, most know that fights can lead to further charges and an increase in sentences and that's something nobody wants.

There's the occasional prisoner transfer throughout the morning, but not really anything too serious to mention. I ask Vick how Toby Manning has been and she says he's been bearable, mostly keeping to himself. Shortly before the lunchtime muster is called, the prisoners return from the gym, elevating the noise level in the unit considerably. They look to have had a great time in the gym and hopefully have worn themselves out.

The control room calls for muster and the crooks stand by their doors after Vicky calls it over the P.A. Once they're standing quietly, I grab the muster sheet and begin to walk along the cells, completing the tick and flick. The unit is surprisingly quiet. No-one speaks, coughs or whispers throughout my trek along the tiers and I don't need to shout when I announce for them to 'break off'. I add my numbers, then compare with Vicky and Will. Our numbers match and when control calls for the numbers over the radio, I call it in. After a few minutes of waiting, count is called correct and the prisoners line up for lunch.

Each unit has their own kitchen and counter from which to serve meals from. The old meal halls you see in the movies are not what happens in reality. Not here anyway. An officer attends the prison kitchen an hour or so before each meal and collects a trolley. He wheels it back to the unit and hands it off to the kitchen billet who finishes the cooking process in the unit oven and then sits the trays in the bain-marie. When the prisoners' queue in front of the counter, the billets dish the meals out. It's a simple enough process and is carried out quickly and efficiently.

If I thought the unit was quiet during muster, then I was mistaken. Now, with a plate of food before them and forks busily shoveling said food in, the unit resembles quiet time at a day-care centre. Pure silence.

Eventually, the prisoners finish their meals and wash their individual dishes. The kitchen billets finish cleaning up and the shipping officer wheels the empty trolley back to the kitchen. While most prisoners return to their cells for an afternoon nap, some break out the table tennis gear, while others begin a game of pool, or 8-ball. One jumps on the exercise bike while a couple of others begin to work out on the gym equipment. A game of poker commences at a table near the officer's station; five crooks taking places while one keeps bank on a sheet of paper. The "bank" is normally based on gambling canteen items and can include anything from soft drinks to toothpaste and everything in between.

It's a relatively quiet afternoon in the unit and fortunately for us, no real drama. There is a minor commotion when two prisoners have a difference of opinion on whether Superman or Batman should have won in the movie, but it's sorted quite quickly. Of course, Superman should have won.

When we walk out of the unit a few hours later, I remind myself that any day that you can walk out after your shift, is a good day.

## THURSDAY, AUGUST 2

I'M ROSTERED in Admissions today and work with 2 other officers in the urinalysis room. I've worked in here a few times before and always manage to have a laugh at some point. The antics the prisoners get up to in here can be quite amusing and I'm hopeful of laughter instead of stress. Robert Nixon is already in the room and is taking inventory of our stock levels. Jason Smith is our third officer and he sits in the booth (see July edition).

Our list is quite extensive for the day, having 40 names on it. There has been quite an influx of drugs into the prison in recent weeks and testing prisoners gives management knowledge on which drugs are making their way in as well as which units are being targeted. Drugs isn't just a community epidemic; prisons are huge markets as they contain many vulnerable customers.

Jason begins calling units with names almost as soon as count is called correct and it doesn't take long for prisoners to begin arriving. Having them arrive quickly is often a good sign for us as it means they are just as keen to get things over with as we are.

"Anyone ready to go?" I ask the first three that walk in. One nods at me and I lock the other two in a separation cell that sits off to one side of our urinalysis room. As I close the door, another two prisoners enter the area. I lock them into a second cell then escort the first customer through. To be honest, I don't know how some of them can piss so easily in front of three officers staring at them intently, yet they even manage to hold a conversation whilst aiming their stream.

The first crook of the morning, Dale, knows the routine pretty well, having been in prison for the past 11 years for armed robbery. He is pleasant and one of those crooks that makes the day pass with ease. I conduct the strip search, handing each piece of clothing to my offsider, check his genitals and inspect his mouth. Once finished, he gets dressed then grabs a sample jar. He turns towards the toilet bowl and holds the jar at the ready. A few seconds later we hear the familiar twinkle and I give Robert a wink, who begins filling out the book. Once Dale is finished, he screws the top on and hands me the sample. I bag it and seal it with tamper-proof security tape. Once I finish my process, Dale signs the security tape to acknowledge its security then signs Robert's book. The whole process is over in less than 5 minutes and Dale heads back to his unit.

I go to the first holding cell and drop the trap, asking for any volunteers. No one is ready and I check the second cell with no luck. A third group of prisoners enter our area and two from the four are ready to piss. I wave one to the side and lock the others in a third holding cell. Just as I enter the piss test room, cell 1 begins to hammer on the door.

"I'm ready to piss," we hear the crook yell.

"You'll have to wait for a minute. Just doing one," Robert yells back. There is an immediate response as a loud crash echoes through the area; the crook kicking the door. It's not something that fazes us too much as it's just a way for the prisoner to save face amongst his peers; giving us a bit of stick for not jumping to his call.

We focus our attention to the current client and, like the first, is keen to get through the test quickly and painlessly. A few minutes later, he too, is on his way back to the unit. I go to the first cell and bring Mr Impatient out for his turn. He grins as he exits the cell and makes his way into our room. He begins the strip process but I can see that he isn't quite as forthcoming as the first two. I slow the process down and carefully check each piece of clothing he hands me. They all come up clear and I direct him to do the rest of the dance. Showing me the inside of his mouth; behind each ear; his armpits; his fingers splayed; his balls and scrotum and all the other bits where things have been concealed in the past.

To my surprise, it all checks out and I beckon him to grab a jar. He does and turns towards the toilet bowl, the only bit of privacy he's given. The concave mirror hanging just above him is our only ability to see the proceedings and any attempts to adulterate the sample. It's not an easy angle to keep watch, but we try as best we can. As he stands in front of the bowl, I seen his hands moving about and try and see what he's up to. I can sense he's doing something but for the moment, let him be. He grunts a couple of times, straining to urinate. We don't see or hear any urine but he suddenly holds the jar up to us.

"This enough? It's all I got," he grunts at us. Again, I get the sense that he's trying to intimidate us by giving us attitude. The specimen jar is maybe a quarter full. I wink at Robert.

"Nope. Need it at least half full, man," I said to him.

"What? But that's all I got. Fuck me, I can't get anymore."

"Sorry man. Rules are rules, yeah?" I reply but he doesn't like my answer.

"Come on, Boss," he says, turning towards me.

"What's that?" Robert said, pointing at the crook's crotch and I immediately see the issue. Protruding slightly from the prisoner's penis is the end of a black straw. It appeared that he had filled the straw with piss and then inserted it down the eye of his shaft. Once he was pointed at the bowl, he managed to massage it back out far enough to take the end cap off and empty its contents into the jar. That was why we didn't hear any piss hit the bowl and also why there wasn't sufficient fluid. The straw didn't hold enough.

The crook looks down, sees the issue and throws the specimen jar he's still holding, at me. I duck and it goes sailing over my head, exploding as it struck the wall. There isn't enough piss to spray anyone and Robert's already grabbing his wrist, twisting it sideways. I lunge at them and grab his other wrist as we bring him down to the floor. I hear a code Alpha as Jason makes the call before rushing out of the booth and coming to our aid. Before we knew it, the room is filled with half a dozen officers and the crook is cuffed and taken to an adjoining cell. He screams and carries on but knows it's pointless. He'll be charged for his attempt to adulterate and probably lose some entitlements but that's about it.

Back in the room, the three of us resume our mission to get through the list. We finish 15 and have 7 locked in cells by the time lunchtime count is called. The afternoon turns into a marathon of piss collection as we process one after the other. There's only really one other crook worth mentioning and that was Ben Tassel, also known as Big Ben.

Big Ben, as his name implies, is a big man. Weighing in at around 420 pounds, he struggles to walk and needs constant rests when walking anywhere other than within his unit. Unfortunately, piss testing Big Ben comes with a minor issue. For one, he can't reach his dick, which in itself, is almost "non-existent". The issue is he can't hold his dick and a jar at the same time. Once the strip search is complete, including having him lift every individual fat flap, Ben is required to grab a jar and piss into it. He takes one from the box and faces the bowl. And thus, begins a 10-minute groping dance of him trying to reach around far enough to grab his dick, and once he has a firm hold of it, to then get his other arm far enough under to catch the urine. There is A LOT OF GRUNTING involved. A LOT! There's also a lot of wheezing and holding breath and exhaling and jiggling this way and that. Unfortunately for Ben, there are no officers willing to volunteer to hold the cup for him. There are some lines we just don't cross.

Eventually, as Ben is slowly making his way back to the unit, we tag and bag his sample.

A couple of hours later, the three of us head out of the gate, grateful for the end of another shift. I've definitely seen and smelled enough piss for the rest of my life but know I'll be back to do it all again soon.

## MONDAY, AUGUST 6

It's a new week and I was hoping to have a nice cushy unit job today, but as I enter the gate, am asked to fill in for another officer who called in sick. Their allocation? Piss Testing. I groan inside as I slowly make my way back to the urinalysis rooms. I wasn't expecting this and normally need to psych myself up for it, but I hope for a couple of good officers to make the day go a bit easier.

As I walk into the rooms, I see Robert already there. I bump fists with him, glad to see one decent officer. My hopes for a second decent officer are all but extinguished when I see Tony Malone (see June and July editions) sitting in the booth. Robert sees my expression when I see Tony and he begins to laugh, a loud bellowing that makes me crack my own smile. Tony looks out at us and waves nonchalantly.

The list proves to be better than the previous time I was in here; only 27 names on it. The only downside is that they are all protection prisoners, meaning they need to be escorted to us. If no-one is able to escort them to us, then we will need to get them ourselves and that can take up valuable time. I scan the names and see that a few of them are repeat customers. A couple of names stand out as being difficult to deal with, but we'll deal with them when the time comes.

Count is called correct and Tony commences calling for the prisoners. He lets us know which are on their way up and ten minutes later we have 7 crooks in 2 separate cells. Even protection prisoners need to be separated from each other.

The first customer is a fresh entry, having only arrived in the jail the previous week. He's a young kid of maybe 18 or 19, in for sexually assaulting a drunk girl at a party. He looks much younger than his age, the other prisoners burning him at every available opportunity. I watch as Robert takes charge of the strip searching for the day, leaving me to fill out the paperwork. I act as his backup or spotter when not busy so that we have two sets of eyes on the prisoners.

The kid, Cooper, finishes his strip, his face vacant and nervous. He grabs a sample jar and stands at the toilet bowl. We wait for a minute or two and nothing happens. We already know the reason, having experienced it on a regular basis with other customers. The kid's got stage fright, and judging by the look on his face, it's not likely to diminish any time soon.

"No go, kid?" I ask and he just looks at me with contempt. "Alright, come on. I'll give you a glass of water and stick you back in the cell for a bit." I lock him back up and another prisoner bangs up, wanting bladder release.

The process repeats itself, over and over again. Some can go, some cannot. Some give attitude while others just take care of business and get on with their day. It really doesn't make a difference to us. If you piss with attitude, you're still pissing and that's all we really care about; crossing off names. And if you don't piss for any reason, then you are given what's called "a dirty", which is classed as giving a positive sample. So pissing is always the better option. For those that know they've taken drugs in recent days, the temptation to try and smuggle a clean sample is almost a no-brainer, considering the consequences. Some prisoners may be eligible for parole if they stay clean, while others might be trying to gain a special privilege. Every case is different and we collect samples regardless of reasons.

We have a pretty productive morning and are able to cross over half our names off. 16 are done by 11.30 and our afternoon should be a quiet one with only 11 names left to process. Tony calls up one of the units and tells us there are no escorts at the moment. We can either wait or get them ourselves. Robert and I choose the later and head to Loddon North. The unit is almost at the other end of the prison and we have to manoeuvre down several corridors to reach it. We pass the gym and wave at the officers in the station as a basketball match is played out. Aaahh, nothing quite like life in jail.

We could hear the yelling from within the unit before we even opened the first of two doors. Half a dozen voices were screaming at each other over what appeared to be a card game gone wrong. Two officers were standing in the station, watching the shouting match unfold before them, both looking flushed with nerves. They heard us enter the unit and looked relieved. They were both quite new to the jail and had maybe 4 months experience between the pair of them.

"You boys OK? I asked as we neared them. One of them grinned at me.

"They're fighting over a bottle of Coke." The difference between a bottle of Coke on the outside and inside is unfathomable. Outside it's just a drink that costs maybe a buck. Inside, it can represent a debt; someone's pride; a prize for winning a game of some sort. If you lose a bottle of Coke to someone and you don't pay up? It could get you stabbed. You promise someone a Coke for protecting you? They could turn on you as well as whomever you were seeking protection from in the first place. You could trade that bottle for tobacco, drugs, clothes, toiletries, protection, friendship, sexual favours or whatever else you deemed of value. Things take on a whole new level of value behind the walls. And the worse thing you can do as an officer, is look at that bottle as just a bottle. See it for what damage it could do and then act accordingly.

"Guys!" Robert yelled, interjecting. "What's the problem?" Four prisoners began answering him at once, all trying to talk above each other. Robert held his hands up, waving them down. "One at a time. Steven?" he asked the closest one.

"Both boys got a straight flush, 9 to King. Jack got all Clubs and Bob got all Spades."

"And both think they won," another crook said, grinning. "Do you know who won?"

"One of the long termers who was standing up on the top tier, watching the proceedings, spoke up. "They both won. Suits are equal in Poker." I began to nod my head, pointing at the wise man on the shelf above us. One of the victors began to protest.

"That's bullshit. I fucken won that."

"Just split the deck, highest card wins," Robert suggested and they both nodded unenthusiastically, neither wanting to forego their winnings. But both agree to the new terms and Steven does the honours of shuffling the cards. They both split and both pull 4's. The second round they both pull 8's and I wonder if a higher power was involved. Then Shane, the younger of the two, barely out of his 20's pulled a 3. He threw it on the table in disgust, knowing defeat was now seconds away. Ken reached for the cards, a huge grin spreading across his face. To our surprise, both crooks began to jump up and down in victory when Ken pulled the Ace of Hearts.

"I win," he yells, then looked surprised when Shane also began to cheer. "What the fuck are you cheering for? You lost."

"No, I didn't. Ace, 2, 3, 4"

"Queen, King, Ace, Dickhead." I groan, wishing I could take the Coke for ourselves. I look at Robert and he's grinning, shaking his head. The rest of the prisoners that are watching the charade, crack up and begin laughing, the sound sending me into a giggle. I wave at the group to quieten so I can be heard.

"I've got a solution. Since you're both on our list to be piss tested, whoever pisses more, wins." The unit now breaks out into more gales of laughter as well as some heckling. It's funny to watch. To our surprise, both prisoners actually agree to our proposal and we escort the pair back to the urinalysis rooms a few moments later.

When we reach the rooms, Jack agrees to piss first and we lock Bob away. We take Jack into the room and Robert goes through the usual process of the strip search and Jack enthusiastically dances through it.

"OK, grab a jar," Robert tells him. He grabs not one, but three, removing the lid from each, then lining them up carefully. He grabs the first, closes his eyes and his face becomes a solemn blankness reminding me of a Jedi master meditating. After a couple of seconds, I hear the familiar gush of piss on plastic as he releases. He watches intently and as he fills the first, grabs a second jar then continues. The second is filled shortly after and he continues while transitioning to the third.

The last few drips trickle into it as the jar sits about three quarters full. Jack smiles a huge Cheshire grin and hands Robert one of the jars.

"Fair effort," my partner says as he secures it. Jack signs the deed and we escort him back to the unit, after checking to see whether Bob was ready. We drop by Loddon South and pick up a couple more prisoners whom we escort back, then wait for them to need the urge.

We watch the clock and as the time passes 3, we all know that there will be no extra crooks to process today. Given that they have a maximum of 3 hours to produce, our finishing time of 6 doesn't give them enough time to meet max amount available. The 3-hour time limit is set by the hierarchy and we are required to follow it to the letter. Prisoners are given one measured cup of water on the hour, up to 3 cups maximum. If they don't produce a sample in that time, they are escorted back to the unit and a positive result is noted on their file.

To our surprise, Bob who is a long-termer, asks us to note a dirty on his file and just escort him back to the unit. He can't go and doesn't want to wait 3 hours. We grant him his wish and don't wait around for the heckling in the unit when we reveal that Jack is the winner. He begins strutting around the unit with his arms raised like a prize-fighter but settles down when he sees the look on Bob's face. He's smart enough to know when to quit.

As we walk out of the prison an hour or so later, I wish the other officers a good night. Today, has been a good day.

# TUESDAY, AUGUST 7

I ALWAYS GET a kick out of working in Visits, the place I'm rostered in today. It's different to working in a unit; the atmosphere being more jovial. I don't know whether it's because there are members of the public around or whether it's because the prisoners seem a lot happier. I just find it a more jovial place to work. I walk into the back area and check out the list of visits for the day. It's a fair number but see that a couple of good heads are working with me which will make the day go by much easier.

Tom Grady enters as I finish reading, followed close behind by Rachel Finning. Having a female in the stripping area isn't so bad. Although she is unable to be totally hands on, she will be invaluable running the show and also de-escalating situations as they arise. Being a happy place can be deceiving. When things kick off here, they tend to kick off quick. Mostly because of how close the prisoners come to their own outside realities when friends and family visit.

Our list is made up of Mainstream in the morning and late afternoon with Protection in the middle of the day, just after lunch. As Rachel begins to be notified of which visitors have arrived by the reception staff, we prepare for our first round of customers. It's not long before they start showing up, most happy and pumped to see loved ones. I can only imagine the stress they must suffer, not seeing family for long periods of time, but then remind myself that they are here because of choices they made and I push the thought aside.

"Who's got me?" a prisoner asks as Tom and I stand in front of him.

"You can choose your own stripper," I say with a grin on my face. He appreciates the joke and points to me. Tom pretends to be wounded and he beckons at another prisoner to follow him into the adjoining strip room. I conduct the strip and hand the prisoner his visit's overalls, a one-piece suit designed to restrict the ability to conceal any contraband their visitors may have managed to smuggle in. The suits have a long zipper that is sealed along the back and then cable-tied shut. It's a simple process and complete within a few minutes.

We process 8 prisoners within 10 or so minutes and once the last one enters the visits area, we are left alone to wait.

"Got another half a dozen or so on the way," Rachel informs us and within 5 minutes another two enter our area. As they walk in, I see one of them walking slowly and looking down at his feet. He has his arm crossed in front of him as if holding something close to his chest. It's not the sort of demeanour you'd expect from someone about to see family. I signal to him to follow me and he does.

We begin the strip and he takes his shirt off. He appears to avoid eye contact with me and any conversation I try to instigate is met with short one-word answers. He keeps holding his arm as if in pain.

You OK, Brady?" I ask, trying again to get him to talk but he shakes his head. My instinct tells me that whatever is wrong only happened recently. I go through the motions of the nude dance, checking his bits, front and back. As he begins to turn, I see a small mark on his side, no bigger than an ant; tiny. I see another one further around, down by his waist. I almost shrug it aside but then look at the bigger picture as he stands with his back facing me. A very faint bruise is beginning to bloom around each dot and that's when I realise that he's been stabbed. I gesture to him to get dressed.

"Who stabbed you, Brady?" I ask and he looks at me in surprise.

"I can see the stab wounds mate, let me know now so I can call a code and get you help." He shakes his head, tears now visible in his eyes.

"I can't, Boss. They said they'd kill me."

"No one is going to kill you. But we need to get you looked at." I see him peer through the gap in the door behind me and when I quickly turn my head in that direction, see the prisoner in the opposite room gesturing at Brady. When he sees me, he drops his hand and looks away. "Was it him?" I ask, stepping between the door and Brady, blocking the line of sight. He slowly begins to nod, now visibly shaking. I don't know whether it's from shock, fear or both but the shaking doesn't look good. I press the duress button on my radio and call a code Mike (medical emergency). I get Brady to sit on the seat and wait for the nurses.

When the nurses arrive and tend to Brady, I pull the Supervisor and one of the T.O.'s aside and tell them about the other prisoner that was gesturing at the victim. They immediately leave and head for the control room, to view footage of the pair walking up to the visits building. I stand by the door and continue to watch as the nurses assess him. They call for a stretcher and ask for an ambulance to be called. Once Brady is on the stretcher and wheeled to the medical wing to await the ambulance, I head to the front area and keep an eye on the other prisoner. He appears to be visiting with a mate of some kind. They are laughing and eating chocolate as they converse. The prisoner keeps glancing over at me then whispers something to his visitor; both men breaking out into gales of laughter.

I continue to watch the pair for about half an hour, until the front-end staff tell me that the prisoner's visit only has 5 minutes to go. I phone control and inform the Sup and he tells me that he's on his way.

"Looks like he stabbed him in the gym corridor. Staff are there now looking for the shiv," he tells me. I hang up the phone and quickly head out the back, informing the other officers of the Sup's comments. To my relief, three T.O.s enter the area just as the prisoner returns from his visit and they immediately order him into the strip room. I watch as they conduct a thorough strip search, including a close examination of his rectum. By close, I don't mean someone placing their eyeball at the entrance to his rectal entrance; rather getting to fully bend at the waist and spread his cheeks, four sets of eyes looking for any evidence of a foreign object.

We don't see anything and the prisoner dresses himself. Once finished, the T.O.s escort him out of the building and into the Admissions area to await further developments. The Police would already have been called and would arrive to assess the available footage and interview both parties. They wold also take any evidence that is available; particularly the shiv that is found dumped in a bin that's located near the Visit building's entrance. It's a crude one consisting of a 6" piece of oven rack with masking tape wrapped around its base for a handle. Brady would have been stabbed with at least four inches of metal; enough to pierce internal organs.

Lunchtime muster is called shortly after and once it's correct, we begin our afternoon, processing protection prisoners. There are only a few and the afternoon sweeps by quickly and drama-free. For the most part, protection prisoners can be a lot less painful; most just wanting to serve their time quietly and hassle-free without much fanfare.

Once we see the last of the protection prisoners escorted away, Rachel begins calling mainstreamers back up and it doesn't take long for our area to, once again, be overwhelmed with obnoxious comments and loud demands. Thankfully, they are all in good spirits and enjoy their visits with loved ones.

When we walk out of the prison a couple of hours later, the Sup tells me the reason for the stabbing; the two were cellmates and Brady had taken a shit in the middle of the night, after suffering an upset stomach. Go figure.

# FRIDAY, AUGUST 10

TODAY, I begin a 3-day weekend, working in the Dispensary on a nice 8 hour shift instead of the usual 12. This is probably one of the most favoured locations for the prisoners that attend here; its where they are administered their methadone and Buprenorphine, or Bupe for short. It's an enclosed area that is situated beside the medical wing and run by four officers. One runs the book, ensuring an up-to-date log is kept of all incoming and outgoing prisoners. The second officer performs pat-downs of the prisoners as they line up for their doses. They are also responsible for monitoring that prisoner's sleeves remain pulled up to prevent them from diverting their medication. The third officer is assigned the post of watching prisoners consume their medication and having open mouths presented for inspection after they finish. The fourth officer is back up for any of the other officers.

It can be quite a volatile area as the prisoners that attend here see this as the one highlight of their day; getting their dose. I'm joined by Patty and Thelma, both women aged in their 50s and both veterans of the prison for well over a decade. Our fourth officer is Tom Grady. We all walk in around the same time and begin our morning with a coffee and catch up. Tom informs me that Brady had returned to the prison the previous day and was back in his unit. The prisoner who stabbed him was interviewed by the police and taken to Murray South, one of the two management units. What a way to be punished; a single cell with a TV, all meals through the trap, his washing done for him every other day; a true punishment for his crime. He would also face police charges but they would be laid at a later stage.

Count is called correct a few minutes later, so we finish our coffees and take up our positions. Thelma runs the book while Tom handles the pat-downs. I stand next to the nurse's window where I can inspect open mouths for the day and Patty stands behind Thelma where she has a good view of the room. Thelma calls the first unit and requests their crooks to be sent up. Shortly after, we are greeted by a line of around a dozen excited prisoners, all boisterous and enthusiastically exchanging banter.

They all place their ID cards on the counter in front of Thelma then move along. Tom begins patting them each down, then once he's finished, they follow a yellow line that's painted on the floor. There is an iris scanner next to the nurse's station and the first peers into the scanner and waits for it to respond. After a couple of seconds, a female computerized voice begins to talk.

"Please look directly into the scanner." Then, after the machine clicks as if it's taken a snapshot, it announces, "thank you. You have been identified." He then shuffles to the window, greets the nurse with an excited grin and awaits his dose. The nurse hands him a card to sign, then a wrapped straw and a cup containing his red methadone. He takes it, peels his straw and slurps the liquid, ensuring he gets every last drop. Then he adds some water from a jug that sits on the counter, swirls the water around the cup and sips the rest of it. He throws his cup in the bin and flashes me his open mouth, then walks into a waiting room. Prisoners are required to wait a full 10 minutes before returning to the unit. It's Patty's job to monitor the times for each prisoner and release them when the 10 minutes is up.

Not all the prisoners that come up are Methadones. A few will be Bupes and these prisoners have a different course to follow. When they arrive, their first port of call is to be patted down. They are then handed a one-piece overall and once they have it on, have the zipper that is located on the back, cable tied to prevent opening it. They are then handed rubber gloves which they put on. Only then are they allowed to attend the nurses window. Bupe is given as a tiny strip, almost like a fresh-breath strip. It's placed under the tongue and left there for ten minutes, or until it's completely dissolved. It's the easiest medication to divert and is also the most sought after. Bupe is one of the more common drugs that's smuggled into the prison. It's easily manipulated behind or between teeth or behind the gum line, and officers need to be especially switched on when it comes to Bupe diversion.

There are no Bupes in the first lot of prisoners, but looking at the book, I see that there are two in the next lot. Once we send the last of the first group back to their unit, I make sure there are enough overalls available, then unlock one of the waiting rooms so we can separate them from the other prisoners. They will not only need to be isolated while we wait for their Bupe to dissolve, but they will also need to be closely monitored for any sneaky mouth movements or touching their mouths with their hands. When they do attempt to divert, it's usually done in the blink of an eye.

The second lot of prisoners, 14, enter the area and begin the process. Once we identify the Bupes among them, I hand each a set of overalls and cable tie them shut. Once all the methadones are done and sitting int their waiting room, we allow the Bupes to get their medication. Once they have their strips firmly under their tongue, we walk them into the separate waiting room and begin the observation. Ten minutes feels like an hour. Every mouth movement is scrutinized as we watch them fixedly. Thankfully, these two only have single doses. Prisoners are sometimes given double doses, each dose given after the previous one has completely dissolved. It can be a long and tedious process, especially if there are multiple dual doses in a day.

Patty and I watch the prisoners as time ticks by. When the 10 minutes are up, the crooks approach us and we inspect their mouths, instructing them to lift their lips, move their tongue from side to side and give us a clear view of every part of their mouths. Only after we're satisfied that their dose has completely dissolved, do we release them from their overalls and send them back to their unit.

If you think that once the prisoners have left our area, their doses have been safely ingested, then you are sadly mistaken. As I've written in the past, life behind these walls is harsh and often unpredictable. Monitoring the prisoners for adverse side effects isn't the only reason we make them sit and wait for 10 minutes. There is another reason and it is one that we, as officers, are more akin to understand. Our hope is that most of the methadone will have been absorbed into the body by the time the prisoners leave our area. It has been noted that in the past, it's not uncommon for prisoners who have consumed methadone to be dragged aside; sometimes behind a wall, bush or into a cell. Then once privacy is confirmed, the prisoner is forced to vomit in a bag or container of some sort. Once the prisoner has finished vomiting, they are let go so the other party can then consume the vomit. It is, of course, one of the more extreme measures taken to obtain another prisoner's 'done, but the method is not uncommon.

Our third group of prisoners arrive; all 22 of them. The obnoxious comments begin almost immediately as they enter through the doors and for the officers, another round of meds begins.

Most of our units are finished by the time lunchtime muster is called. Our rooms are empty of prisoners so there is no count to be called in for us. We take the opportunity to conduct a quick search of the area and replenish water, overalls and cups. We also take the break for a coffee and spend the time talking shit. Just the usual officer chit-chat that is about nothing in particular. Count is called correct and Thelma calls for the next unit to send their 'dones, who arrive less than 5 minutes later. Thankfully, it's a quiet group of only 8 methadones and 1 Bupe. They each put their card on the counter for Thelma then subject themselves to a pat down. Once the first has his eyes scanned, he fronts the nurse and speaks to her through her tiny Perspex window, while the others line up behind him. We separate the Bupe and Tom gives him a set of overalls. Once he has them on, the zipper is cable tied shut, he puts on the gloves then waits patiently for the 'dones to finish receiving their doses.

Sometimes, certain units can be extremely painful to deal with; prisoner's non-stop obnoxious comments, refusals to comply with instructions and basic bad attitude; other units can be sheer bliss. Avoca, the boys that are currently occupying our rooms, are of the latter variety. Our last unit to be called, Maribyrnong, is the complete opposite of Avoca. It has double the numbers, has double the attitude and the prisoners are just plain arseholes. They aren't even the happy-go-lucky obnoxious variety. As we see out the final prisoner from Avoca, we hear Thelma call for Maribyrnong to send their crooks up. A look passes between each officer. It's the kind of look that says "it's showtime."

When the 15 prisoners begin to file in, led by an angry islander called Tui, the energy change in the room is immediate. Tui stands around 6 foot 3 and easily weighs close to 200kg. He is a bundle of bad attitude and his demeanour is clearly one of "I don't give a fuck." He stands in front of Tom, eye-balling him as Tom begins the pat down. Once he's done, Tom moves on to the second prisoner, a Sudanese named Badr. Like a lot of Sudanese, he's tall and skinny and he looks down at Robert with contempt written all over his face. Badr has a history of assaulting officers inside the prison and Police outside the prison and isn't intimidated by anyone in uniform. On his last visit to prison, he hot-watered staff in his unit because they wouldn't give him a single cell, despite none being available.

Badr watches me as Tom pats him down then continues eyeballing me as he waits for the eye scanner. I tell myself that it's only 10 minutes until we see the back of them, just 10 minutes. None of the officers speak as Tom continues pat downs. Tui sips the last of his methadone, throws his cup in the bin and begins walking past me, his mouth closed.

"Mouth open, please," I say to him and for a moment he just stops and stares at me. I stand my ground, looking at him in a perpetual stand-off. After a few seconds, he opens his mouth and continues past me. Once he's seated, I watch as Badr takes his cup from the nurse, snatching it up without a word of thanks. I frown as I see my tax dollars get slurped up. Once he's done, he too, attempts to walk passed me without showing me his mouth. I ask him the same as I did Tui, Badr throwing his arms up in a "what are you gonna do" gesture and I repeat my request. He finally opens his mouth then mumbles something under his breath.

As I stand there, watching each prisoner go through the process, I remind myself that these guys are the real deal. They aren't the fictional characters you see on TV or the simple fine evaders and fraudsters you see in other units. These guys are the violent, aggressive persons you see on the nightly news who assault police, conduct violent home invasions, steal cars from people in the street, often using weapons such as baseball bats, machetes and knives. The prisoners now standing before me wouldn't lose any sleep over assaulting an officer; male or female. These are the ones you need to be fully alert of, never taking your eyes off them and always remaining aware in their company.

We all breathe a lot easier as we send them back to their unit, Badr giving us a final glance over his shoulder as he walks out the door. The reality is, though, we get to do it all again tomorrow.

As we walk out an hour later, I remind myself that any day you can walk out of a prison under your own steam is a good day.

# SATURDAY, AUGUST 11

SATURDAYS ALWAYS FEEL different for me. I don't know what it is, considering the same number of officers come to work and the line to get scanned in is the same. It's just that something always feels different on a weekend. I guess it's just the vibe, knowing that it's the weekend. A good aspect of doing a 3-day weekend in the Dispensary is that the same officers work there, so I know that the team I have working with me is a decent one.

We walk in together just as we walked out the previous afternoon and go through the usual morning prep. Once our lunches and personal belongings are stowed away, we wait for count to be called correct. It's good practice to shuffle the duties of each officer on subsequent days and Robert and I switch roles. Patty jumps on the book and Robert is happy to stand by the nurse's window, leaving me to get hands on with the prisoners.

Count is called correct and Patty immediately phones the first unit while I begin to glove up. During our brief coffee catch up, we decided to phone for Maribyrnong first, getting through the riffraff at the beginning of our shift rather than at the end. It turns out to be a good move as the crooks don't look nearly as mean as they did the previous day. Tui even greets Thelma with a grin. I give him a pat down and move him along. My personal thoughts on dealing with volatile prisoners is not to give them a reason or excuse to cause trouble. I know that some officers love eyeballing them right back, as if they feel a need to uphold their own authority. I personally see it as nothing more than ego flexing and so avoid eye contact all together. I remain my own person through every encounter I have with them, regardless of who they are or what they are in for. I greet each prisoner I come in contact with and ask them the required questions, depending on the situation. I have always found that it is best practice to remain neutral in one's opinions, thereby acting in an unprejudiced manner.

I pat each prisoner down, those wearing long sleeves, I ask to roll up. A couple question me but I have the same response for each of them.

"You know the rules. It's not your first time. Roll them up please." They know that if they persisted with their objection, they would miss out on their little prize at the end of the queue; their methadone. There are always a couple that are nice until they get what they want and then give officer's some stick once their methadone can't be taken away, but most remain constant.

We happily see the last of them out the door as Patty phones for the next unit who come bouncing in mere minutes after the last group leave. If only they would come as quick when they were called for piss tests.

We restart the process and I give each prisoner a pat down. There are 9 methadones and 1 bupe in this lot and I separate the bupe and begin by handing him his overalls. Once the dones are dosed up and sitting in the waiting room, I gesture the prisoner to the nurse's window to receive his strip. He follows my instructions and just as he is about to take his bupe, I see something that raises my awareness. I see another prisoner in the waiting room make eye contact with him and raise his eye brows a couple of times in quick succession. I know it's a signal of some sort and immediately keep an eye on the bupe crook. There is only one reason for the signal and that is to remind the bupe crook of his requirement; to divert his dose and keep it for whomever has ownership of it. I watch him intently, looking for any sudden mouth movements or a wandering tongue. There are plenty of hiding spots in a mouth, especially if he has missing teeth or cavities. He doesn't notice me watching and sits in an adjoining waiting room. From where I am, I can see his side profile and can only see one side of his face. If he slides the strip to the other side of his mouth, I may not see it. I see the other prisoner make eye contact with him again, and watch as he gives him the eye-brow gesture. I also see the bupe crook nod slightly, as if confirming the diversion. And then, like a total amateur, he reaches into his mouth with his fingers, reaches down into his shoe and lifts the leg of the overall to expose his sock.

I try hard to stifle the laugh as I approach the room. I signal to Robert to help me and he follows as I enter the room where bupe crook is sitting.

"Just going to conduct a quick strip search," I say and he looks at me in surprise.

"Why?" he asks but his expression tells me that he knows.

"Just routine. Is there anything on you that you shouldn't have?" I ask and he shakes his head. He stands, turns his back and I snip the cable tie. He then removes the overalls and I hand them back to Robert who inspects every inch of it, both inside and out. Then he strips his prison greens, his shoes and finally his socks and shoes. I hand the shoes back to Robert then inspect each sock. Hidden in one of them is a half-dissolved strip of bupe. I hold it up and the crook frowns, his eyes glancing over my shoulder.

"Don't worry about them. They can't see us," I say, knowing who he's looking for. "The Sup will let you know what happens from here. Ever been caught diverting meds?" I ask and he shakes his head a second time. "Alright, no worries. You can return to your unit." I hand him his socks and he begins to dress. As I walk past the waiting room door holding the 'dones, I look in and am greeted by a very angry looking eye-brow raiser.

Once all the prisoners have left, I phone for the Supervisor of Tambo East and inform him of the diversion. I also alert him to the other prisoner that was gesturing to the diversion. The information is important because it helps identify crooks that have a tendency to stand over weaker prisoners. The Sup will also notify the Intelligence unit who will note it down and keep it on file. One thing that will be high on the priority list is to ensure the safety of the prisoner caught diverting. He may face retribution from those after his bupe and it's our duty to ensure his safety.

We continue our work until lunchtime count and we all enjoy a quick chin wag and a cuppa. It can get quite exhausting when you are focused and alert for hours on end and it's a real luxury when no prisoners are around.

The afternoon goes smoothly and the good news is that it's just a run of the mill afternoon. We finish shortly after 2 o'clock and head home. Today has been a good day.

# SUNDAY, AUGUST 12

Sunday always feels more relaxed than any other day of the week; even Saturdays. And the best thing about Sunday? The breakfast cook-ups. Most units throughout the prison will have their cook-ups with each officer assigned a specific ingredient depending on what everyone chooses to make. There's always a selection of bacon, eggs, mushrooms, avocado, pancakes, pikelets, waffles, sourdough bread, tomatoes, fresh fruit, hash browns and a selection of juices. I mean, seriously. Are you hungry yet?

I bring in a bottle of orange juice and a bottle of apple juice, while Robert brings bacon and eggs. Patty has a bag of freshly sliced mushrooms, avocado and tomatoes while Thelma brings a deliciously thick cut sourdough loaf. As soon as we arrive in the Dispensary, I turn on the frying pan and prep the ingredients. I love cooking and am usually the one tasked with it.

Half an hour later, we're all chomping on bacon and egg sandwiches with a variety of sides. There isn't a lot of conversation in the tiny kitchenette as we fill our mouths with breakfast goodness. We all love our food and know that this brief moment of culinary bliss is only a tiny bubble when compared to the rest of the week and we intend to make the most of it. Count is called correct at 8am but none of us are in a hurry to call any units. We have priorities and the prisoners aren't it. Other units will be going through the same process as us so no one annoys anyone else during this time of food tranquillity.

It's a little before 9 by the time I swallow the last of my breakfast. I wash it down with a mouthful of OJ and toss my dishes in the bin; another bonus. No dishes to wash. We spend a few minutes cleaning the things we used then pack the leftovers up and stow them in the staff fridge. There is sufficient for lunch and maybe then some.

I wish I had something exciting to share with you today but even the crooks see Sunday as a day of relaxation. Not a lot happens and we process the units by 2 o'clock. The only minor thing that happened was a code Mike just after lunchtime muster. A prisoner "slipped" in the shower and had to be taken to hospital by ambulance. His so-called slip gave him a fractured right eye socket, a loose tooth on his left side and a cracked rib that was also on his right side. Those shower stalls can be deceivingly bouncy. When officers reviewed the footage, it revealed 3 prisoners entering the injured crook's cell just before the so called "fall". All 3 will face charges in the coming days.

But for us, today was a good day.

# THURSDAY, AUGUST 16

AFTER WORKING THE WEEKEND, I have a short week to work consisting of just 2 days. Sometimes, it really does pay off working in a prison; the rosters are pretty awesome. Today I'm working in Tambo West. Stephen Jacobs is already sitting in the officer's station as I enter the unit and am about to greet him when I see the third officer of the day coming out of the toilet. My heart sinks seeing Tony Malone wave at me as he walks back to the station, not bothering to look at me. I wave back unenthusiastically and take my bag to the staff room.

There are some places in the prison where you don't mind working with someone like Tony. Don't get me wrong, I don't not like him for mild or petty reasons. His demeanour and his abrasive attitude is just not suited to places like Tambo West. When he works in the urinalysis area, Reception, the medical unit or places of low prisoner flows, he can be quite useful. But here, in a volatile main stream unit? A place filled with angry prisoners who have so many weapons hidden and have kettles ready to boil bucketloads of boiling water? I'd rather work with Charles Manson standing beside me. Unfortunately, some people are not only a danger to themselves but also to the officers working beside them.

Once my things are packed away, I head back to the station and shake hands with my compadres. I take a quick look at the unit roster and see a few familiar names. Main stream units can be divided by several factors but most notable is which gangs each unit comprises of. Warring bikie gangs can be sent to specific units to keep them separate; some units can be predominantly islanders, Asians or African gangs. Some units can be a mixture, such as this one.

I notice one name in particular that surprises me. Badr, the methadone crook from Maribyrnong. It seems he was transferred overnight for reasons yet unknown. I check the handover log and find that it hasn't been filled in for the past week and a half. It truly astounds me how officers can work in a unit for a day, then give the next day's staff absolutely no information as to what's been happening, such as observations, transfers, codes or any sort of tension. A well-worded handover means the incoming officers can have their facts right before unlocking 5 dozen prisoners for 12 hours. Without one, you may as well send them into the unit blindfolded.

"You wanna take the clipboard?" Tony says to me and I nod, following him as control calls for morning numbers. He opens each trap and calls the number of prisoners in each cell to me. I also note that he doesn't greet any of them as he conducts his checks. Like I said; abrasive. When we finish the last cell, Tony heads back to the station as I count up the numbers. When I get back to the station, I note the final number from the previous night, matching the two. This morning's number is one higher and I remind myself of the overnight transfer. I call in the number and we wait for count to be called correct.

"Attention all stations. Count is correct at 8.02," control calls a short time later and I head for the upper tier to unlock the cells. Stephen unlocks the lower tier and before long, prisoners are filling the unit. Washing machines begin to whir, toasters begin to pop and the chatter builds.

Monday morning can be quite busy, especially if the weekend staff were all blow-ins (not regular unit staff). I hadn't checked the previous day's muster but when I do, am surprised to find out that regular staff were in fact rostered in the unit; surprised because of the lack of handover notes.

If the prisoners weren't angry enough before, they certainly are after I tell them that the gym was closed for the day. According to my emails, there had been an incident in the unit the previous day and as a consequence, the Sup had cancelled gym time. An officer had been shit-bombed by an unknown prisoner huddled amongst others as he exited a routine cell search. When the perpetrator failed to come forth, the Sup cancelled gym for the rest of the week; a hard-hitting consequence to those that used it religiously. It could also prove to be a painful decision for the person responsible, as retribution can be swift.

The only good thing I can gather from the Sup's email is that the staff from the previous day would have already told the crooks the gym consequence so I knew that the surprise and anger they were now displaying was purely just for a bit of theatre.

The med trolley arrives for morning meds and Stephen makes the announcement. He also heads for the med room and begins chatting to the accompanying officer. The prisoners immediately begin to line up in anticipation of their pills. The phone rings and when I answer it, am greeted by Gary Hanson from the Urinalysis room. He's after two prisoners from the unit and a quick check of the muster confirms their presence. One I already knew, the second I check for. I look around and see both sitting at a table near the station.

"Badr and Adonis. Need to go to Admissions, lads," I say to them and they both look at me suspiciously.

"What for, Boss?" Adonis asks but I shake my head.

"They don't tell me those things," I reply. I know some officers happily tell prisoners that they're required for a piss test but it only makes it harder for everybody'. The first port of call for a crook, after finding out he's required for a piss test, is the water tap in his cell. And they will stall for as long as possible. The other department that is within Admissions, a department that is popular with crooks, is Property. It's where they can obtain any special buys that they've ordered; such as new runners, stereos, fans and what not. So, if they have a current order in the system, they almost skip out of the unit to get their purchase.

I can see the two of them whispering to each other, both glancing in my direction.

"Now boys," I repeat and they begin to move. I fill out their movement slips and they head out. They pass Stephen, still chatting to the other officer as the prisoners continue receiving their meds. I look across and frown at Tony who's sitting on the other side of the station, reading a newspaper.

Once the med trolley leaves, the usual myriad of activities slowly commence around the unit. A card game here, table tennis, a game of pool, board games and of course the fitness equipment. Every unit has at least a treadmill, an exercise bike and a home gym. Everything is used and used well, the home gym normally a hive of activity as prisoners vie for a spot.

There are a lot of duties to complete as an officer as well. Apart from monitoring the unit, there are tier walks to conduct, as well as random cell searches; unit musters to update; prisoners to move along and their newly available single cells to allocate; cells prepped for new incoming prisoners; file notes to write; the daily routine of musters, medical appointments, classes and work allocations. It's a never-ending line-up of jobs that stretch from morning to night.

I look at the list of moves for the day and see that there are 3 prisoners leaving our unit; one who's being transferred to another prison and 2 who are moving to another unit. I show the names to Stephen and he calls the transferring prisoners to the station and informs them of the moves. They all happily wander back to their cells and pack up. Outgoing moves happen in the morning while incoming moves are an afternoon activity.

As if on cue, prisoners begin to arrive at the station as soon as the 3 prisoners exit our unit, all asking the same question. Who gets to move, as 2 of the 3 cells are single. I bring up the current single cell waiting list and hold it up for all to see. A mix of groans and cheers erupt in the group as the winners view their names, quickly running to pack their belongings. I can only imagine the sheer relief it must

# FRIDAY, AUGUST 17

Today I was rostered in Tambo East and when I arrived in the unit saw Tony Malone sitting in the officer's station. We shook hands as I entered the station and after I put my things away, checked my emails. Our third officer, Paul Bennet, entered the unit a short time later. They didn't greet each other. Instead, Paul grabbed the clipboard and beckoned me to follow.

"Can you drop traps?" he asked and I was happy to oblige. When we finished and were back in the station, there was very little talk while we waited for count to be called and I could sense something brewing between my two offsiders. Whatever it was, I hoped that they were professional enough to keep it outside of work as it's bad practice to show prisoners anything but a united front.

Count is called correct about 10 minutes later and I head out to commence unlocking the cells. Tony remains sitting in the station, blank-faced. Paul looks at him for a moment, then shakes his head and heads for the top tier while I unlock the bottom. Within minutes, the unit is a bustling throng of activity as prisoners exit their cells and begin their morning rituals of breakfast, laundry, catch-ups and officer-pestering. The latter is normally prisoners itching to get to the gym and this morning is no different.

I begin to write movement slips for around 20 prisoners and once finished, watch as they exit the unit in an excited group, looking like a bunch of kids off to a movie cinema or carnival. As they exit, I see the medical trolley arrive and enter the unit dispensary window. I'm about to greet it when I spot a handwritten note sitting on the counter in front of me. It takes my interest because it's not uncommon for prisoners to drop notes on each other.

When a prisoner drops a note, it's taken quite seriously because it's an anonymous way for prisoners to give officers handy bits of information. Most of the time, notes are written to inform officers about a prisoner that is bound to be stabbed if he remains in the unit. This is one of those notes and concerns a crook by the name of Jester Williams, a young 22-year old, in the unit for burglary and assault.

I check his file and it looks like Jester has only been in the unit for a few days. Some prisoners can be targeted by other prisoners because they are weaker, are accumulating debts for protection, drugs or canteen or are trying to stand over other prisoners. Jester, however, is none of these and judging by the tone of the note, could be in a lot more danger of retribution if the threat is real. The note doesn't go into specific details but what it does say, is pretty clear.

"Jester attacked my friend's mother on the outside and if he stays in the unit, he'll get stabbed"

I check the muster sheet and see which cell Jester is in and see if he's sharing with anybody. The unit muster shows him to be in cell 38 and in a single cell. 38 is on the top tier and I look up and see the cell door still closed. I ask Tony to go up and lock Jester in, showing him the note, while I phone the Sup. He looks at the note, reads it, then grins.

"That's a shame. Bash a crook's mother and then end up in here with them," he says. He doesn't move and for a moment, looks as if he has no intentions of going. I look at him, raising my eyebrow and he finally moves. As he ascends the steps, I phone the Sup and wait to be answered. Just as Tony reaches the top of the stairs, there is a sudden loud screaming from the end of the tier and I look to see a prisoner running from the open door of cell 38, a bucket in one hand.

I reach for my radio but hear Paul already calling a code foxtrot. Tony stood frozen at the top of the stairs, apparently unable to move, as I call for the unit to go into lockdown. I don't need to use the P.A. as my adrenaline is charged enough to amplify my voice. Most prisoners remain where they are standing and I holler a second time as I run up the stairs, agonizing screams coming from the cell in question. Paul begins to lock crooks into cells as I run towards Jester's cell, cautious of any wayward feet that may be intentionally stuck out to trip me.

When I reach cell 38, Jester is sitting on his bunk, his hands held out in front of him as if admiring his nails. To my horror, I see that it wasn't just a simple case of getting hot-watered. The bowl of boiling sugar syrup had hit him square in the face and then run down his naked torso coating every inch of his skin with a sticky gloop that began to instantly burn and solidify. He'd tried to wipe the syrup from his eyes but only managed to rub the melting skin clean off. His forehead, nose and cheeks were all now little more than exposed muscle tissue, the skin dangling down in long strips. He was trying to scream but there was no voice, just hollow chokes coming from deep within his chest as if his tongue had been ripped out. As I entered the cell, I could actually hear prisoners laughing behind me, totally amused by the permanent scarring this kid had just received. The sweet smell of the syrup filled the tiny cell as I watched Jester shaking uncontrollably, his skin almost mirror-like.

Without thinking, I turned the cold tap in the shower on and grabbed his hand, pulling him to his feet and pushing his face beneath it.

"Don't touch your face," I yelled at him and when he tried to reach up again, I held his hands down. One prisoner poked his head in through the door and gave an animated giggle. His head suddenly disappeared as Paul grabbed him from behind and pulled him back out, ordering him to his cell. They stood eye to eye for a moment before the crook backed down and walked away, still grinning.

When the staff arrive a minute or so later, the rest of the unit is finally locked up and to my surprise, see Tony back in the officer's station. He'd failed to back either one of us up. The medical staff arrive moments later and immediately begin to work on Jester. An ambulance is called and there is an eruption of banging and door kicking as he is wheeled out of the unit. Loud cheers accompany the banging, as well as shouts of "Dog", "Rat" and "Mutt".

As I go back to the station, I confront Tony, sitting in one of the chairs.

"What the hell was that? No back up?" He looked at me like I'd taken a piss in his cup of tea.

"I hurt my ankle on the stairs," he replied, but I could see he lacked the conviction to believe in his own lie. Unfortunately, arguing gets us nowhere and I sit at the computer in disgust and begin typing my report. It's all I can do to stop myself from simply screaming my frustrations at him.

When I finish my report, I email it to the Sup, then head back upstairs and go to cell 38, still standing open. There are no other officers besides us and there's no reason to keep it open, especially with the gym crooks due back in an hour. I lock the cell and answer a couple of trap taps as I walk past. It's the normal questions you'd expect; when are we being let out and how long are we locked up for; the usual stuff. No-one asks about Jester's welfare and it doesn't surprise me. For the most part, a lot of them don't care and those that do, won't stick their neck out to highlight the fact.

The gym crooks arrive back in the unit just after 10, already aware of what had transpired in their absence. The prison telegraph line works very well in these types of situations, sometimes more efficiently than phone calls between officers. They are all still excited and as we lock each away, ask when the unit will be unlocked. That question is answered when the Sup rings a short time later. The unit is to remain in lockdown and wait for the arrival of Police who will conduct an investigation into the assault.

The lockdown remains in place for the rest of the day. The Police officers don't arrive until after lunchtime muster and stay until just after 6. We deliver meals to the cells via their traps and escort the nurse to those that require medication during each med run. The prisoner responsible for the assault is removed from the unit and taken to the admissions area to await transfer to another unit, but I don't find out which.

I walk out alone at the end of the shift. For one thing, I'm still pissed off at Tony for his lack of back up. Paul was still in his mood from the morning and I don't know the reason for his beef with Tony. I'm not interested as I have enough on my plate trying to deal with him myself.

# MONDAY, AUGUST 20

WAS CALLED in for overtime and got to work in the urinalysis room again. You know how some days you come to work and you just know that you're going to have a shit day? Today was not one of those days. Today was one of those days where you just feel the sunshine in the air and the positive energy from all those you come into contact with.

Miguel Foster is my main offsider today and Chris Upton is sitting in the booth. Both are funny guys to work with and their positive energy and sense of humour is something that makes the day a real pleasure to get through, despite our surroundings. Although we have a substantial list of names to get through, having these guys beside me is half the battle won.

I won't bore you with every single prisoner we piss tested as there really isn't that much to tell. There were two moments worth mentioning though. The first was when we tested a regular junkie named George Blakely. He's in his early 30's and has been in and out of jail since his early teens. He's also a regular meth user and, given his current mental state, may have actually fried his brain the last time he was out. Prisoners whose brains are completely fried from drug use can be extremely unpredictable and need to be treated with extra caution.

Miguel had gone to answer the door knock coming from George's cell and when told that George was ready to piss, unlocked the door. George came into the piss room and went through all the requirements for the strip test. Once he grabbed the jar, he lined up in front of the toilet and put the jar on the shelf above the sink. Then, as if polishing some ornate copper vase, he spat into the palm of his hand and began polishing the knob of his dick.

"George, what are you doing, bud?" Miguel asked. George looked at him groggily, then smiled.

"I need to warm it up. Can't piss without warming it up," he replied, looking at Miguel vacantly. Miguel shot me a glance but I just shrugged. George was rubbing the head faster and faster and for a moment, I though he was going to give us a white sample instead of yellow. But when he grabbed the jar and began to trickle piss into the jar a few moments later, the look on Miguel's face was gold. I struggled to contain my laugh, not wanting to wind George up, but bellowed with both my offsiders once the crook was safely back in his cell. It was the strangest method of pissing I have seen, to date.

The second noteworthy incident came from a prisoner called Eugene Prince. He was a relatively new prisoner, aged in his mid-20s. He'd arrived with a group of prisoners and then put into a cell with 2 others. Miguel and I processed prisoners as they needed to piss and when it came time for Eugene to be processed, led him into the room.

As I was conducting the strip searching for the day, I gestured Eugene onto the mat and faced him. He began to remove his clothes, one piece at a time and when he removed his jocks, the 3 of us began to choke on fits of laughter. Eugene just stood there, red-faced and wide-eyed. After a few seconds, another officer peeked in at us, curious about the roaring gales of hilarity. Once he saw what we were seeing, he also began to cackle.

"What?" was all the crook could bring himself to ask. He was standing before us, naked, his hands cupping his genitals. It wasn't his genitals we were laughing at. What had tickled our funny bones was the carefully tied finger that he had cut from a rubber glove and had filled with a clean urine sample, probably purchased from one of his unit buddies. He had tied a piece of clear fishing line around it and then tied it around his waist. As he was standing in front of us, the urine-filled finger was dangling in mid-air between his legs, looking like a magician's floating-finger trick. It looked as if he'd tried to sticky tape it behind his ballbag but the tape had loosened, leaving the finger dangling beneath him. Once he got his laughter under control, Miguel pointed out the obvious.

We confiscated the finger, expelled the urine and put it into evidence. The prisoner was charged and returned to his unit. The rest of the day went without a hitch and we completed all the required tests we were tasked with.

We were still laughing when we walked out later that afternoon.

Today, was a good day.

# TUESDAY, AUGUST 21

WRITING about the day that was today makes me shudder with revulsion. I have never, I repeat NEVER, been as repulsed as I was today. Some prisoners just have that kind of effect on people. Let me explain.

Today I was rostered in the medical unit. It houses prisoners that require ongoing medical attention, or those who are too frail to be housed in a unit because of their inability to look after themselves. There are approximately 40 cells, each housing as many as 3 prisoners, depending on their needs and classification. A total of 4 officers man the unit, with duties including searching cells and prisoners as well as escorting nursing staff on their rounds. Main stream prisoners are still kept away from protection prisoners by remaining locked in cells until each classification is given their runout. Generally, either protection or mainstream are given a runout in the morning and the other in the afternoon. Each subsequent day is rotated so prisoners are given alternating times with which to use the outside chook pen.

Today, I had the pleasure of Ricki and Thelma to help me, as well as a quiet man called Vincent Tremaine. The medical unit is seen as a pretty quiet area of the prison and not a lot of excitement happens. There can be the occasional altercation about medications and dosages but generally speaking, it's a pretty good area to work. Or so I thought.

The medical wing also houses a number of monitored cells; cells that have active cameras monitoring each prisoner they contain. These cells are normally utilized to monitor prisoners that have been deemed a risk to themselves and thus put on suicide watch. Suicide watches are classified by the severity of the prisoner's threats of self-harm and are called S1, S2, S3. S1 requires a prisoner to be monitored and physically viewed every 15 minutes, S2 is 30 minutes and S3 is every hour. Having a number of "S watches" can make or break the day, depending on how active the watches are and how serious their threats are. A lot of the time, prisoners use suicidal threats as a form of bailing from a unit. Others use it as a way to get attention or to simply be a pain in the arse. Some, however, can be quite serious and have to be monitored to ensure their safety.

As I enter the wing, I'm greeted by Ricki and Thelma, already setting up for the day. I see a familiar yellow folder on the bench in front of them. It's a suicide watch folder. I head straight for it, looking at the name and the classification. Its an S1, which isn't good but not what gives me instant dread. What deflates me of every bit of positive energy I had walking in, is the name at the top of the page; Robert Coleman. Thelma and Ricky see my shoulders slump and giggle a little. Painful is the only word that accurately describes Robert Coleman.

Robert Coleman is a long-term gay prisoner, aged in his mid-60s, that is mostly housed in protection units. By gay, I don't mean any disrespect. The reason it is of importance to know of his sexual orientation is because Robert not only likes to provide sexual gratification to willing prisoners, but he also likes to keep semen samples in a row of named cups on his window sill. He's also the carrier of Hepatitis, Venereal disease and Aids. Whenever I know that Robert is in a unit, I know to keep a pair of disposable gloves very close.

I put my things away while waiting for count to be called correct and when I come back out to the station, see Vincent sitting quietly off to one side. I greet him and shake hands, asking about his family.

He smiles and tells me about his 6-yo grand-daughter's weekend birthday party. As he finishes telling me about the wonderful cake his daughter made, control calls count correct and I begin to unlock the mainstream prisoner's cells. Thelma is already busy on the intercom, talking sternly to Robert Coleman who is adamant that he was due to be released today and if we don't let him go, he would sue all of us. He also wanted to know when his bucket of KFC would be delivered as he'd ordered it quite some time ago.

The mainstreamers begin to exit their cells with most heading for the chook pen. The sun is out and most are looking at a quiet chat in the sunshine. Some sit and watch TV while a couple of others remain in their beds. A nurse comes out from their station and asks for an officer to accompany her on her rounds and I happily volunteer.

Unlocking cells and standing by as the nurse attends each of the patients is quite a simple task that doesn't involve much effort. A few of the prisoners offer some conversation and I happily respond. As I unlock each cell, the same mixture of damp sweat, bed farts and industrial cleaner hit my nose and I try and stand just inside the doorway, out of the breeze. None of the windows open for obvious reason and with the aircon switched off, airflow is kept to a minimum. But smell is a funny thing, as it's only really noticeable for a few seconds before your body becomes used to it. At least that's what I thought.

Once the nurse is finished visiting the patients, I return to the station where Thelma is still engaged in conversation with Robert. He's still wanting his KFC bucket but is now also wondering where his lawyer is. Getting fed up with his constant buzzing, Thelma tells him to stop pressing the intercom or he will be disciplined. He doesn't care. As soon as he hears the connection break, he presses the intercom button again, forcing us to answer. All voice traffic is monitored and you do need to watch what you say, especially as he is an SI.

The day was going along absolutely wonderful. The sun was out; there was good conversation between the officers; the crooks were happy. And then, in a split second, it just all went to shit. Literally.

Robert stripped naked and waved his canvas gown around like a chequered flag, cheering loudly, as if riding a horse in a rodeo. Then, just as we were getting ready for lunchtime count, he squatted in the middle of his cell and took a shit. A decent one, too. He was still buzzing up as soon as we hung up and as soon as he dropped his crap, pressed the intercom and asked us to come and smell. When we refused, Robert decided to use some of his faeces as hair wax, giving himself a head full of short spikes. But that wasn't what bothered us. What he did next, did. Robert turned the shower on and plugged the drain with his canvas gown. Prisoners flooding their cells is not uncommon, occurring at least once or twice a week. But when you have faeces mixed in, as well as a prisoner that is diseased, things get a bit dicey.

Just as we were about to call the sup to get the water turned off, a code Alpha was called. The officer sounded distressed and two of our officers ran out to help; Vincent and Ricky. I was in talking to the doctor about the dangers for us from the flooding when the call came through and thus remained while the other two bolted. Less than 30 seconds later, a code Charlie was called. A code Charlie is an order to lockdown the entire prison. It's mainly called when resources may be stretched thin and unable to respond to a second incident, if one was to be called. I began to lock the mainstreamers back into their cells, securing our wing.

As I returned to the station, a smell hit me. It was thick shit that filled my nostrils and as I looked around, saw that there was water coming from beneath Robert's cell. I ran and grabbed a towel, rolled it tight and threw it against the cell door. Then I grabbed a second and a third, rolling each as tight as possible before jamming them against the crack. I opened the trap, the thick stink hitting me instantly.

ROBERT!" I yelled, but he was dancing with his back to me. "ROBERT! TURN THE SHOWER OFF!" He either didn't hear me or refused to listen. He didn't turn and he didn't turn the shower off. Thelma called out to me and I closed the trap and went to her.

"Sup's just tied up at the code. 3 crooks stabbed another crook.

They reckon there's blood everywhere." I groaned, knowing that the lockdown would remain for most of the day. Once the scene was under control, the prison would remain in lockdown until the Police had been and finished their own investigation. And that could take hours. A lot of hours. I looked back at the water still leaking through the towels. I went and grabbed a thick blanket, wound it up tight and jammed it against the already soaked towels. It blocked it but I knew it was only for a matter of time.

Robert continued singing and dancing around his cell, the water continuing to rise and I could see that it was above his ankles. The drain was still working to an extent, but nowhere near fast enough to stop it from flooding the hospital floor. Thelma called for the Sup again and he said he'd send someone with the key to the mains. But we were going to have an issue and it was one I saw from a mile away. If we turned the water off to Robert's cell, how many other cells would it affect? And how would the nursing staff react to it? The other issue we had was that the prison was running at capacity. There was nowhere else for Robert to be taken and even if the T.O.s would enter the cell, there was nothing to stop Robert from doing it again. It would appear, that we were stuck with him.

After about an hour, the shit-laced water began to leak through the blanket, the water slowly creeping across the linoleum floor. The depth of the water was a couple of inches as it worked its way around the unit. The smell was unbearable with most people gagging. I can't begin to tell you just how bad the smell was. I'm almost convinced that as I sit here, writing this for you, I can still smell it.

It turns out that the prisoner that was stabbed, died within seconds of the attack. He was 27 and a father of 2 young children. He had drug debts that he tried to escape from but even after being transferred to a protection unit, it wasn't enough to save him. The 3 prisoners that attacked him with shivs made from toothbrushes, stabbed him 42 times. One officer tried to approach the gang during the attack but one of them held the shiv up to him and told him to stay away. Officers aren't allowed to carry weapons of any sort and thus all the unit officers could do was watch. When the T.O.s finally rushed in, they sprayed the group with capsicum spray and cuffed the attackers. They'd only taken 55 seconds to enter the unit from the initial call but it was long enough for them to do the damage. All 3 were taken to separate units and held in holding cells.

The police took a couple of hours to turn up and worked well into the night. The police interviewed each prisoner, then returned to the unit to continue their investigation. The deceased prisoner was removed from the prison just after 3, around the same time that someone finally turned up with a key to unlock the mains cabinet. We'd had a couple of prisoners mop the water up and that had kept it to a minimum but the smell was there to stay. No amount of air freshener would kill it.

It was just after 6 that a psychiatric nurse finally turned up and talked Robert down. He agreed to take a cake of soap and wash the shit from his hair. He took his clothing from the drain and picked up any remaining pieces of shit and flushed them. He was handed a mop and bucket and he cleaned his cell as best he could.

By the time we finally walked out of the prison, our nasal passages feeling like they'd been permanently scarred, Robert was asleep on his bunk. The smell in the unit remained.

Today was definitely not a good day.

## WEDNESDAY, AUGUST 22

I WAS SENT BACK to the medical wing for another day and much to my delight, saw Thelma and Ricki already in the station when I walked in. I don't know whether it was just my nose, but the smell from the previous day remained. There was, however, some good news. Robert had been moved to another unit during the night. According to the nightshift officer, Robert began to get extremely abusive during the night and had smeared faeces into the speaker grating of his intercom, rendering it useless. As prison protocol requires every cell to have a working intercom, and as there were no other available cells within the medical unit, Robert was moved into another unit. Let's just say that when the news was relayed to us there may have been a couple of low-key high fives between us. We also found out that the Police officers remained in the prison until nearly 1am. The attack was caught on CCTV and was clear enough to identify each of the attackers. 2 of them had been long termers, in for 15 and 22 years, but the third was a 21-yo that was in for a minor break and enter. All 3 would now be facing murder charges.

The day is pretty much a no-event. Other than the usual rounds with the nurses, the day plods along as it normally does in a hospital.

By the time we walk out, our noses have begun to lose the previous day's stench. It was a good day.

## SATURDAY, AUGUST 25

I WAS ROSTERED in Thomson East today. It can be quite a challenging unit to work in and my nerves are eased slightly when I see my offsiders. One is Chris Upton and the other is Toby Richards, a good friend of mine. Both officers have years of experience and are known to keep level heads when it comes to incidents. As I enter the unit, there is a code Mike called by control. It's for Tambo East and I find out later that the crook had been told by a night officer that he was being transferred to another jail this morning. A good way for crooks to prevent their transfer, particularly if they want to remain in their current abode, is to feign a medical issue. Sometimes it works and sometimes it doesn't. The prisoner in question actually ran at his cell wall and knocked himself out. He had accumulated extensive drug debts at his destination and really wanted to avoid the place. After being attended to by the medical staff, the crook was taken off the transfer list.

The 3 of us talk shit for a few minutes as we prepare for the oncoming shift. Once our things are all stowed away, I grab the ligature knife and muster sheet and follow Chris as he heads for the first cell. Toby is a regular in the unit and is already on the intercom with prisoners asking their usual morning questions. Questions like whether they're on the bus; whether they are transferring to another unit; available billet jobs; single cells that might be available, that kind of thing.

Chris begins to drop traps and call out numbers to me. One if it's an occupied single cell and 2 if it's a double. We finish the bottom tier and climb the stairs to the second tier when a prisoner begins banging on his cell door. It's the 3rd door along from us and I follow Chris there. It's a two outer and we find that one of the crooks has fallen off his bunk. His cellie tells us that he was having a seizure or something and rolled onto the floor, hitting his head. I call a code Mike and we wait for staff to arrive.

It doesn't take long before a number of staff and the duty supervisor arrive. When they do, Chris cracks the cell and brings the upright prisoner out and gets him seated on a nearby chair. There's a fair bit of blood on the ground and it appears as though the prisoner split his scalp. He is conscious though and when the medical staff enter the cell, they begin working on him immediately. Prisoner Sexton has a history of epilepsy and staff suspect he had a seizure while up on his bunk and simply fallen to the floor. Several staff are asked to carry him out of the cell and onto the stretcher while the duty sup calls control to order an ambulance. Sexton is stretchered back to the medical wing to await his ride into town.

Once he's left the unit, control calls for the resumption of muster numbers and Chris and I finish our count without further incident. Count is called correct a short time later and our day begins with the unlocking of the unit. I'm halfway around the top tier when the sup calls out to me. I hadn't heard him come back into the unit, so am surprised when I see him standing at the station. He waves at me, gesturing for me to come to him, which I do.

"Don't unlock 37," he said, leaning in close. I look at him curiously. "Sexton had a stab wound in his back. They think he was attacked by his cellie. Let the rest out for the time being and if need be, we can lock them down after." I do as he asks and unlock the rest of the top tier as Chris finished unlocking the bottom. When I return to the station, a few prisoners are already congregating and asking questions about why 37 remained locked. They are such a curious bunch.

Because there's no actual footage, the investigation relies on statements from the prisoners involved. It doesn't surprise me to learn that Sexton is refusing to talk. It's not uncommon for crooks to keep tight lipped, even when they're the victims. It's a prison code kind of thing and if broken, cam lead to much more serious repercussions. But our suspicions allow us to keep the prisoner locked down for the rest of the day.

As I've said before, Saturdays have a very different feel about them. Apart from the excitement from the morning, the rest of the day is nothing but pure routine. I could write it down and tell you about the med trolley turning up; the gym time; meals; lunchtime muster; poker games; table-tennis games; the laundry being done; but that's not what you're here for, is it?

Sexton returns to the unit later in the day. His cellmate is eventually picked up by the T.O.s and transferred to another unit with the matter pretty much closed due to neither crook talking.

As far as we're concerned, today was a good day.

## SUNDAY, AUGUST 26

Some days, you just know when you are going to have a crap day. Not necessarily an eventful day, just a crap one. Before you even set foot inside your work, the energy surrounding you is just screaming for you to turn around and go home. Today was one of those days.

As soon as I arrived at work and saw that I was working with Tony Malone, I knew that I should have stayed in bed that morning. There had been an incident the previous night. Rats had managed to chew through some pretty important cables that provided power to the CCTV system. Every camera in the prison was on the fritz and as the control room had no clue as to what was happening around the jail, Tony and I were tasked with driving the perimeter security vehicle around the outside perimeter of the prison; to ensure there was no-one trying to climb over the fence and no contraband was thrown into the jail. It meant that I would be sitting in a car with someone that I not only had no respect for but also had nothing in common with.

We headed outside and located the security vehicle; a Ford Territory. I was lucky enough to be handed the keys and was more than happy to take the wheel. We would be doing nothing more than driving around in a big circle, watching for anyone approaching the massive concrete wall from the outside. Unfortunately for us, if anyone did want to get contraband over the wall, a drone would probably be the better option, especially since they have a range of up to 5 km.

The day wasn't exciting. There were no crazy car chases or us shooting drones from the sky. There were no escape attempts and for the most part, I got to drive in silence as my passenger decided to nap for most of the day. I didn't mind. For me, it meant that there were no uncomfortable silences and not much forced conversation.

Today wasn't a bad day as such; it was just crap.

## THURSDAY, AUGUST 30

It was a hectic day working in Murray South, which is one of the management units. I guess it depends on what you favour from a work environment that determines whether or not it's considered good or bad. Personally, I think it comes down to your own choices as well as the frame of mind with which you approach the work day. Today was busy; very busy.

Being a management unit means prisoners are locked down for up to 23 hours per day. They are entitled to a single 1-hour run out which is normally in one of the 7 chook pens, scattered around the unit. Prisoners also receive their meals through their traps and have their laundry washed by unit staff. There are visits to facilitate, medication rounds, prisoners to be escorted to medical appointments and tele court, as well as countless other things that come up. All the duties are handled at unit level and rely on 7 officers to share and complete. One officer normally runs the book which means they don't move from their location unless urgently needed.

Thelma is running the book today and we also have Bob, Pete, Rickie, Chris and Mario. Pete and Mario are regular officers in the unit and we generally follow their instruction to ensure a smooth day. They are, after all, the brains of the outfit.

As soon as count is called correct, Mario asks Chris and I to stock up the rations trolley as today was rations day. It was also canteen day in the unit, which meant that at some point during the morning, a stores person would deliver 44 bags of shopping that each prisoner has ordered on their weekly shopping list. Once they are delivered, officers take each bag to the prisoner's trap and count each item out, ticking it off on the order form. Believe me when I say that if items are not counted out and marked off, every order will be missing items; not that prisoners would ever take advantage of the system. Please note my sarcasm.

Once the trolley is filled with disposable razors, sugar rations, coffee rations, toothpaste, shaving cream and toilet paper, Chris and I begin going trap to trap, giving each prisoner their goods. Most seem pleasant enough despite their predicament and are happy to be topping up their supplies. One prisoner refuses to come to the trap and we close it and move on. When we're done, we stow the trolley back where it came from and return to the station. Bob and Pete are busy escorting the first of the run outs and Mario is busy planning the 3 visits that are scheduled for the unit. The visits are held within the unit, in a side room which houses both contact and noncontact visit booths. Chris and I go and help escort prisoners to their designated chook pens.

Another aspect of working in the management unit is the constant burning of prisoners; or staff, depending on the prisoners doing the burning. Today seems to be 'pick on Murray' day because they haven't stopped yelling abuse at Murray Toomey, a protection prisoner that was brought into the unit the previous day. He has a history of lagging on other crooks, particularly those that he owes drug debts to.

As Chris and I escort our first prisoner to his chook pen, Bob and Pete pass us to grab their next crook. They wait until ours is safely locked away, then go to the cell and begin the process. The prisoner has some rubbish he wants to throw into the bin on his way past and Bob gives him the OK. It was all going so well until the crook was a few feet ahead of his escort. It was all the space he needed and he seemed to move with such incredible speed that it was all over by the time I registered what had happened. Although the hooting from the other prisoners was enough confirmation that Watson had succeeded in whatever he had planned. He'd been carrying a rubbish bag, supposedly filled with rubbish. When he was a few feet ahead of his escorts, he reached into the bag, pulled out a milk carton and threw the bag behind him, temporarily slowing the officers walking behind him. He then ran at full speed to Murray's cell, wedged one side of the milk carton underneath the cell door, finally jumping on the carton with all his might.

I can only imagine the resulting stream of piss and shit that shot underneath the door, covering everything in the cell with a thin coat of nastiness. The ensuing scream of horror, followed by the distinct choke of dry retching, is what set the rest of the unit off in a gale of laughter and loud cheers, their cries of jubilation echoing across the unit. Some began to bang their cell doors with fists and boots in a unified cheer of victory. Inside the cell, Murray began to vomit.

Murray had been sitting on the floor cross-legged and folding some washing that had been handed to him. He was facing the door and had virtually no time to react once he realised what was about to happen. The mixture of piss and shit that was jettisoned under his door was a direct hit, striking the crook directly in the face. He told us after, that a little had squirted into his mouth and he needed to see the nurse. We all understood his concern, although he didn't appreciate the new nickname the unit had bestowed upon him; Shit Storm.

The shit bomber ended up losing his run out and was transferred to another unit, although he did walk out with his chin held high, the other crooks giving him a farewell parade of cheers. Murray was taken to another cell and allowed to shower, a new uniform handed to him. Once he was cleaned, he was taken to the medical wing for some tests, and then returned to his cell to begin the clean-up.

The visits were all finished by 2 o'clock and once the last of the escorts was finished, Chris and I went trap to trap to dispense the canteen. An almighty roar erupted when the crooks saw the shopping bags, their weekly sugar fixes now only moments away. It's a relatively simple task and there are only a couple of genuine mistakes which we mark off and subsequently report back to stores. The missing items are usually delivered the next day if they're in stock or credited if they aren't.

The day comes to an end when control calls for lock-up count and Mario does a brief handover to the nightshift officer. As we walk out of the prison, I actually appreciate the busy day. It passed with relative speed, some humour and some new experiences. Today was a good day.

# FRIDAY, AUGUST 31

It's the last day of the month and unlike a sales job trying to reach its monthly target, the day has no real significance to us in prison. Dates only have a meaning to those that are serving time, as a date may mean their release, back into the arms of their loved ones.

Today I'm rostered in the sally port. This is the big roller door you see from the outside and is a giant airlock that has roller doors at either end which are controlled from a fortified control room. Its main purpose is to act as a safe entry and exit point for vehicles such as transport buses and trucks. Both roller doors cannot be opened at the same time. It's also where supervisors will walk prisoners through as they are being discharged.

Usually this part of the prison is operated by the control room staff as well as two officers directly in the sally port. My offsider today is Ross Newton, a control room regular. Ross has been at the prison for almost a dozen years and is quite friendly to work with.

The workload in the sally port comes in peaks and troughs. As each vehicle enters, we wait for the roller door to lower then give the vehicle a thorough once over. A heart beat monitor is attached to it and once activated, we wait for it to come up negative, a process that takes around 30 seconds. We also climb into each cabin to ensure no contraband is brought inside. Cell phones or iPads usually remain in the sally port and are locked inside temporary lockers.

Other than discharging prisoners, there is virtually no prisoner contact in here. Occasionally we might hear one or two try and yell something at us from within the transport buses but it's usually too muffled to make out. There's a log book to maintain as well as confirming the correct numbers of prisoners that enter and exit the prison; the number of which we pass on to the control room staff.

There isn't really any particular drama that happens in this part of the prison. The work is usually completed with relative ease and we greet each driver with a smile and handshake. But, being the last day of the month, I was glad for one final story that I could share with you; something to make you smile, as we come to the end of the book.

At around 3.30 a prisoner was brought up by the duty sup. He'd served two and a half years for burglary and had finished his sentence. Usually, the process for a discharge is that they are brought into the sally port and one of us will identify the prisoner. His details are entered into the log book and then, much to his and his family's excitement, the outer roller door is raised and he runs out into the arms of his family who are anxiously waiting on the other side. And most of the time, we are happy to see them leave. But every so often, a prisoner arrives who you just wish would suffer a little bit of karma.

We could hear the crook giving the sup quite a bit of stick from beyond the inner roller door.

"Can we walk faster, Fatso?" I heard him tell the sup, a lovely man by the name of Phil Hanson. Phil was the kind of man that always had a kind word to say, no matter who you were. He always smiled and he was always friendly, greeting everyone with a warm handshake and a smile. He was a little on the larger side as he limped; the leg injury from a long-ago motorcycle accident. "For fuck sake, can we get there today? I got places to be," he added. There was a loud banging on the roller door as the crook smashed his fist against it. "Come on, let's go!" As the roller door began to wind up, we could see the pair come into view from the feet up. The prisoner was dressed in Nike runners, a pair of black jeans and a black t-shirt that had a woman in a bikini printed on it; a sharp dressed guy you could say. As they entered the sally port, Phil came to me, shook my hand and asked me how I was. "Yeah, yeah, let's go," the crook continued.

"Painful?" I asked Phil and he smiled at me, his grin growing wider.

"Not for much longer, mate." There was a twinkle in his eye that made me a little curious, but I took the paperwork to confirm the prisoner's identity. I held the page up, compared the photo and asked him his name.

"Already been through this like a dozen fucking times," he began but I dropped the paper to my side and just looked at him. After almost a minute, he finally got the idea.

"Name?" I repeated.

"Mitchell Lawson," he replied and after I asked him a few other questions, confirmed his Id. I turned to the control room window.

"One out," I shouted and just as the roller door began to retract slowly up into the ceiling, Phil shot me a wink that, at the time, seemed to match his Cheshire grin. The prisoner wore a huge smirk and began to walk towards the opening. Just as he reached the boundary between sally port and outside world, he turned back to us, shot us the bird with both hands and began to cackle with laughter. The sup would normally turn and leave at this point but Phil stood his ground, that Cheshire grin never faltering; instead growing wider.

"LATER, FUCKERS!" the crook called back to us, then turned and began to walk out. At that exact moment, four police officers rounded the corner and surrounded the crook.

"Mitchell Lawson?" one asked. He nodded, the humour draining from his face. "I'm Constable Riley. This is Constable Smith and Constable Jackson from the New South Wales police and they have an outstanding warrant for you. Put your hands out in front of you." The laughter that I heard come from Phil, who was still standing beside me, filled me like Autumn sunshine. The three of us stood there as we watched karma work its magic.

He'd had an outstanding warrant for assaulting his pregnant girlfriend but had fled to Queensland before they were able to execute it.

Once he was apprehended and charged here, the warrant was put in waiting, ready to be used once he was released from prison.

Seeing the look on his face still makes me smile as I write this. It was a funny thing to witness and a story I will surely share many times.

When I finished my shift a couple of hours later, I reminded myself of just where I worked; a maximum-security prison; a place that really did provide a different experience with every single working day. Today was a fantastic day.

# AUTHOR'S NOTE

THANK YOU ONCE AGAIN, for sharing my day-to-day stories of life in the prison where I work. Yes, it's scary. Yes, it's unpredictable. But it's one of those jobs that you can never underestimate. It's one of those jobs that can never be matched for brutal honesty and reality.

Think you can do it? Why not give it a go. A 3-day-week with a fulltime income and enough stories to last a lifetime.

I have decided to write a fictional novel in the coming months. It will be about maximum-security, with all it's brutal truths and hopefully something that will interest you. It will be called "The Final Alibi" and I hope you keep an eye out for it.

AS ALWAYS, I thank you for your continued support.

Simon King

# BOOK 4

# INTRODUCTION

WELCOME to the fourth instalment of Prison Days. I must say that each month, I wonder whether I will have enough material to complete another book and every month the prisoners come through for me. Come through in spades, in fact. Should I ever doubt them? And as long as people buy them, I'm more than happy to keep sharing the insane behaviour that seems to be a part of life behind the walls.

BUT TWO THINGS have really turned my experiences upside down this month and I don't think life can ever be the same. The first thing that really made my month was the return of an old friend. You read about him in the June edition of Prison Days and I was very happy to see him return.

THE SECOND EVENT that left the prison staff reeling in shock was the loss of one of our own and is something that I will reveal to you within the following pages. But I will say the shock from losing one of our own, is one that will never diminish.

. . .

So, are you ready for another journey behind the razor wire? Ready to hear the stories from beyond the walls?

## SATURDAY, SEPTEMBER 1

WAS CALLED in for overtime and to be honest, it's a great way to start the month, with a few extra bucks in next week's pay. I had a choice of several areas but decided to work in Loddon South. It's a protection unit and one that houses quite a number of loud, obnoxious crooks that, if you were to put a label on them, I would call painful. A large number of them are in protection due to drug debts which they owe to gangs within the prison. Others are there because they have given up information on prisoners, while a few are there simply because they fear the main stream units and have taken measures to ensure a move to protection.

While some protection units house paedophiles and mainly sex offenders, other units will house no sex offenders, their populations made up entirely of what main stream prisoners call "Rats". These rats are those who will share information with officers and move into a cushy protection unit. As an officer, I can tell you that there is very little difference between a non-sexual offender protection unit and a main stream unit. There are plenty of assaults, rapes, murders, stan-dovers and smuggling that makes me wonder why some crooks will go to such extreme lengths to gain access to protection. It makes very little sense and yet it's a never-ending cycle.

The unit smells of mouldy rubbish as I walk in through the airlock. It's quiet as everybody is still locked down. Three officers are standing in the officer's station and wave at me as I enter. I wave back at them and take my belongings into the staff room where I put my lunch in the fridge and stow my bag in the cupboard.

I head back to the station and greet the 3 officers. Robert Nixon, Jason Smith and Tom Grady are all hunched over one of the unit logs. After shaking hands with each of them, I crane my neck to see what they are so engrossed in. It turns out to be the handover log, a book that is filled out by the previous day's staff. It is supposed to be filled out each evening, especially when specific events need to be highlighted to incoming staff and it appears that a significant event took place in the early evening. It must have happened just after I knocked off from duty the previous day because I didn't hear anything by the time I walked out.

There had been a significant assault in the unit; 3 prisoners attacking 1 other. All 3 were armed with shivs and attacked the victim in the open unit, visible to everyone. The entire incident had been captured on cctv and would provide pretty conclusive evidence when the time came. The victim had been taken to hospital, where he remains. The 3 attackers have been transferred to the management units and will be interviewed by police throughout the day. Both Robert and Jason were in the adjoining unit the previous night and had rushed in to help lock the unit down. Based on what they were saying, there was a lot of blood that had to be cleaned up. I listened as the 2 told us their war story with enthusiasm. It sounded scary and I understood their eagerness to share.

As I have mentioned before, normal officers do not carry weapons of any kind. We do not carry batons, or firearms or even pepper spray. You may think that a bit crazy considering the environment we work in but then you'd be forgiven for not remembering the most important part; the prisoners outnumber us at around 20 or 30 to 1. It would take very little effort for a group to overpower an officer and take their weapons. Although extreme, keeping weapons of any type away from prisoners is common practice. And as we all know; prisoners already have access to enough weapons of their own making without us adding to them. Some officers struggle to safely hang on to their security swipe cards long enough without losing them; I shudder at the thought of giving them weapons, as well.

Just then, the radio comes alive as control calls for morning count. Tom and Jason grab the muster sheet and begin going trap to trap to conduct our count while Robert checks his emails. The phone rings and I answer it. It's Thelma who is in the dispensary and asks whether I could send the unit's methadones to her once count is called correct. I agree and hang up.

The boys return to the station and once the numbers are added up, call the number in to control. Minutes later, the count is called correct and I make my way to the top tier to unlock our prisoners. It's a quick process of inserting the key, twisting the handle open and twisting the key back, thereby unlocking the door without actually opening the cell door. The top tier takes about 5 minutes and when I'm done, return to the station.

Sleepy heads begin to emerge from their cells, each heading to a specific spot in the unit. Most make a sprint for the kitchenette, grabbing their bread and lining up for a go at the toasters. There are several and each is a 4-slicer, increasing the speed of each prisoner's breakfast. There is a calm atmosphere in the unit but all of us know that things can kick off in a split second and remain vigilant as we each begin a required task.

Jason heads for the door as I announce morning methadone's to make their way to the airlock. Being a protection unit, every move has to be escorted by an officer which means one of us has to accompany the required prisoner to wherever they are needed throughout the prison. Some officers see this as a bad thing; I, however, love the idea of not being stuck in a unit all day. It can get pretty stale, sitting in a station with a bunch of guys for 12 hours. Getting the occasional escape means fresh air, a bit of exercise and above all, a break from the non-stop barrage of unit noise, which can include endless questions and requests from needy prisoners.

24 prisoners leave the unit with Jason and once the doors close,

their excitement now out of the common area, the unit quietens considerably. I check my emails and once finish, check out the list of random cell searches we have to do. There are 3 for us, allocated at random and I check the cell numbers against the muster. All 3 seem to be pretty straightforward crooks and I wave the list at Tom.

"Fancy getting your hands dirty?" I ask and he nods. We head off to the first cell and knock on the door. It's not that we need permission to enter, it's just seen as a small bit of courtesy if the prisoner is in the middle of a toilet break or something. We wait a second then open the door with a key. It's empty and I turn around to scan the unit for its owner. He isn't around and think he's probably off to the gym. Tom and I go in and immediately begin to search things. It's not like you see in the movies, where everything is upended and thrown on the floor, then trampled to bits. We take our time, ensuring we not only pay attention to the finer details, but also to avoid needle-stick injuries. The last thing either of us wants, is to be stuck by a real or make-shift needle that's just been used to inject drugs.

Needle-stick injuries are probably one of the most common injuries for an officer to get while on duty. It can come as easily as reaching into a dark place where you can't see, or sliding your fingers under edges of a bunk or shelf. Once you are stuck by a needle, the wait to see whether you are infected by a disease is 3 months. Think about that for a moment. 3 months of not knowing whether you have aids or hepatitis etc. And while you wait those 3 months out, there's no kissing your wife or husband; there's no intimacy with your partner; there's no kissing your children. You are anxiously awaiting the results for 12 longs weeks. I have never personally suffered a needle-stick injury and (touch wood), hope I never do.

Tom takes the clothing shelves, picking up each piece, shaking it out, then roughly refolds each piece and returns it to the shelf. Socks are unfolded; books are opened and the pages flicked through. Magazines are checked thoroughly and, as Tom is about to discover, can be a great hiding place for another sort of contraband.

There is a pile of magazines on a shelf above the clothing and Tom takes them down. Maybe half a dozen or so car mags are put o the small table and he begins to flick through them, one at a time. The first 5 don't reveal anything, but in the sixth, he hits pay dirt. The first few pages on either end are nothing special yet, hidden amongst the inner-most pages are torn out pages of hardcore porn. The porn has been ripped out of another magazine, then hidden amongst the pages of the car magazine. There are almost two dozen pictures showing everything from anal sex to blowjobs and beyond. It may not be considered as much on the outside, but in here, it's pure gold. The porn could be rented out for a night to fellow prisoners for drugs or favours, or even smuggled to a sex offender's unit for a time. Sex offenders would pay big money, real money, for this type of stuff.

"Great find," I say to Tom as he confiscates the magazine. We finish our search and find no other contraband. We exit the cell a short time later and head for the next, one on the upper level almost directly above the first. The door is open and the owner inside. It's Max Turner, a small-time crook in for parole breach. He has extensive drug debts and his appearance is enough to tell you that he's a full-blown junkie. This is probably the biggest cue for my partner and I because a junkie's cell can be filled with real and make-shift needles.

Once we've conducted our strip search and find nothing on his person, Tom and I commence our search. It doesn't take us long to find our first bit of contraband. There's an old plastic coffee jar on the top shelf and it's filled with pens; the clear variety as they are the only type allowed. This strikes me as odd considering there is no paper, no books and no other hint of reading or writing material. A jar filled with pens just looks out of place and as soon as we shake the pens on to the bed, we find several with needles hidden inside the plastic ink reservoirs. We find 7 in total and carefully place them back into the jar and remove the lot.

There's nothing else found inside the cell and we move to the next one, just 3 doors down. It's also occupied, but by 2 prisoners. We knock on the door then open it to find one on his knees in front of the other one who's sitting on the bunk. The sitter has his erection sticking straight up at attention, the saliva from the first prisoner running down its shaft. The one on his knees is already getting to his feet, his face a glowing beacon of embarrassment, while the other pulls his trackpants back up with a wide grin. For some, embarrassment does not come easy.

"Sorry boys, search time," I said and we strip each of them in turn, finding nothing out of order. Once they exit, we commence with the search and although thorough, find nothing out of place.

Once we get back to the officer's station, both Tom and I write reports for each of the cells, bagging and tagging the evidence, then notifying the supervisor. It isn't long before lunchtime count is called and, with nothing exciting happening, it passes without incident. The afternoon isn't really anything too interesting. If you've read the previous chapters of this series, then you already know the procedures that occupy the afternoon. Everything runs smoothly and the afternoon glides by. The only small bit of excitement is when the owner of the first cell returns, a crook who'd actually been at work for the day in one of the factories. He heads to his cell and by the time he reaches it, I've caught up to him to give him the bad news on his porn. He's a long-termer and an experienced prisoner. He doesn't show his disappointment, only a grin to try and play the loss down. He enters his cell and closes the door once I finish talking to him. As I walk away, I hear the dull thud as he punches his wall, clearly upset about the loss.

As we walk out a while later, I remind myself of the importance of reminding one's self of the little things that matter during the shift; like watching out for the needles. Sometimes it's the small pricks that can ruin your whole day.

Today has been a good day.

# SUNDAY, SEPTEMBER 2

ANOTHER OVERTIME SHIFT FOR ME, which means a nice chunk of spare change in my pay packet this week. I'm asked to work in the medical wing and I look forward to a quiet day like it usually is. Although whenever I enter the unit, I still smell the overpowering stench of Robert Coleman (see August Edition), the memories of that day firmly entrenched into my brain. But the stench of shit is not what greets me as I open the inner door to the unit. I'm happy to see Thelma and Vincent (both from August Edition), both great officers to work with, and I know that for the most part, it should be a good day. They tell me that Doris Reading is doing a cook up and should be ready shortly. I slap my head, realizing that I forgot that it was Sunday.

I put my things away, then head to the kitchen to find Doris busy cooking a feast on 2 electric frypans and 2 sandwich presses. I give her a hug then hand her a tenner for my share of the food. She refuses it and I thank her with a kiss on the cheek which makes her blush a little. She doesn't look 62 and the blushing colour in her cheeks makes her look about 40. I head back to the officer's station and chat to the two about usual things. We only have one S3 in an observation cell and he's been very compliant. Sometimes, the suicide watches use threats to kill themselves as ways to bail from a unit. They become almost immediately compliant once they are given a suicide rating and put into an obso cell. I can see him sitting on his bunk as I check the CCTV monitor. He appears to be reading a book and sipping a coffee.

Shortly after, the four of us are also sipping coffee and eating bacon and egg rolls. The smell is amazing and Thelma even brought some delicious cloudy apple juice to wash it all down. It's a highlight of what turns out to be just an ordinary day of checks and escorts as we walk beside the nurses as they conduct their hourly rounds. A couple of times, patients vent their frustration when being woken for a jab here and a finger prick there, but overall, it's a pretty decent way to pocket some extra money on pay day. Rather than bore you with less than interesting stuff, I'll just tell you that it was a good Sunday and a great day to walk out of when we finally did 12 or so hours later.

Today, was a good day.

# TUESDAY, SEPTEMBER 4

I COME in and am directed to the kitchen for a couple of days. One of the normal staff members has taken some overdue annual leave and I get to fill in. It can be a great place to work, especially considering there's a very good kick-back; Food. I can already smell the first kick-back as soon as I walk through the door, fresh eggs and bacon sizzling on one of the large hot-plates. The cook waves at me and points at the food with an equally warm smile which I respond to.

Once my bag is put away, I grab a couple of slices of still warm bread, freshly baked that morning by the hired help. The prisoners do a lot of the prepping for the day's menu, as well as most of the cooking, under the watchful eye of a couple of qualified chefs. The 3 officers that work in the kitchen, just as we do in the rest of the prison, are there purely as deterrents. There are a multitude of things that can be used as weapons so it is imperative that we keep a very close eye on the proceedings. Everything from butcher's knives that are chained to tables, to slicing blades on a deli slicer. Any of the vast number of kitchen utensils the prisoners use on a daily basis are counted, checked and rechecked. Perimeter walks are conducted as well as walks along each of the tables. Its always a good reminder that, when you walk amongst the criminals, keep an eye on the length of chain on the blade they are using at the time.

My other two offsiders are already there, having started a couple of hours before. Two staff have an early start, while a third officer works a shorter shift, not only arriving later, but also finishing earlier. The rotating roster has its good points and bad points and for me, it's a definite win for the day. It makes no difference in my pay as I'm paid a salary, so being rostered on a short shift is just one of the great benefits of working here.

Sam Howell is already downing a bacon-heavy sandwich, waving a hand at me as I shovel some goodness onto my own bread. John Simons, the other officer, is gobbling a sandwich while overlooking the bakery section, four prisoners busy baking the prison's supply of bread. I walk over and shake hands, a quick chin-wag to catch up on any gossip. It's another thing that can be very active in prison.

The prison gossip train is one that is always active and always fully loaded. And it's the very thing that we love, that is responsible for it. The roster. Because people work very different shifts to everybody else, unless you are close to a particular officer and know them personally, you never know what they do or where they are. I remember a time when I went on annual leave for a month and when I returned to work, very few people realised just how long I had been away for. They simply put it down to the roster.

Once we finish our breakfast, I take over the supervision of the bakery and assume a post in one of the nearer corners. I ensure my back is close to a wall to prevent anyone from walking behind me; prevention being better than cure, if you know what I mean. If I don't give them the opportunity then I can avoid most issues. I remain at the post for a couple of hours as I watch giant mixing machines working mountains of dough which are in turn put into baking tins and placed in the industrial ovens. It's a giant production line that ends with the guy that mans the slicing machine, bagging each loaf once done.

Everyone works in silence, a few comments and jokes thrown out here and there. Each joke is met with a sudden burst of laughter which ends just as quickly. The prisoners each work their stations to ensure the line remains productive with each person having a set quota to reach. They work one of two shifts and once they reach their numbers, are allowed to leave. once they've been wanded for metal and also given a pat-down for any goods that may have found their way into pockets, they are returned to their units.

It's mid-morning by the time the first issue arises. A loud barrage of swearing suddenly erupts from the far end of the kitchen, the expletives flying thick and fast. As I go to investigate, I can already see the issue as a prisoner holds his hand close to himself, the chopping station behind him. He's managed to slice his finger and as he holds it up for me to see, blood trickles onto the concrete floor.

"Alright, hold it close," I said and reach for a roll of paper towel sitting on a bench. I hand him a large chunk of it as I hear Sam call a code Mike. Within a few minutes the staff begin to arrive, quickly followed by the nurses. They assess the wound and determine that it requires stitching and ask for the crook to be escorted to the medical wing. A couple of staff members offer to take him and we return to our previous positions, work resuming without hesitation.

When lunchtime count is called, a lot of the crooks begin to pack up their stations, their shifts ending once the count is called correct. It's effectively a changeover of the work crews and Sam and I facilitate the wanding and pat downs once we finish counting up our numbers. I grab the hand-wand and begin scanning the prisoners one at a time. It's a pretty important time as any number of metallic items could be hidden, to be used as weapons once properly fashioned into whatever weapon they had in mind. Sam is conducting pat downs and as I finish with my last one, look at the prisoner he is currently checking. I nearly burst out laughing when I see the insanely huge bulge in the front of his shorts. I tap Sam on the back and when he looks at me, point at the "discreet" package. The crook has an animated grin as he realises that he's been busted. He doesn't kick up, understanding that he's been caught and will be sacked from his position. His haul? A dozen sausages that he's managed to stuff into the front of his underpants; raw and without wrapping, the only package being his own.

He hands them over and then follows us into a private room where we now conduct a full strip search. This reveals a small bag of coffee hidden in his shoe; a bag of sugar in his other shoe; half a dozen slices of bacon in one armpit, again without wrapping. As he turns and bends over, I see the end of a plastic bag protruding from his anus and he laughs as he slowly tugs on it when asked. It gradually escapes the confines of his arsehole and when we finally unbag it, discover half a dozen small balloons which later turn out to contain ICE.

For us, the ICE is a valuable find and could mean that one of the deliveries that had arrived that morning, could have been the source of contraband. The intelligence squad will use this information and track whoever had made deliveries that morning, comparing it to previous finds and deliveries. Every bit of information helps and once we phone the sup with our find, complete our reports, which we send out to everyone who needs it. The crook is not only fired from his job, but also separated into a management unit until the risk is determined. He may have been the mule and once the owners of the drugs find out he's been caught, may come calling for payback which can be thorough.

The afternoon shift arrives about half an hour later and the processes restart. Although the bakery section closes after lunchtime count, there are still plenty of stations to watch as prison meals are prepared by the hundreds. Each unit will send their respective billets up to get their unit's meal trolleys and then return them once the meals have been served.

It's a casual afternoon, highlighted by another cut finger, a code mike for someone with back pain, and one small altercation that resulted in a thrown saucepan that crashed into a wall. It's dealt with quite quickly and tempers eased.

When I walk out alone a few hours later, I'm whistling, happy to be going home. Today, has been a good day.

# WEDNESDAY, SEPTEMBER 5

I'M BACK for another day in the kitchen and another short shift. There's an extra skip in my step as I walk through the door, knowing that after tomorrow's shift, I have a 3-day break. I'm off on a road trip with my wife and I can not wait to leave this place behind, even if only for a few days. Sam and John are already in as I arrive and I grab breakfast after putting my things away. I check the menu board as I chomp down on a bacon and egg sandwich and see that one of my favourite foods is being made today; donuts. The prison has a rotating menu, which means that the same food is served week in week out. Fridays is fish and chip day, for instance, and Mondays is always tuna casserole day. Wednesday's dessert is donut and, for someone with a sweet tooth, the best dessert day of all.

The prisoners are already busy preparing the batter and heating the fryers. The bakery is still in operation, Sam overseeing the area. I go and stand near the donut boys and watch as they bring the doughy mess into a beautiful reality. Trays and trays of donuts need to be prepared, with each prisoner receiving one for dessert that evening. That means hundreds of them need to be made and I'm just the man to watch over them. I stand and watch, finishing my breakfast, when there is a sudden uproar from the other side of the kitchen. Two

Asian prisoners are yelling at each other in Vietnamese, their words not making any sense. But sometimes language isn't really needed when you can see the issue as plain as day. One has not kept up with demand and the other is telling him to pull his finger out of his arse. The quicker they fill their quota, the quicker they finish and this one clearly wasn't too fussed with his speed level. Sam goes over to them and settles them down as John walks over as back-up. The situation is quietened down almost immediately, neither prisoner wanting things to escalate. Sometimes the best thing for an officer to do is just make their presence known. It's not about running in and waving your arms about. If it can be taken care of now, on their terms, then the chances of repercussions later on in the unit can be dramatically reduced. And that's a win for everybody.

All the donuts are finished and packed by 2 that afternoon and when the last of the trays has been put on the trolley and wheeled into the cool room, the moment of glory arrives. One of the cooks, carrying glory before him, sets a loaded tray of hot jam donuts on one of the benches, waving one arm back and forth across the dish like a game-show host presenting a grand prize.

"Enjoy," he says and steps back as a rush of bodies push past him, mine included, a jumble of eager hands reaching for the sweet-smelling reward. There's enough for everyone to eat their fill; five hot jam donuts finding their way into my belly. It's the highlight of an otherwise simple and quiet day. Some days are just not filled with the stuff that fills pages and sells books, but for us, those are the days we appreciate the most.

As I walk out a couple of hours later, the sweet taste of jam still lingering on my lips, I find out that I'm back in the medical wing in the morning. I drop by to see how it is going in there on my way past and am pleased to hear that it has also been a pretty quiet day in there as well. Hopefully, tomorrow will be the same. Today has been a very good day.

# THURSDAY, SEPTEMBER 6

When I return to the medical wing the next day, I'm greeted by that all too familiar hint of shit that I know will never disappear after that horrible day the previous month. It's like its permanently entrenched into the floors. Vicky Temple and Scott Jones are already in the unit and we greet each other with handshakes all round. Behind us, in their own little area, 2 nurses are having a heated debate and, by the sounds of it, are not likely to agree anytime soon. It's unclear to us what it's about and, as long as they don't start to tangle each other physically, we don't get involved.

The morning muster is finished within a few minutes and once count is called correct; I unlock the first lot of prisoners from their hospital cells. They begin to shuffle out; half out into the courtyard to catch some early spring rays, the other half pacing up and down the corridors. A couple flick the TV on whilst another one jumps on the treadmill. I return to the station and check the day's moves, looking for any names that are currently residing in here. There are no names that match and I close the list down and engage a prisoner in conversation. He's standing close by and he asks about one of my tattoos. It's a black circle surrounding something that resembles a strange letter

K; it's the symbol for "Ka" from the Dark Tower series, by Stephen King.

"Is that like a peace symbol?" he asks, pointing a finger at my forearm. He's a fairly new prisoner, aged in his late 30's.

"No," I said, shaking my head. "Do you read, William?" I ask and he ponders for a bit.

"Sometimes, not much though."

"It's a symbol from a book by my favourite author. Ever read any Stephen King?" He shakes his head.

"Watched the Shining once. Scared the shit out of me," he said, laughing a little. We talk for a bit and he listens while I explain the meaning of the symbol. I always appreciate talking to prisoners when they are interested in what I have to say. He asks me more about the story of the Dark Tower and I give him a brief rundown of the 8-book odyssey. It's one of my favourite subjects and one that I enjoy talking about. It's rare that I meet people interested in Stephen King and when I do, I try and help them understand the amazing breadth of his work, often misunderstood as being just horror.

It's a good hour before William returns to his cell and I begin locking the prisoners up shortly after. It's time for the next group to come out for their time out in the open and the changeover is quick and efficient. The new group almost mimics the first, some going outside while others congregate around the TV and treadmill. The whole process repeats itself a couple more times throughout the day, each change over running smoothly and quickly. There are some places within this prison that are just meant to be laid back and this is one of them.

Having a couple of easy days in a row is somewhat of a blessing as I know that it won't last forever. It never does in this place and although I know there's drama in the future, I try and enjoy the peace while I have it. It's an enjoyable day and when I walk out a few hours later, look forward to my upcoming road trip.

Today was a great day.

# MONDAY, SEPTEMBER 10

It's quite hard to walk back into the prison after an amazing weekend away. But as we all know, no matter how long the holiday, they always come to an end and reality resumes all too quickly. I head to Thomson east, a main stream unit housing a variety of prisoners including one significant group from a motorcycle gang. I won't name them but as is common knowledge, there are a large number of outlaw motorcycle clubs and when thrown together in a room, don't tend to play well together.

The unit is quiet as I enter and I immediately pack my things away. I head to the officer's station and as I sit, hear the door open as 2 other officers enter the unit. A massive smile begins to grow on my face as I see a familiar face walk in. It's my friend Kon Giopoulos, an officer that almost died in the prison a couple of months ago (see June edition). Today is Kon's first day back and I exit the station to greet him. We hug it out and he tells me that he's glad to be back. It's been a long road to full recovery but he's been given the all clear and here he is.

Normally, officers are put on light duties upon returning from an injury. Kon is not one to take on any form of light duties. He's a very proud man and working units is what he does. The other officer,

Thelma Wallace, is also a veteran of the place. I'm in very good company and look forward to the day. As we enter the station, a sudden commotion erupts in a cell on the upper deck, almost above us. We can hear the crooks yelling at each other, accompanied by the flat cracks of slaps and punches. Thelma follows me as I head upstairs, go to the cell door and drop the trap. I look in and can see two prisoners appearing to cuddle each other, blood dripping from one of their mouths. I kick the door a couple of times and get their attention. They immediately release each other and head to opposite ends of the cell.

"Guys, what's going on?" I ask.

"Caught this fucking rat stealing my chips," one of them yells, pointing at the other prisoner. Thieving, as contradictory as it sounds, is a definite no-no and for the prisoner accused of the crime, will almost certainly mean a unit move. Not only will the commotion have been heard by adjoining cells, but the crook who accused him will almost certainly tell his mates. The one accused, looks to be no older than 20, small and meek. His name is Bobby Thomas and he's only been in prison for a couple of days. He hangs his head in shame, the bag of chips in question, lying crushed on the floor between them.

Thelma heads back down the stairs and phones the Sup. Once she has clearance, she returns and between us, we unlock the cell to remove the thief for his own protection. Kon is already on the phone to the Vacancy department and after informing them of the details, is given a new unit for the crook. He's off to a protection unit and once count is called correct, will be moved before the unit is unlocked. I hope for his sake; he learns to keep his fingers to himself. He's likely to have them cut off in here, if he doesn't learn quickly.

We finish our count and, once Control calls count correct, arrange with Loddon South to send their transport officer to come and get this kid. Kon and I head back to his cell and take the other one out so the kid can pack his things up. We give the other one a chance to put his things up on his bunk to ensure nothing else is stolen. Kon and I stand watch as the kid packs and, once he's done, hand him over to the transport officer. He exits the unit to a chorus of dog-whistles and cheers.

Once they are safely out, Kon and I begin to unlock the unit, prisoners exiting their cells and heading to their respective activities. Some head to the toasters for breakfast while others head to the laundry and begin their washing. A few head to the officer's station and others begin using the gym equipment. There's no gymnasium today so the prisoners will keep busy on the unit equipment, which in itself, is quite adequate.

Thelma is standing in the station and is already inundated with questions by the time Kon and I return. As we begin to facilitate requests, the morning medication trolley enters and a lot of the prisoners begin to form a line in front of the dispensary window. The line is quiet and for once, everyone seems to just want to get their meds and get on with their day. There's only one little flare up when one of the newer prisoners tries to get his medication without his ID card. But when the rest of the crooks begin burning him, he quickly retreats and goes back to his cell to get his card. When he re-joins the back of the line, he stands quietly, his head staring at the floor.

Once the med trolley exits after the last of the meds are given, the unit settles into it's usual routine. 2 prisoners are transferred out to other units and 1 transfers in. There are a couple of cell re-shuffles and most of the work is completed by the time lunchtime count is called correct a few hours later.

The afternoon goes by as we watch several prisoners play cards; a table-tennis match; several prisoners play pool as well as the usual line-up of fitness exercises. It's around 2 o'clock when Kon and I agree to conduct our random cell searches. We are pleased when 2 of the 3 cells allocated for searching prove to be vacant and when we approach the third, see that it's occupied by a quiet Asian, named Tran. He is about as straight as they come; in jail for drug smuggling.

Many Vietnamese are in our jail and for 99% of them, it's due to drug smuggling. After we strip Tran and search his person, we let him leave and we search as best we can. The cell is so clean that we struggle to fault anything. Every bit of surface is clean and free from dirt and dust and there is nothing out of place. After searching fruitlessly for almost 20 minutes, we exit the cell and return to the station.

The games continue and for us at least, it's another afternoon that we can take it easy. The prisoners behave themselves for the rest of the day and as we exit the prison as a group a couple of hours later, I'm glad to see my mate back at work. It's been a long time without him but I can see that he's happy to be back where he belongs.

Today was a good day.

## TUESDAY, SEPTEMBER 11

WOKE up feeling very ordinary and decide to utilize a sick day. I remain in bed for the rest of the day and enjoy a 3-day break.

# FRIDAY, SEPTEMBER 14

THE SALLY PORT is not one of those places that people will actively volunteer for, yet for me, it still remains one of the few places where I feel like I'm not part of the prison. For one thing, there is absolutely no prisoner contact, unless of course, the Day Sup escorts one out for his discharge. It is also a place where you have very little staff contact, the only "faces" from the prison being shadow shapes behind reflective glass that watch you from the control room. Other than that, it's basically trucks and buses and the drivers of each that you deal with.

Today was a day where I literally felt at home. And I only had today to go before I was going away for a few days to drive interstate. My wife and I were heading up the coast to visit her Dad for a few days. He'd been doing it tough after falling quite ill and we decided to both take some annual leave and head up to see him for a few days.

The morning rush of court buses coming in and out of the prison was well and truly under way by the time I arrived for my shift a little after 5. The night officer, some new officer I'd never met before, waved at me and then disappeared almost as quick. Some people just weren't born with the basic courtesies of life. But I wasn't too fussed; instead, I was happy to be there.

Once I put my things away, I waited for control to raise or lower the roller doors at either end of the area. I could see movement through tiny little slits in the metallic roller shutters and heard the voices of people from both sides. The inner door made a sudden crumple of disapproval and a second later began to retract; slowly winding itself up and up and up. It revealed a bus carrying prisoners to court. Once the roller door had reached its pinnacle, the bus slowly rolled forward, creeping over several CCTV cameras that were embedded in the floor. I watched the monitor as it drove over the cameras and then, once I was satisfied it was all clear, gave the thumbs up for control to bring the roller shutter down again. Only when it is secured does the driver and offsider exit their vehicle.

"Morning Simon, we have 5" the passenger calls out to me. I wave back, flashing a smile at her. They both approach and I enter the cabin of their truck, ensuring they have no hidden passengers or contraband inside. I also confirm that they are carrying their phones and iPad. The book marks their incoming belongings and this need to be married up on exit. Anything left behind is considered smuggled contraband and can carry charges as well as instant dismissal. It's definitely not the way you'd want to lose your job.

Once their cabin checks out, I do a quick walk around of their vehicle and check that all the doors are secured and latched. An unlocked door is considered a major security breach and again, carries very harsh penalties. The bus checks out and another thumbs up to control begins to raise the outer roller shutter. It slowly trundles up its tracks as the two officers return to their cabin. I turn to the control window and hold up 5 fingers to signify the number of prisoners onboard. Once the door is fully raised, they start the bus and slowly drive out. Another bus is already waiting outside the door and the drivers wave at each other as they pass and the incoming bus enters the sally port. It too drives over the cameras embedded in the floor and the process is repeated. Incoming buses are processed a little different though.

As the door trundles shut again, the officers exit their vehicle and are themselves searched for any contraband. They are wanded with a hand-held metal detector and remove their boots for inspection. I check the cabin and also ensure the doors are secured. Once I'm satisfied that the bus is clear, I give control a thumbs up as well as signalling a closed fist to them. This means that the bus is empty and is carrying a count of zero prisoners. As the control room keeps a tally of the prison count, it is imperative that they maintain a clear understanding of how many prisoners are coming in and out of the prison; a count that is directly dependant on me.

There are about a dozen morning trucks for me to check during entry to the prison, and then recheck during their exit. It's a process that I will repeat multiple times throughout the day and one that one gets very familiar with as the day wears on. As well as court buses, there are delivery trucks that need to be thoroughly searched. Delivery trucks can be seen as one avenue of introducing contraband, such as any type of modern technology, drugs, alcohol and tobacco. It's probably fair to say that multiple movies and TV shows have gotten this part right. Unfortunately for us, smuggling small things in can be very simple as we are limited with what we can actually search. Anything sealed, such as food containers, is out of bounds as these items have been factory sealed at another location. And yet every day, things will make their way in and be freely distributed right under our noses.

The other thing that happens in the Sally port, and as read about with rather comical results (see August edition) are when prisoners are discharged from prison; when they have completed their sentences or are granted parole. This can result in various different experiences, from the good as you watch joy and relief on a first-timer who might actually use the prison experience as a genuine lesson and never return; to the ones that like to flip you the bird as they tell you to "keep the fucken bed warm, Dog". But in the end, it really makes no difference. Stay out, come back, it doesn't matter one way or the other.

There are quite long stretches of time between buses and trucks at times and it's these times where, if you have some, can catch up on other things; be it reading a book or magazine, drawing or writing. I think you can guess what I do during those times, the results of which you are reading right now.

There are a few codes throughout the day, mainly code mikes called for unwell prisoners that require medical attention in their respective units. There is one code foxtrot but I don't find out the details due to my isolated position. For me, it's actually a good thing as I use it as a break from the shit; for you, I guess, not so much.

If you think that there's action on a daily basis, at every site in the prison, then I'm sorry to say there's not. Very little "drama" happens in the Sally port. It's just a day of processing and searching; of idle chit-chat and minor introductions to new drivers. But for me, it also serves as a tiny break from the stresses and awareness of what the rest of the prison still endures.

For me, the day is a good one.

# THURSDAY, SEPTEMBER 20

My first night shift in quite some time and my heart sinks down into my feet as I realise that I'm in Murray South for the night. Of all the management units, this one was the absolute worst. Comprised of 3 separate areas in the one building, the station is placed in such a position that all the cells, except the ones located in solitary, can see everything you do, thanks to some ventilation mesh that's embedded into each cell door. You are watched by close to 60 sets of eyes from the moment you enter the unit and, if the prisoners are in the right frame of mind, can burn you for hours.

The day-staff greet me as I enter the unit, all happy to be within minutes of the end of their shift. Jason Parker takes me through the highlights of the day and also shows me the 2 watches I have. Both are S2's, meaning half-hourly observations throughout the night. The other 4 staff commence their lock-down counts as I stow my things away. It doesn't take long for control to call the count correct and within mere minutes of showing up, I'm left alone.

From the way the crooks begin yelling, I know that it's going to be a long night. They either burn one of their own or burn the night officer; it's usually one or the other and if the night officer isn't a regular face that they know, that's who cops it. I can tell you from experience, it's not easy. The abuse is raw, nasty and very, very personal. They yell everything from raping your mother, wife or sister, to hot-watering you when you give them their breakfast in the morning. If you ever find yourself in this situation, the best advice I can give you is to ignore it. I know it's not easy to do, believe me, I really do. The irony is that I'm actually sitting in the very same unit, during a night shift, as I'm writing this passage for you about the night in question (and yes, I'm writing this while being burnt). It is just baiting, the crooks hoping that they get a reaction because, if they do, they know they have you. Do not give in.

"Aye dog, shoulda brought your mother with ya," one yells.

"Were your parents related, ya fuckin mutt?" yells another. I can turn a television on if I choose, but I'd rather spend my spare time writing. It allows me to focus on other things while riding the abuse. If I cave, the abuse will never end. And so, the night begins with me checking my emails, while keeping an eye on the CCTV monitors of the main areas. I can also hear abuse from the solitary area and can hear them burning some poor fool in there. The target was transferred into the unit just a few hours prior and it isn't long before he caves.

It's less than an hour into my shift and the intercom buzzes. When I answer it, a quiet voice slowly creeps out to me.

"Boss," he whispers.

"Yes, what's up?" I ask.

"I can't guarantee my own safety," he said and I groan inside. It's not a genuine cry for help or threat of suicide; it's a bail. He just wants to get out because of the burning. I know this because he is whispering to me. The reason he's whispering is because he doesn't want anyone to hear his call for help. If they catch wind of his attempted bail, the burning will increase ten-fold.

Even though I know it's nothing more than an attempted bail, it isn't my call to judge. I have neither the qualification to make that assumption, nor the authority. As far as I'm concerned, the threat is as real as any other.

"Sit tight and I'll get someone to come and chat with you. You'll be OK for a few minutes, yeah?" I ask and he says he'll wait. Of course, he will. It takes me a few minutes to ascertain the night psych's whereabouts, but when I do, request their attendance.

The night psych, Walleed, arrives a few minutes later and I escort him to the cell. I stand by as he attempts to talk to the crook through the trap but the other prisoners have cottoned on to what's about to happen and commence an assaultive barrage of abuse that is so loud, the nurse is unable to hear the crook's voice. Although he tries for several minutes, it's an impossible task and he eventually beckons me out into an adjoining office. He asks me for alternatives and I ask him to sit tight while I contact the night supervisor. When Clare arrives, I give her a rundown and she calls for extra staff to assist. Once we have almost half a dozen officers, we escort the crook to a room that's located in one of the other sections. He is now comfortable enough to speak with the psych and once he does, admits that he just wants to get out of the unit. Clare tells him that the prison is full and it will be impossible to remove him now; he'd have to wait until the morning. But he shakes his head, determination in his eyes telling us that he'd rather do something stupid than return to his cell.

The psych beckons us out of the room and the crook is left sitting at the table, his hands cuffed in front of him. There's only a table with attached seats so he's unable to use anything against us. The nurse begins to explain the situation to us and as we listen, I see the crook stand, walk near a wall and begin slamming his head into it; low flat thuds emanating out to us with each impact.

"It's not gonna change anything," the nurse says through the door and the prisoner stops and sits back down. He knows how to play the game and that's exactly how I've come to see it; nothing more than a silly game of chicken. Prisoners know how to manipulate the system to their needs and this is one of those ways.

"Just escort him to the medical unit," Clare says. "We'll have to move someone out of one of the observation cells and into another unit for the night." And just like that, the crook wins the game and is escorted out. As he exits the room, the unit erupts into a crescendo of abuse and dog whistles as the other prisoners let their feelings known. The crook keeps his head low as he's led out and, just like that, it's just me and the remaining sets of eyes again.

It's another couple of hours before the unit begins to settle down, a couple of "under the door" conversations going on here and there. They leave me alone for the most part and that suits me fine. It gives me the headspace to do some writing. It's just after midnight before the unit is silent, except for the occasional cough, bed fart and flushing toilet.

The rest of the night progresses slowly as I tap away on my keyboard. Clare visits around 2 in the morning and, after a brief chat, she continues on her rounds. The day staff begin to arrive a little before 7 and after a brief handover of the previous night's events, I bid my temporary goodbyes and head out.

I hate that unit, but all things aside, I'm walking out and that means it must have been an OK night.

## FRIDAY, SEPTEMBER 21

As much as it pains me to write this, and I mean this sincerely, I hate telling you that I returned back to Murray South for a second night. If the previous night was bad then tonight can only be described as a complete fuck up, from start to finish. I can already hear the shouting well before I enter the corridor that leads up the unit entrance, feeling like I want to rip my heart out and nail it to the fence for the night; maybe grab it back if I walk past here in the morning.

Jason is sitting in the station as I enter and I hear a couple of crooks greet me, prison style. But their greetings immediately evaporate, like water off a duck's back; Jack is grinning at me and it's the type of grin that quickly births a groan in my throat.

"Got a new arrival coming. He's about five minutes away and just in time for you," he said, the sarcasm biting me like fingers on a chalkboard. I was already wound up, not only from the previous night but also just by being back in here now.

"Oh yeah? Is it Ricky Gervais? Coming in to entertain us for the night?" I said, my own sarcasm sounding deflated and weak.

"Toby Manning," a voice from behind me says and as I turn around, see Vicky Temple enter the station. Her grin matches the one sitting before me perfectly. I hear an internal thump as my heart hits the floor and begins convulsing. What can I say about Toby Manning? (see August edition) Painful, hard work, a handful, irritating, messed up; and did I mention painful?

"Thanks, guys," I said and put my bag away, sitting down in one of the chairs and watching as two other officers begin evening count. The voices from within the cells are still enthusiastic, as they continue their conversations about lost girlfriends, stolen cars, and one on the bottom deck that was explaining to a couple of others how to break into a particular model of bus. Go figure.

When count is called correct twenty minutes later, the day crew make their way out of the unit, telling me to have a good night with sarcastic grins and little snickers. It might be a little facetious, but there's no malice intended on their behalf. All of them had been in my situation before; each having served their own night duties in here.

The phone rings almost immediately and I'm advised that a couple of Tactical officers are escorting Toby up now. I acknowledge the call and hang up. His cell is on the bottom deck and one of the closest to my station and so, I head over and unlock the door. The prisoners already know about the move; the prison telegraph transmitting faster than phone calls between officers at times.

"Toby is coming," one yells, and although there are a few laughs and howls, I can hear their own apprehension. Like I said, Toby can be very painful and, as you'll read soon, not just to officers.

The doors open a few minutes later and a grinning Toby walks in, flanked by two officers that tower over him by at least 18 inches. He's about 5'6, 32-years old, and is thin and wiry. Although he used to have hair, he's now bald, thanks to some manipulation by his case workers. You see, one of Toby's habits is to bronze up (look up the meaning in the prison terms section at the beginning of this book if you're unsure of what that means), and at times, enjoyed using his own shit as hair wax and giving himself "poohawks" as he called them.

He flashes me a grin as he walks in and shows me his now vacant gums; his teeth all removed due to decay.

"Hello Mr King," he says as he heads for his unit.

"Hey Toby," I said, recognising the grin only too well. Toby's IQ is around 30, having the mental age of an 8-year old. This makes him very susceptible to influence from the other prisoners which, I hoped, would work in my favour. They also began to greet Toby under their doors, yelling things out to him. Toby heard them and I could see his head lift a little higher, his shoulders drawing back a little as he walked proudly into his cell like a regular idol. As the tactical boys follow him in, Toby turns on them and his voice instantly turns to one of hatred and threat. He holds his cuffed hands out to the officers, beckoning them to uncuff him.

"Take these off, you fucken maggot," he said to them, his voice loud enough to carry out into the unit and I can see the delight on his face when the prisoners begin to cheer him, egging him on for more. As he sees me standing outside the door, he grins again. "What are you looking at, dog? Fuckin dog." The unit erupts into gales of laughter as the officers remove the shackles and exit his cell. As they close his door, I hear him spit at them, but the door slams home before it hits anybody.

"Fuckin dogs," comes from within the cell as Toby begins to kick the door, the loud booms exploding in my ears. They are so loud that you think your brain is rattling.

"Leave him with you," the officers say to me, the same shit-eating grin on their faces as were on the day staff before them. I thank them in my own sarcastic fashion and see them out, once again, alone with my crooks.

The banging and shouts from Toby continue for a while, and pretty soon the other prisoners grow tired of it. It makes it not only hard to hold conversations, but the banging is loud enough to make watching television almost impossible. I can hear a couple of the prisoners telling Toby to stop but it's like trying to talk to a rabid dog. I dial in his intercom and try and get his attention. For a moment I only hear him kicking and panting, still yelling the same abuse at the now-gone officers that walked him up. He thinks he's impressing the other prisoners, but unbeknownst to him, they are starting to get pretty pissed with him. When he finally hears me on the intercom, he stops the kicking and I hear him walk over to the speaker.

"What do you want, Dog," he shouts, still trying to play to his audience. I try and calm him down, asking him how his day was, but he doesn't listen, resuming his abuse. It's no good and I hang up. He presses the intercom and starts shouting as soon as I answer. I hang up again and he presses the button again, and again, and again. I have no choice but to answer the call as the intercoms are not only seen as an emergency device but are also 100% monitored by a government department. I begin to hear more prisoners call on Toby to shut up and once he hears the calls, finally begins to quieten. I hang up the intercom but he immediately re-calls. I call the Night Sup and explain the situation. He gives me the OK to leave the intercom open with the volume turned down until he's asleep. Calls from other cells can still be received, but Toby's connection needs to be broken before they can be answered. As a new call notification comes in, I hang up on Toby and answer the next call in line. They are simple calls such as handing out toilet paper, requests for food which are denied, and the ever-present request for coffee; again denied.

Once they finally give up trying to get me to hand shit out, I leave the connection to Toby open and finally check my emails. It's nearly 10 o'clock and it feels good to have the unit quiet. Conversations are still progressing around the place but, for the most part, they leave me alone. Just as I'm about to close the email program, I hear a faint sound that I recognize immediately. I turn the intercom up a bit and listen.

"Gonna flood up, Cunt," I hear Toby say, the familiar rush of a shower in the background. It's a game he knows only too well and one that I have been known to play a few times; crooks like him on one side, and officers with no choice on the other. I go to the water cabinet that's next to his cell and, once I open it up, begin to turn the taps off that supply water to his cell. I know what will come next and, although I'd rather keep the shower running, it's something that I must do. I hear the water begin to slow, then quit completely, Toby kicking the door a couple of times in disgust. "Think that's gonna work, Dog?" he yells and I return to the station, ready for round 2.

It's almost midnight by the time the unit is finally completely quiet, the only sounds being the low TV sounds emanating from various cells. The prison has (I know, I know) a special movie channel that plays latest-release movies 24-hours a day and some prisoners, especially those that are confined to their cells for 23 of those 24 hours, prefer to watch TV by night and sleep by day. I turn my own TV on and begin flicking through the channels. I come across a Gordon Ramsay thing and begin to watch. What can I say; he's the only one on TV that speaks my kind of language. I watch as he goes into some idiot's cool room and discovers boxes of rotten produce and mangy chicken. I try and sit a little closer to hear and then the intercom pipes up. It's Toby again and I answer him, expecting the worst.

"What's up, Toby?" I ask.

"I need some toilet paper, please."

"OK, I'll bring you some." I grab a roll from one of the cupboards and walk to his cell door. I raise the viewing window first, to make sure he isn't standing there with a cup of piss or something. I shine my torch in and see Toby standing just inside the door, his grin wide and full. At first, the dark patches on his face don't register with me and I'm about to open the trap to hand him the roll. Fireworks suddenly explode in my mind as I take a second look and shine my torch directly into his face. His face, head and shirtless torso are covered in thick, brown shit, the little bits of corn he must have eaten the previous day, smeared here and there. The smell hits me then, even through a couple of inches of steel.

"How do you like that, Dog?" he yells and begins kicking the door again. Bang, bang, bang. A couple of other crooks begin to shout for him to shut the fuck up but he doesn't stop. I return to the station and call the Sup. It's not really asking for help, just more to let them know what's going on, just in case things kick off. As I hang up, other crooks begin banging their own doors, shouts now telling Toby to pull his head in. It takes another hour to quieten things down enough for me to be able to hear him on the intercom. He still isn't talking sensibly and I have no choice but to leave the line open and once again reduce the volume. It's almost 3 by the time I hear nothing else from him. The soft snores that come through the speaker, tell me that he's finally given up.

By 6 that morning, Toby has awoken and apologized for his behaviour. He knows that his case workers will be told of his behaviour and, just like an 8-year old, wants to make good before they find out. I turn his water back on and he agrees to shower the shit off himself and clean up his cell. When I serve breakfast shortly after, his clean smile greets me and I hand him his toast. Day staff begin to arrive and I clap each on the back and tell them to enjoy. As I grab my things, I make my farewells and walk out without looking back.

Another shift in that shithole finished and I couldn't be happier as I walk out. It is after all, my weekend.

## TUESDAY, SEPTEMBER 25

TODAY I WAS in Visits and although I was in a very good mood when I came into the prison, it didn't last long. I'm OK working with people who don't understand the finer points of being in close proximity with people who have a propensity to deal with situations that don't go the way they think they ought to, with violence and abuse. You know; people who know what can set a prisoner off and try and avoid those things in order to maintain a relatively safe environment. What I'm not OK with, is working with people that will go out of their way to stir shit up; to wind a prisoner up and look for a reaction. What those people are known as, are arsonists. The reason being, that if you work with them, you'd better carry a fire extinguisher in your back pocket so that you can put out all the little spot fires as you follow them.

If you have been following my writings, then you're probably expecting me to write one name in particular; Tony Malone. He can be, as we know, quite painful. But no, the name is not Tony Malone who, in this case, I probably would have preferred with me today. The name of the thorn that was in my side today is Brock Livingston. He'd only graduated from his induction course a couple of weeks prior and although fresh into the prison, apparently had six years' experience at another facility. I'm not one to doubt, but to be honest, didn't believe it.

As I entered the building, Robert Hall, a 45-year veteran, greeted me as he went about setting up the book. A new officer followed close behind me and when I introduced myself, he told me his name was Brock.

"Pleased to meet you," I said, offering him my hand. Robert and Brock also shook and we stowed our bags in the staff room. Once our bags and lunches were put away, we headed back into the strip area. We agreed that Robert would run the book until lunchtime and then I would take it over. I didn't mind running the book as it broke up the day a bit. And staring at naked men for 6 hours was much better than staring at them for 12.

"Why do I have to strip the whole day?" Brock asked.

"Because you're the junior today," Robert said, looking at Brock over the rim of his reading glasses. You could see by his expression that he didn't like the answer but unfortunately that's the rules. New officers get to practice their stripping skills while still settling into the job. Robert wasn't always as accommodating as me and would often throw new officers in at the deep end. It was his way of seeing whether they would sink or swim. This was after all, maximum security. It wasn't a place where you needed to be led around by the hand, being shown the ins and outs of everything that went on. Some things you just had to figure out yourself. The thing about stripping is that it brought you into close proximity with prisoners when they are at one of their most vulnerable. That meant you quickly learnt how to interact with them, whether they were in a good frame of mind or bad. Robert had heard that Brock came directly from a youth justice centre. This was a very different environment compared to 16 to 21-year old inmates.

Robert Hall had been a correctional officer for most of his life. Currently 68 years old, he started his career in maximum security back in 1973, a couple of years after I was born. He's a lovely man with a great sense of humour. He could be hard when he needed to be, but generally, was the kind of officer that didn't have anything to prove. He'd pretty much seen it all and the crooks had a certain respect for him. He was nearing retirement age and he'd told me a few times while working with him, that he didn't look forward to ending his career. His wife, Eileen, had passed away a few years ago and, with no family around, didn't really want to "sit around home alone" as he put it. The problem was, Robert was beginning to slow down considerably and he had troubling hearing. Some of the newer prisoners were giving him a hard time when he didn't hear what they were saying, especially when he asked them to repeat themselves.

Control signals a correct muster and Robert calls the front to see which visitors had arrived. Once he receives the list, he begins notifying units of which prisoners are required to attend. It's one of the few times where prisoners don't need to be asked twice about attending somewhere. Visits, the gymnasium and methadone are probably the only times that prisoners will skip out of a unit, anxious to get to their destination.

Whilst waiting for the prisoners to turn up, the phone rings and we watch as Robert answers the call, his face growing blank and grey. Brock watches him, then leans in to me to ask what the issue was. I didn't need to wait for Robert's explanation. I knew what the call was about and it was one of those things you try to avoid.

Robert hangs the phone up and checks his list. He runs his pen down and when he reaches the intended target, taps it repeatedly.

"Watson, box visit." Brock looks at him, confused. "His missus scanned positive for meth," Robert continues.

"When a visitor scans positive to drugs, and if they can't find any during the subsequent strip search, the visit can continue but has to be converted to a box visit," I tell Brock. His face lights up with recognition as he begins to understand. I watch him as I see his mind begin to tick over. Finally, after almost a full minute, he finally comprehends the consequence to changing the visit from a contact visit to a non-contact visit.

"Holy shit, he's gonna be pissed, ain't he?" he finally asks.

"Yes, he is," Robert says and looks at Brock sternly. "Maybe let me tell him and you stand back." Brock looked at him for a moment, considering his options. He took a step back and lent against the wall.

"I could do it. I'm not stupid," he mumbles but we ignore him. It's not a situation we want or need and deciding on who will tell the prisoner that he might not be able to hold his child or girlfriend or mother is not something worth debating over. Robert and I both know that the best way to deal with the situation is to simply deal with it head on and not try and sugar coat it. If we don't make a big deal of it, chances are, neither will the crook. I'm about to share this with Brock, but the door opens and four prisoners walk in.

"Boss," the first one says, greeting Robert and dropping his ID card on the table in front of him.

"Morning, boys," Robert replies and ticks each of their names off. The box visit isn't among them and I signal the first prisoner to follow me into the strip room. We go through the usual process and, as we finish, I see Brock stripping another prisoner in the adjoining room. I motion to another prisoner when the door opens and two more enter our area. I follow the crook into the strip room and just as we begin the dance, I hear Robert speak the words that are dreaded in this particular area.

"Sorry son, it's changed to a box visit."

"What? But why Boss?" the prisoner asks, his voice already frantic.

"I don't know, but your visitor will be able to shed light on it. They don't tell us what happens out the front."

"But Boss, I haven't seen my missus in weeks. Please, not a box visit." His voice is starting to crack but, looking over my shoulder, I can tell he won't go much further. His shoulders are slumped, his head down, almost defeated. If he was going to become aggressive, he would be up on his toes, his shoulders high and arms ready to strike. Aggressive prisoners don't tend to stand still and look like they need to be seated. They are up, loud, maintain eye contact and almost bounce on the spot, ready to strike. Recognizing body language is an important part of the job and as I have said in previous chapters, an officer's biggest weapon is his mouth. But, as in many examples of sheer stupidity, it can also be the greatest betrayer; especially on an inexperienced officer with a bad case of attitude.

"Dude, wanna shut the fuck up? Get in here so I can strip ya," were the words that I heard next. Not from Robert but from Brock. He had the intelligence level of a door handle and I'm pretty sure you know what happened next. Watson turned and within a split second was in Brock's face.

"You shut the fuck up, screw dog," he screamed, spittle flying from his lips. Brock's face turned crimson as I saw him look at me, his fingers starting to fumble for his radio. "Rip your fuckin tongue outa your head, cunt." He kept his hands down by his side and I saw Brock begin to raise his own, defensively. I saw another crook turn and take a step towards the two men.

"Sit down, Jason," I said to him and he looked at me with apprehension. "Brock, let it go," I said, turning back to the two. Robert sat in his chair, completely surprised at the stupidity of the newer officer. But Watson was fired up and I could see he was about to explode. And then, as if still in doubt about the volatility of the prisoner, Brock made the second mistake of the morning. Rather than use a clearance strike to keep the prisoner back, Brock grabbed Watson around the throat with one hand and tried to pull him forward. He actually wanted to go toe to toe with a crook that had been actively pumping weights for four years straight.

I was left with no choice but to hit the duress button on my radio and call a code alpha as Watson grabbed Brock by the shirt and half picked him up, smashing him back into the wall behind them. Robert yelled for the other prisoners to get into one of the strip rooms and locked them in, preventing them from joining the scuffle. I yelled at Watson to step back and let Brock go but he wasn't listening. Instead, he reached up and grabbed Brock's throat with both hands, his hands as strong as vices. With little choice, I brought my fist down on Watson's forearm as hard as I could and broke his hold on Brock. He turned on me in a split second and took a step towards me, his fists at the ready. I instinctively performed a clearance strike as he took yet another step towards me, deflecting him to my side. All it would have taken then was for someone to give him a slight push and Watson would have stumbled into an open strip room where he could have been locked up until he either cooled down or the Tactical Officers removed him. Either way, it would have been a closed case with a simple report.

If only things had of happened like that. But like I said, inexperience can be traitorous in this place. Before I could react, what happened next played out in an almost slow-motion movie; a movie I was helpless to stop. I watched as Brock was rubbing his throat; the look on his face more embarrassment than anger. He was looking at the floor and appeared to be calm. Watson was trying to regain his balance, rubbing his forearm. Robert was standing opposite to me, shaking his head. I heard the door open as officers were getting ready to assist. Then, without the slightest warning and moving so fast, Brock took two steps forward, pushed me aside and wound his fist back. He pistoned his punch straight out, connecting with the back of Watson's head. His push had knocked me off balance as I stumbled backwards and I saw Robert lunge forward much too slowly, unable to stop the attack.

I saw Watson's eyes flicker, roll upwards, then close before he hit the floor as officers piled into the room, some grabbing Brock and dragging him back. I saw a look of bewilderment in Robert's face as one of the other people called a code mike.

The commotion that followed can only be described as shocking. The strip rooms had a small side window down the side of each door. The crooks that had been locked away watched the whole mess unfold and were going ballistic in their room. One of them had punched the window, smashing it and opening up three fingers on his hand with blood pouring down the white door. All three were screaming and the room was echoing so bad, my head felt like it was rattling from the noise. I looked down and saw Watson shaking uncontrollably, the seizure gripping him tightly. He'd hit his head on the floor when he fell and blood was pooling to the side of his face.

It took a good twenty minutes for everything to be brought back under control. The nurses arrived within minutes and were treating

Watson, who had stopped seizing by then. Several tactical officers brought the 3 crooks in the strip room under control and the one with an injured hand was off having it fixed. Brock was taken up the front where he would be required to complete an officer's report. Robert and I were also now filling out our reports while everything was still fresh in our minds. The prison remained operational but the Visits centre had been closed for the time being as we tended to our reports.

"I should have stopped him," Robert suddenly said as we sat, breaking the silence, the clicking of the keyboards suddenly stopping.

"It wasn't your fault, Rob," I replied. "You handled it exactly the way it should have been. Brock fucked up." But Robert shook his head.

"No, I should have known he'd act that way. I knew Watson would kick off. I should have handled it better. And I could have stopped his punch. I was right there." He paused, wiped his eyes and looked at the ceiling. Then he looked at his hands as he held them in front of his face. "Too dam slow these days. Maybe my prison days are over."

"Rob, you're fine. You're an amazing officer. No-one could have stopped Brock except Brock. Don't beat yourself up over it. Seriously." He nodded and after a moment resumed typing, his fingers slowly clicking the keys as they danced across the keyboard. I looked at him a second longer, his face looking tired and weary.

The visits centre was reopened just after lunch time muster was called correct and we received a replacement officer, Tom Grady, to fill in for Brock. The Supervisor had dropped in to check on our reports and told us that Brock had been suspended pending an investigation. He said that it didn't take long for them to make the decision based on the security-camera footage.

A lot of visitors had decided to go home by the time visits resumed and as such, our afternoon passed with very little fanfare. There was another code alpha in Tambo East which turned out to be a disgruntled crook who was looking forward to a visit from his brother. The brother turned out to be the "not hangin' around' kind of guy and as such, missed the visit. The prisoner was taken to one of the management units and prison life continued.

Robert is very quiet as we walk out a few hours later. His head is low and he looks as though his thoughts weigh heavy on his shoulders.

"You OK, Rob?" I asked as we walk. He looks at me and shrugs his shoulders.

"Everything has to end sometime, I guess," he said in a low voice.

"You're a great officer, Robert. You can't beat yourself up over someone else's fuck up. I'll see you tomorrow, yeah?" I said and held out my hand. He took it and shook, smiling at me.

"Thanks, Simon."

I run into the Sup out in the carpark and he tells me that Brock is looking at a pretty straight forward charge of assault. The video footage did not look good and he would be a very lucky man if he got off. I can share the outcome with you now as I'm writing this a couple of months later.

Brock was sacked from the prison a couple of days later and it was Watson that asked for him not to be charged. He said he brought it on himself and Brock was only defending himself. To me, Brock took a cheap shot and punched a prisoner in the back of the head. There is no justification in attacking a prisoner when he has his back turned unless that prisoner is attacking another officer. He could have been pushed into the strip room but Brock punched him square in the back of the head.

I have my own opinion on this matter and one that I won't share. It is up to each person to make their own mind up about what they consider to be appropriate force used in that type of situation. And I'll let you decide whether Brock should have been charged or not. But even in prison, no-one is above the law, whether in an officer's uniform or a prisoner's.

# WEDNESDAY, SEPTEMBER 26

TODAY, I worked in Admissions and although it is normally an awesome place to work, sometimes it can also be quite volatile. Tempers can flare as prisoners go through the processes of being admitted into the prison. As soon as I enter the building, I make my way to the book to check out the list of movements for the day. Depending on the number of transfers, the list alone will determine whether we have a busy day or a slack one.

I greet Jack, the officer in charge of the book today and he returns the greeting with a wave, handing me the list.

"It's an OK morning but the afternoon is pretty ordinary," he says without much enthusiasm. I scan the list and see about two dozen prisoners who are headed to court as well as half a dozen that are transferring out. But at the bottom of the page, where the incoming names were listed, were close to 30 names. Jack was right; the afternoon would be a busy one once the 30 arrived.

The courts are processed first, each one picked up by staff as they are processed well before the prison is unlocked. Admissions is the only area that operates at this time due to the courts and, as such, is a hive of activity. A number of officers help with bringing the prisoners to Admissions while several more conduct strip searches. Others help with loading buses, as each bus is headed to a different court. Courts are spread all over the city and require several buses to deliver prisoners due to time constraints.

I'm asked to help with loading buses, a job I happily help with. I had seen enough penises the last few years and was pretty sure I would see more as the day went on. Besides, "loading buses" meant simply standing out in the compound as the bus staff did the actual loading. We were there as deterrents and in case anything kicked off during the loading process. It wasn't an overly difficult job and within an hour, all the buses were loaded and headed out the gate.

Because of the gap between the courts and when the outgoing transfers arrived, there was plenty of time for breakfast and a catch up with some of the other staff. There was a crowd of maybe a dozen officers as I enter the tea room and conversation is loud and animated. Officers always tend to speak loud and humour is the normal topic of conversation. We tend to pull the piss out of each other as it keeps spirits up. Despite working in such a miserable place, it allows us to keep a smile on our faces.

One officer in particular, Norman Raynes, or Norm for short, is probably one of the biggest pranksters I have ever met. Unafraid of embarrassing anyone, he has a tendency to pull the piss out of anyone; supervisors, managers and officers alike. This morning him and another officer, Eric, are goading a third officer; a muscle-bound fitness freak called Stan Rogers. I don't know how, but Norm always gets a laugh, regardless of how racist, sexist and demeaning his jokes are. While in most places his jokes could be seen as a form of bullying, it's different here. It's different because the people that work in this place have a much thicker skin than most, and tolerating shit is what we're paid for.

Watching Norm walk around the tea room, carrying empty buckets at a ludicrous distance from his sides is just plain funny and you can't help but laugh.

"Is this how you go shopping? Fuck the trolley, just a basket in each hand so you can show off your pecs?" He laughs so hard at his own joke and I think that's probably what most people laugh at the most; his laugh. It seriously sounds like Scooby-Do. He begins arm curling each empty bucket in an exaggerated fashion. "Just checking what I'm buying," and continues his harsh laughing. Eric grabs two more buckets, mimicking Norm. Norm looks at him and heads for him, buckets held out wide. "And when you meet another 'roid queen," he says, waddling towards Eric like a penguin, both trying to pass each other, but their arms blocking the way. "Fuckin aisles aren't wide enough," and more laughter follows. It's funny to watch and just as they begin almost dancing with each other, Tom Grady walks in to grab a coffee. He sees me and waves. Once he has his coffee, he walks over and we have a chat about the previous day's events. We agree that Brock is pretty much fucked. I tell Tom about Robert and how he kept saying he may have come to the end of his career. He shakes his head and claps me on the back.

"He's been around so long; this place will never let him go. It's in his blood. He'll be OK." I'm about to agree with him when control calls for count. We break off and conduct muster; count is called correct about 10 minutes later.

The outgoing transfers begin filing into Admissions 20 minutes later and Admissions staff begin the process of working through each prisoner's property and marking off individual items. It's one of the few times where officers can get an actual idea of hoarding and standovers. A prisoner's items are all individually listed on their property list. If they turn up with four pairs of Nike runners and only have one pair listed, then it's fair to assume they have somehow gotten hold of some extra pairs. Normally, looking at the crook can give an indication on whether they are standing over weaker prisoners or doing "special favours". One of the first prisoners to be processed is a young, skinny guy of about 25. He has long fingernails, a make-shift scarf around his neck made from prison pants and enough bags to fill a shopping trolley twice over. The bounce in his step and the way he shakes his butt from side to side is enough to tell us that the extra property that's about to be found, didn't come from any stand over. He gets most of his property from providing "lip service" to whichever unit is lucky enough to have him.

"Hi Damien," Norman says, greeting the overly happy prisoner. It takes the property officers a good 15 minutes to work their way through Damien's bags, adding new items while confiscating others. He's cheery and not upset when he loses a couple of brand-new pairs of Adidas runners. We all know that it won't take him long to make up for the loss once he arrives at his new home. He's stripped and allowed to dress in his private clothes for the trip west.

The rest of the group are processed and before long, the buses are once again being loaded. It's a relatively pain-free morning and before I know it, lunch-time muster is called. If only every day was as structured as today. It really does make the day go quick.

The start of the afternoon stretch begins with an amazingly slow couple of hours. With no one to process, we are left with nothing to do except wait for the incoming bus. At approximately 2.30 we are told that the bus has broken down and will be at least another couple of hours. It's time we have to spare as there is nothing happening other than the occasional prisoners returning from court. I grab a book and hide away in a corner of the building. It's a great couple of hours as no codes are called and the afternoon is smooth sailing.

The moment the bus turns up, shortly after 5, the commotion begins. It's understandable for the prisoners to be pissed as they've been crammed into their individual cells for almost 6 hours, pissing into urine bags and eating fruit sticks. I inform the billets to warm the meals up and then I head out to help with the unloading.

The groans are almost instant from the moment the doors are opened. Each cell houses a maximum of 4 crooks and we unload a cell at a time. They are identified, then led into a holding cell, where most make a beeline for the toilet. For some, the idea of pissing into a bag, less than 12 inches from the heads of 3 other prisoners, is beyond impossible and so the waiting can be daunting.

With two transfers cancelled, the remaining 28 prisoners are taken off and put into holding cells with very little fuss; all except one. Dane Reynolds, a new prisoner who only arrived in the system less than a month ago is volatile from the get-go. His abuse starts the minute the door is opened and he refuses to identify himself. We eventually separate him into his own holding cell and let him stew a bit. Although he still has access to a toilet and is fed a hot meal, he's informed that due to his uncooperativeness, he'll be processed last. He is led to the furthest cell from where we are working because we know exactly what will happen once we lock him in. The second the door is closed on him, he begins kicking the shit out of it, each bang booming through the halls. It's almost deafening and we know he'll continue until we process him. I can not describe just how loud the noise is, but if you compare it to a rock concert in your bathroom and imagine the beat bouncing off the tiled walls, that's how loud the sound is.

With the banging in our ears, we begin the process and create a production line. The prisoners are individually strip searched then interviewed; have their property processed one at a time and then see a nurse to ensure they don't have any immediate concerns. The time taken to finish each prisoner can take some time and is totally dependant on not only how cooperative they are, but also how much property they have. It's almost an hour before the first couple are finished and taken to their new units.

Dane is still banging his feet on the door as we reach the half way point and as all cells are monitored by CCTV, the book person can see what he's up to. As I walk past to grab another couple of prisoners, I stop and have a look at the monitor.

"How's he doing?" I ask Jack and he shakes his head.

"He's been punching the walls. See the blood spots?" he says and points to the monitor, at an area of the wall that looks like it's been drawn on. "That's not graffiti, that's this dickhead's blood." And just as I'm about to continue, I see Dane begin headbutting the same spot on the wall, the dark patch growing bigger and darker with each bang. "Oh fuck," Jack says and gets up, pushing past me and heading to Dane's cell. I follow him, my radio held at the ready to call a code. He'll need a code mike at the very least.

As we near the cell, we can hear the dull thumping from inside. Jack drops the trap and calls out to Dane.

"OI! DANE!" he yells, trying to get his attention. For a moment he doesn't get it, but then he kicks the door himself and I hear Dane yell back.

"GET ME THE FUCK OUTA HERE, DOG!" he screams. Jack suddenly pulls back as Dane spits at him through the trap, saliva and blood shooting through the small window. It isn't a good situation and Jack pulls his radio to call a code alpha. The spitting is classed as an attempted assault. As the crook is also hurting himself, a nurse and a supervisor will need to determine if he'll have to be restrained. If he does, then the Tactical boys will enter the cell and restrain him. Thankfully, it's left to the sup to make the call and I'm glad he's the one getting paid the sup's wages.

When the sup and nurse arrive, the sup drops the trap and starts to talk to him, at first receiving no reply. But his calm voice soon gets Dane talking and before long, he's calm enough for the door to be opened. The Tactical boys enter first and cuff him, Dane holding his hands out in front of him compliantly. Once he's cuffed, the nurse enters the cell and does her assessment, the Tactical boys standing close by in case of any sudden moves. The headbutting seemed to have taken the fight out of him as he quietly sits and lets the nurse do her thing. Once she clears him, he is escorted to a desk and interviewed then led to property. Because of his actions, he is only given the bare necessities such as underwear and toiletries. He understands that he'll be transferred to a management unit and will need to remain there until he is cleared for a main stream unit.

As Dane is led out by the Tactical boys a short time later, we continue processing the rest of the crooks; just 4 remaining. It doesn't take long and before we can say "Yahoo, the day is through," the last of the prisoners is walked to his unit, effectively finishing our day. We are all in good spirits as we head out of the building and walk down the corridor towards the front gate. It has been a long day and I can't wait to get home.

"Simon, wait," I hear from behind me and I turn to see Donna Murphy running up the path. Donna is the HR manager and her serious tone raises my pulse a little. As she nears, I can see her face, serious and flat, almost vacant.

"Hey, Donna," I said as she reached me. To my surprise she asked if I could follow her into a nearby building, into a vacant office. Once there, she closed the door and asked me to sit down. The one thing I like about Donna is that she never beats around the bush; straight to the point whether it's a good one or bad.

"I've just received word that Robert Hall has been found dead in his home. He apparently hung himself. Henry Tully was supposed to work with him in Avoca today and when he didn't show, called his neighbour. Apparently the 3 of them know each other. Anyway, when there was no answer, his neighbour let himself in and found him. I know you worked with him yesterday. Did he say anything to you? Was there anything that might have, you know, pushed him over the edge?" My heart sank into my feet as my stomach felt like I'd just swallowed a brick. Images played out in my mind like slow-motion movies as I tried to comprehend her words. She must have seen the shock on my face because she reached forward and squeezed my hand. "I'm sorry," she said. I wouldn't call Robert a close friend but he was a workmate, someone who'd I'd known for a few years and worked with in the prison numerous times. It hurt to hear a man of such incredible experience, end his life because he felt no longer worthy of his place. It made me incredibly sad.

I told her about the previous day's incident in visits and logged into the computer to email her the report. It didn't exactly solve the problem for her but gave her a small indication, especially once I added what he'd said to me. Once Donna had finished with me, she walked me to the door and I walked out alone.

Today, was definitely not a good day.

# THE FUNERAL

ROBERT'S FUNERAL was held a week later and attended by a couple of hundred people. He had spent a lifetime within corrections and I was happy to see so many of his past and present colleagues attend his farewell.

Some, like me, came dressed in uniform, and it was very inspirational to listen to the stories many of them had to tell about Robert. Once the church service was complete and Robert had been cremated at the Crematorium, a lot of people attended one of the local bars that Robert used to go to.

We spent the afternoon sharing war stories and drinking to the memory of an old mate. I was incredibly sad at how his life had come to an end but will never forget him. To me, he is a fallen hero and one that deserves to be remembered for the years of service he gave. He helped to keep the nightmares behind bars.

I hope you found peace, old friend.

**R.I.P.**

Robert Hall
June 1st, 1950 - September 25, 2018

# AUTHOR'S NOTE

IT HAS BEEN another tough month in Maximum Security. But as I write the conclusion on yet another chapter of this series, I look across at the pile of notes I have for the upcoming chapters and can see that there is no slowing down. In store for you in the next Prison Days, October edition, is an attack on an officer that will leave him fighting for life; a Governor's time will finally come to an end; an officer is caught in a very "delicate" situation with a prisoner, and a number of prisoners fall victim to a rather "urgent" problem. The usual assaults, rapes and fights will also feature again and I'm sure you will find October to be as entertaining as the rest.

Thank you again for your continued support and I am always happy to hear from you at prisondays@yahoo.com or on my Facebook page @prisondaysauthor

FINALLY, if you are interested, I am writing a fictional story based on some of my experiences in maximum security. Join my Facebook page to receive further updates as the project comes to life.

Thank you again for your continued support and I hope I don't ever see you while I'm at work, in a maximum-security prison.

Simon King

# BOOK 5

# INTRODUCTION

It is a Saturday night, or should I say Sunday morning, 12:57 in the morning to be precise; and the unit is echoing with the endless screaming of prisoners continuously "burning" each other. It's just another shift for me, sitting alone in the officer's station of the hardest unit in the prison. Is it fun? No. Is it exciting? No. It's mind-numbing as I listen to the constant bantering of first one lot of prisoners yelling abuse at each other, followed by the other group.

The intercom kicks in occasionally as individual prisoners buzz me, asking how much longer the yelling is going to continue. I tell them that I don't know. Some nights it stops around 10, other nights at 11. Some nights it begins to fade around 1. Tonight, seems to be one of the late ones where no-one wants to sleep. It's cold, almost freezing in fact.

Personally, I just want to tell them all to shut the fuck up, but I know I can't. I am nothing more than a passenger, forced to listen and monitor. I've turned the unit lights off and I'm hoping that they might get the hint but the longer I sit here with the voices continuing to roar, hope quickly fades to despair. This is what Maximum is all about. It's not about going toe to toe; seeing who can yell the loudest. For us officers, it's about knowing when to speak and when to shut up. Having the prisoners burn each other is actually a good thing; as long as they are abusing each other, they aren't abusing me, and that's a win. It means they leave me alone and I can sit here and talk to you instead.

I'm in awe at the realisation that this edition marks the fifth outing. It's already been five books and there is still so much to share. This month has been another crazy journey through the darkness that is life behind bars. Several prisoners have been stabbed; plenty of assaults; one prisoner that thought he was ready to die while another was mistaken for Superman. There's so much to get through and I know you can't wait to read about it. If you do like my war stories, then please don't forget to leave a review. Books without them really do fade into the vast abyss that exists on the internet.

Now, hang on tight as I unlock the door, and follow me inside. Please try and stay close, there are teeth behind these walls; teeth that bite.

## MONDAY, OCTOBER 1

IT'S the first day of a new month and I'm relatively happy as I walk in through reception. I'm greeted by the Reception staff and proceed to be scanned and checked. I see my friend Kon a few spots ahead of me and call out to him. He turns to me and flashes his big Greek grin at me.

"Where are you today?" he asks as I finish grabbing my bag and follow him into the key room. It is a controlled airlock with only half a dozen officers allowed entry at any one time. It's quite a tight space and we form a line in front of the thick glass window; it reminds me of a bank teller, one Control Room officer frantically grabbing radios and keys for each officer as they front the queue. Most mornings, the process can be quite frustrating and takes a lot of patience. There are more than a hundred staff that start at the same time and every one of them requires a personal radio and a set of keys. Each set of keys has already been allocated to an officer by the Control Room night staff but mistakes can and do happen and when they do, slows the process down considerably.

The prison also operates some doors with swipe cards and these have an active life of 12 months. Once the expiry date passes, your card is ineffective when attempting to move through certain doors. As I swipe mine, the little light remains red instead of blinking green.

"I'm in Glenelg West," I replied, retrying my card a second time, knowing full well what the problem was.

"So am I," Kon said as he fronts the line and grabs his gear.

"I'll have to catch up with you, card not working." He gives me a thumbs up and shuffles through the other door, leaving me to wait for my card to be reactivated, once I have my keys and radio.

It's a good 20 minutes before I'm finally in the unit, briefly stopping for a chat with Thelma who was on night shift. We pass each other in one of the corridors and she waves me down.

"Good night?" I ask and her frown is immediate.

"Shit. Fucken goose kept bangin up all night. The other crooks gave him quite a burning and he reciprocated by keeping them awake all night. Didn't quieten till almost 4. Where are you today?"

"Glenelg West," I tell her.

"Well, you should have a fun day. They took Robert Bester there earlier this morning. He was one of the Code Foxtrot's from last night. Got smacked around a bit and they took him out for a check-up." Sometimes, prisoners will be shuttled out by ambulance and taken to a nearby hospital for precautionary exams. It depends on the severity but if a prisoner is suspected of having internal injuries then prison medical staff won't take the chance, instead sending the crook out for a more in-depth examination. Unfortunately, prisoners know this and will often, way too often, fake injuries or conditions to either bail out of a unit or simply waste resources. It means nothing to them to tie up an ambulance for several hours by faking a heart attack.

"Great, can't wait. You have a good sleep," I say and we part ways, Thelma heading out while I head in, each of us on opposite ends of the merry-go-round.

I can hear a dull thumping sound as I come through the airlock, Kon standing in the officer's station with Scott Jones. I wave and go and stow my things before returning to the station, the banging continuing with a slow methodical continuity.

"Bester?" I ask as I shake hands with Scott and he nods.

"I got here half hour ago and he was going at it then." A couple of prisoners yell for him to shut the fuck up but he continues, despite the protests from others. I check the muster sheet and get a brief idea of who was in the unit. Being mostly long-term protection meant the main bulk of the unit's population were older sex offenders. There were a couple of young hotheads thrown in for good measure, but overall, it was a fairly quiet unit.

But a unit's atmosphere can change and sometimes the changes can be quite dramatic depending on who is brought in and who is shifted out. Units can go from being classed as "retirement villages" for the staff working there to "Bronx Status" in a matter of a few days. In recent weeks, Glenelg West has been relatively quiet; not quite a retirement home but close enough.

Control calls for count and Kon and I begin the morning round. I grab the muster and mark the cells off as Kon drops the traps, peers inside and confirms each cell's occupancy. We leave the first cell on the bottom tier for last, its sole occupant continuing to beat his war drums.

The trip around the unit is over in just under 10 minutes and as a precaution, we double check on Robert to ensure he's OK. His cell is an observation cell which comes with the added bonus of an in-built camera. Every unit has 3 observation cells, usually reserved for prisoners that are on suicide watch. One of the first things most non-compliant prisoners do is cover the camera with wet toilet paper. Some will do it only as a privacy measure while they take care of their toilet needs, uncovering the camera once finished. But for others, they see it as another opportunity to thumb their nose at any form of authority, often using the camera as a bargaining tool.

Observation cells have two doors, one being the inner door which is a very thick and transparent Perspex, steel bars running across its width in short intervals. The outer door, known as the "outer skin" is thinner than most of the steel doors but still reinforced metal. The outer skin can be safely opened, leaving the inner door secure. Kon unlocks Robert's outer skin door and we peer in at him. He's lying on his back with his eyes closed and one arm over his face. He has his feet planted on the door and stomps each of them in regular intervals of about five or so seconds. He doesn't hear us open the door and Kon kicks the door to get his attention. He opens his eyes and jumps to his feet when he sees us.

"What the fuck you want?" he screams then punches the door. Seeing him move OK, we close the outer skin as he lands another punch, the bang echoing through my brain. It's followed by a kick and then a barrage of punches.

Robert Bester's brain is what you would call fried. Too many date nights with crystal meth has seen him become an almost mumbling psycho that can bounce through emotional states like an earthquake up the Richter scale. He can go from happy to sad to pure rage within a minute. He is extremely volatile and highly unpredictable and that makes him quite dangerous.

We return to the station and add up our numbers, calling them in once finished. It's not long before they call count correct and Scott and I head out and unlock the cells. Within minutes, the unit is a hive of activity as crooks begin their normal routines. Several come to the station and vent their grievances at the new tenant. They know we can't change his allocation to the unit and thus simply use us to vent. It's not something we try and avoid as a good venting now can prevent a blow-up down the line.

The morning runs smoothly as the medication trolley enters the unit and the meds are all handed out quietly with minimum fuss. Robert also requires meds but when we drop the trap for the nurse to give them, he tries to spit at us. He misses and I slam the trap back in place as he restarts his door kicking. The nurse is happy for him to miss out and we move on with our day.

There are 3 prisoners that are leaving the unit today and we inform them to pack their gear. Once they are ready, a fourth officer comes to escort them to Admissions. There are two new arrivals later in the day but after reshuffling a bit, we find a spare single cell available. Several of the prisoners are also aware of the vacancy and don't delay in trying to secure it for themselves. But they know there's a list of offering and once we check it, notify the proud new tenant who happily runs off to move into his new home.

Lunchtime count is called just as I check which cells are up for searching today and I set the list aside, grabbing the muster sheet while Scott announces muster over the unit P.A. system. The prisoners begin to line up and we begin the task of counting the unit. Halfway through, there's a loud crashing from Robert's cell. We ignore it as we focus on count, knowing that it takes priority. When I reach Robert's cell, I open the outer door and watch as he is kicking the metal toilet. I close it again and head for the station to tally up the numbers.

Control calls count correct a few minutes after we call our number through and Kon leads Scott around for the cell searches. The kicking from Robert's cell continues as I begin to adjust the unit muster on the computer, moving departures out and new cell allocations in. Half an hour later the boys return from their searching empty handed. Just as Kon is about to say something, Scott groans.

"He's flooding up," he said, pointing towards Robert's cell. I look and see water running out from under the door. I follow the other two as we head to the cell. Kon opens the skin and drops the trap. Robert is in the process of tearing his mattress apart. Water is shooting from the shower head and the foam from the mattress has clogged the drain.

"Robert!" Kon shouts. No response. "ROBERT!" Kon shouts again and also kicks the door. Robert stops and looks at us, a fire burning in his eyes. "Need you to turn the shower off, man," Kon said but Robert shakes his head.

"I can't."

"Robert, I need the shower turned off. It's flooding the unit. Otherwise I'll have to shut the water off."

"I can't," Robert repeats and when we take a closer look, see the issue. Robert is correct when he says he's unable to turn the shower off. He has managed to tear the shower, including the metal water pipe, completely out of the wall, bits of cement dotted around his floor. He has also managed to tear the sink from the wall and his toilet is sitting at a skewed angle. The strength needed to do the damage that he's caused in that little time is incredible.

Scott immediately calls the Supervisor on the radio and asks her to attend the unit as Robert restarts his assault on the door. The Supervisor enters a few minutes later and immediately opens the water cabinet which sits next to the cell door. The water is shut off and she attempts to talk to Robert through the door. He refuses, continuing to kick the inner door. Eventually she gives up and calls for the Tactical boys to attend. She then calls Murray North and asks them to prepare one of their cells. The rest of us lock the unit down, much to the complaints of the other prisoners. They enjoy a good show but, in this case, we need the unit empty and thus they miss out. The main reason is that as Robert has been quite a pain already, one of the other prisoners may choose to shit-bomb him on the way out.

Unfortunately, he does require running water and a working toilet, and although he may do the same to his new cell, we have no choice but to have him moved. Four tactical boys turn up ten minutes later and prepare to extract him. They prep a large shield as the Supervisor once again attempts to talk him down. His reply is a barrage of spit and abuse and when the Supervisor steps aside, waves her hands like a quiz show prize presenter.

"All yours, boys," she says and walks to the station. One of the boys, dressed in riot helmet and protective suit, walks to the trap.

"Last chance, Robert," he says but Robert stands with his fists at the ready. The officer nods his head and raises the shield, two others lining up behind him and grabbing the protection suit handles that sit on the back of the suit. They will turn into a human train, propelled by three sets of legs, the shield held before them like a battering ram. The fourth officer opens the inner door quickly and the three boys charge past him with grunts of effort. The shield first slams into Robert's fists, then into his torso as his arms crumple at the force of the approaching wall. His legs try and brace him but only for a split second. He is body-slammed almost instantly into the wall behind him, his legs becoming tangled as he falls to the ground. The third officer reaches around and grabs one wrist, pulling it out and down. The second officer pulls his other wrist out and down, pinning his top half down onto the wet concrete floor. The first officer throws the shield to the side and lands on Robert's ankles, pinning his legs as the fourth officer now enters with handcuffs in hand. Robert is screaming every profanity imaginable, struggling hard against his captors as his breathing becomes short and laboured puffs of rage.

Once his hands are securely cuffed, a spit mask is put over his head to prevent him shooting saliva at officers. Then, they pick him up, one on either side of him. While Robert is facing the rear of the cell, the officers face the front, each with an arm through the loops of Robert's arms. When they begin walking Robert out backwards, he's taken off balance, making it extremely difficult for him to struggle as the officer's arms interlock together like a weight-bearing pole carrying a pig carcass off to a bonfire. Robert has no choice but to follow. The unit erupts with cheers and whistles as he is led out through the airlock and I'm thankful to see the back of him.

We unlock the unit shortly after and after answering a few questions from curious prisoners, relax into a quiet afternoon. It has been a pretty interesting day and although one cell was completely destroyed, no officers were hurt. A couple of new arrivals turn up shortly after and are allocated their new cells. The unit billet shows them around as we watch the afternoon unfold. As we walk out a few hours later, I shake my offsider's hands. We are all back together tomorrow, to do it all again.

Today has been a good day.

# TUESDAY, OCTOBER 2

CAME in expecting to return to Glenelg West but halfway to the unit was asked to do some urine testing instead. It's one of those jobs that a lot of people frown about. Me? I don't mind it. It means you can conduct your day freely without having to sit still in a unit station. Plus, there's the added bonus of not having fifty crooks in your face nonstop throughout the day.

Miguel Foster and Chris Upton, two officers I hadn't seen in a while were already in the urinalysis room when I walked in. They were a couple of funny guys to work with and I knew the day would pass without too much pain; prisoners aside of course.

"Going to the funeral on Thursday?" Chris asked and I nodded (see September Edition).

"Wouldn't miss it," I said. He handed me the daily list and I ran my eyes across it, looking for any familiar names that would give us grief. I couldn't see any and handed it back.

We waited until Control called the morning count correct and Chris phoned the first unit for a couple of mainstreamers to come up. It doesn't take long for them to show which is a good thing for us as it means they are keen to get things over with. One we lock in a holding cell then escort the other to the sample room. Sometimes things just tend to 'flow' smoothly, pardon the pun, and this morning happens to be one of those days. Each lot of prisoners are processed within minutes of arriving and head back out the door a short time later. I know it doesn't make for interesting reading for you, but for us it really is a relief.

By the time lunchtime count is called for, our list of 28 is reduced to just 12, the majority already tagged and bagged. The remaining names on the list are Protection prisoners and Miguel and Chris head out to the first unit once count is correct, while I wait behind and prepare the room, ensuring our supplies are all sufficiently stocked. Nothing worse than having a fresh cup of piss and no tape with which to seal it.

The boys return with 4 prisoners in tow and all of them ask for water and time. Chris and I exchange a look that needs no words; protection. I don't know what the reason is but protection prisoners are simply so much more difficult to deal with, both in a unit and out of it. They have an air of need about them, constantly in officer's ears about things they require urgently, as in right now. They have a habit of being in your face for the entire day, complain so much more, require physical escorts whenever they leave the unit and think they are so much more important than regular crooks.

It's almost half an hour before we hear the faint tap from one of the prisoners who's ready to piss. I open the door, usher him out and lead him into the sample room where Chris conducts a full strip, looking for anything that might be used to adulterate the sample. He checks out and once he's half-dressed himself again, grabs a sample jar.

Now, every prisoner that I have ever piss tested, despite some strange methods for warming their dick up, has performed the task as you would normally expect; standing before the bowl and waiting for the stream to begin and then catching the urine in the jar. Imagine my surprise when Jake Bauer takes the jar, spins around and then promptly sits on the toilet with his hand between his legs. When he sees me looking at him curiously, he offers a slight smile.

"I don't urinate standing like some ape," he said as I heard the trickle begin.

"Whatever works, man," I replied, Chris chuckling next to me. After a few seconds, the crook stands, flushes, then pours half his sample into a second jar before sealing both jars and then handing them to me for processing. I seal the lids with security tape and then place them in separate plastic bags which I also seal with tape. The prisoner signs both lots of tape to ensure there's no issues down the track. We prepare two separate samples so that if there's an issue with the first one, the prisoner can elect to have the second sample tested.

"You're all done," Chris tells him and we lock him into a separate cell while Miguel calls for his transport back to the unit. I know it's quite normal for some men to squat while urinating. I've just never seen it done while providing a sample.

Another crook begins tapping on his cell door and when Chris escorts him in, I can tell immediately that he's hiding something. Some prisoner's just have a certain look on their faces when they're up to no good. It's like a smirk that they can't seem to hide. As Chris begins to conduct the strip search, I inspect each piece of clothing but find nothing as Chris continues to talk the prisoner through the process.

Once he finishes the inspection of his private bits, Chris motions for the prisoner to take a sample jar and commence the test. He grabs the jar then turns his back to us and faces the toilet bowl. Chris and I look at each other, knowing that he's up to something even before he begins the routine. I step slightly to my right to try and get a better look from the prisoner's side while Chris watches the convex mirror that is hanging on the wall above the toilet. It allows us to see the prisoner front on but due to the distance and distortion, can prove to be less than helpful at times.

The prisoner stands still, one hand holding the jar under his dick, the other on his hip. He begins scratching his head, then nose. Chris motions for me to look and I step forward a little.

"All good, man?" I ask and the prisoner looks at me.

"Give me a minute. It's coming," he replies then turns his head slightly away. He yawns, covering his mouth with one hand. His hand remains at his mouth and then he yawns again. Chris looks at me, holding his hands up questioningly. 'What's he doing' he mouths to me and I shrug my shoulders, unable to see. His hand is still on his mouth and without warning, makes a retching noise. He bends slightly forward, makes another retching noise, then leans forward and vomits into the bowl as his face turns a crimson red, spluttering as he drops the sample jar. I can see something dangling between his mouth and the toilet bowl and as he tries to reach for it, misses as he vomits a second time. I step forward and before he has a chance to regain his composure, reach in and grab whatever is floating in mid-air.

It's a finger from a rubber glove, tied to a piece of dental floss that's still attached to the crook's dental braces. Chris and I stare at it in total disbelief as the prisoner is still trying to get his stomach under control. He looks at the rubber finger wide-eyed, not because we have it but because it's empty, a small hole sitting just below the tie-off point. Chris erupts into laughter as the prisoner continues retching.

"Hope your donor was a close friend, dude," I said, fighting my own laughter. The prisoner was white as a sheet as we held out the sample jar to him.

"Care to provide a proper sample?" Chris asked but he shook his head. We escorted him to another cell, then contacted the duty Sup. It was a very good reminder that in prison, there's no such thing as "seen it all before".

The prisoner was eventually charged with attempting to adulterate a sample and was given a fine. We continued our day and finished the piss testing with no other exciting stories.

Chris and I laughed as we walked out the gate a couple of hours later, still bemused at the poor bloke's misjudgement of gargling his mate's piss.

Today was a good day.

## WEDNESDAY, OCTOBER 3

TODAY, I was rostered in Thomson East and although some days can feel like they are going as smooth as one could wish for, things can change at any moment in the blink of an eye. In fact, the whole day can run according to schedule and just as you slam home that final door, sure that you're about to drop the curtain on another incident-free day, the proverbial shit can hit the fan. That's what happened today.

The whole day had gone by with relative calmness, the bulk of the prisoners playing nicely together. Myself, Thelma and Robert Nixon, both of my offsiders very experienced officers, had enjoyed a drama-free day from beginning to end without so much as a single incident. Not even a hat worn inside the unit. It was as if everyone just had one of those days where they couldn't be stuffed doing anything other than what was needed.

The medication runs had come and gone with nothing to note; the random cell searches were completed with all crooks willingly opening their doors for us and leaving us to our searches; each muster had come and gone with such quietness that I believed we could have heard a pin drop. Like I said, the day was a non-event as far as we were concerned. Good for us, but unfortunately not so good for you reading this for a bit of excitement.

The afternoon went by with us officers watching a very animated poker match where half a dozen prisoners were playing for a substantial pot which included several bottles of Coke, several large blocks of chocolate and half a dozen bags of crisps. There were also about a dozen Mars bars and one lonely packet of 2-minute noodles.

The final hand was finished just as the 5 o'clock muster was called and the winner hurriedly carted his winnings to his cell, much to the delight of his cell mate who was already eyeing off the chocolate. He kept trying to help his cellie with carrying the goods but had his hand slapped away several times, much to the amusement of the rest of the unit.

Dinner was served on time and with very little fanfare. It was Chicken Maryland for those interested, served with gravy and mashed potato. A chocolate chip cookie finished the meal and once final count was called, the prisoners headed back to their cell doors, patiently waiting as we came around to conduct the final count and subsequently lock them in.

Once all the doors were locked, we all headed back to the station and tallied our counts. Once we confirmed our numbers matched, it was just a matter of waiting until count was called correct and we'd be free to leave. Count was indeed called correct a few minutes later and we grabbed our bags to leave. Thelma was holding the door open as Robert walked into the airlock, both waiting for me to turn the computer off. Just as I grabbed my bag and walked down the couple of stairs out of the station, I heard something. It sounded like a sharp whip crack, followed by the faintest yelp. I stopped, paused and looked into the unit. It was silent again and as I stood, heard Thelma call out to me. I was about to answer her, when I heard another sound, and this time I recognized it for what it was. It sounded like a slap, followed by a low grunt. I dropped my bag and gestured to my offsiders. They came back into the unit and we spread out to try and locate the source of the sounds.

"Here," Robert finally said as he approached a cell on the bottom tier. As I ran over, he opened the trap and peered in. It was the cell of the winner of the poker game and as I approached, had a good idea of what the issue would be.

"Code Foxtrot, Thomson East," Thelma called into her radio as Robert began yelling at the prisoners inside the cell. I tried to look past him, over his shoulder, but the small trap made it almost impossible. As Robert turned his head to say something to Thelma, I saw what he'd been trying to stop. Adrian Kemp, the winner of the Poker game, had his much smaller cellmate, David Bruce, by the scruff and was pushing him against the window. David had been pushed up far enough that his buttocks were sitting on the window ledge. His face looked completely pulverized, both eyes purple and closed. He looked unconscious as Adrian continued to punch David in the face, each time the fist connecting with him, the back of his head would bang against the window. Adrian sounded out of breath yet continued to punch again and again and again.

"Urgent medical care needed. Permission to open cell," Thelma yelled into her radio. Once the cells had been locked and the final count called correct, any opening of cells had to be authorized, regardless of the reason. Thankfully for us, the night Sup was listening and gave us the OK. Robert cracked the door and both of us rushed in, grabbing Adrian's arms as a limp David slumped onto the floor.

"I ain't resisting. Thieving cunt had it comin to him," Adrian said as I cuffed his hands. We walked him out of the cell as Thelma tended to David. I turned to see her place the unconscious prisoner into a recovery position as the first officers burst through the air lock and into the unit.

As we lead Adrian out of the unit, a couple of other prisoners begin yelling but the doors close before I could tell whether they were Supporting Adrian or condemning him. If his statement was true, that David was a thief, then the prisoners would more than likely support him. Thieving is a definite no-no in prison and as I've just described, can be dealt with swiftly and usually with severe consequences. Even in a unit filled with thieves, thieving is never accepted.

Robert and I are greeted by the Tactical Officers who take Adrian and escort him to the Admissions area. He'll face a lengthy wait as the Police will be called out to investigate the crime scene as well as conduct their interviews. Robert and I return to the unit and begin to write our reports alongside Thelma who is in the middle of her own, just as a stretcher arrives. David is lifted onto it and wheeled briskly from the unit to more chants of "maggot", "dog" and "grub".

Once our reports are finished and handed to the Supervisor, we are free to head home, our job finally complete. Although the day was a good one, it really didn't end well.

## THURSDAY, OCTOBER 4

THE FUNERAL of Robert Hall (see September edition). Sometimes, there are days that really impact on one's conscience, in more ways than one. Today was one of those days. I've never considered myself to ever be capable of ending my own life but today proved to me that just about anybody is vulnerable, even those we consider to be the strongest amongst us.

I will remember Robert for who he was and what he had taught me. A man that stood by his principles and tried his best to help those around him. He found himself in a truly dark place and one he couldn't find his way out of. I hope that he has finally found the peace he was searching for.

## MONDAY, OCTOBER 8

TODAY, I returned to Thomson East and found the unit much the same as when I left it, minus two prisoners. As soon as I walked through the airlock, I was greeted by Thelma sitting in the station. Although we both attended the funeral, I hadn't heard from anyone over the previous weekend and thus hadn't had an update o the condition of David Bruce. If he had died, then our reports would be scrutinized on a whole new level as the case, us and our written word would be called to the Coroner's Court. Although I have never been myself, I have known plenty of officers that have, and none of them have had a good word to say of the experience.

Thankfully, David had survived his attack, although still in an induced coma. He had received a severely fractured skull, which had resulted in bleeding on the brain and the medics didn't know just how severe his injuries would be, once he woke up. Adrian had been placed into Murray North and was said to be in splendid spirits. It truly saddens me to know that prison, even the units considered punishment units, are seen as nothing but holiday camps by the prisoners housed in them. Currently, Adrian was suffering in a cell for one; a television including a dedicated movie channel; his meals brought to him three times a day; a complete shopping list including all the soft drinks, snacks and food he can afford; his laundry washed and dried by prison officers; an hour out in the sunshine; all the conversation he can handle with fellow prisoners in adjoining cells. It's definitely not the solitary confinement you might imagine.

Thelma finished updating me as Tom Grady comes walking through the airlock. We shake as he enters the station and update him on the fight we saw. Tom had been on leave for the previous week and hadn't been updated on any of the happenings from the previous few days.

Control calls for count and Thelma and Tom grab the muster sheet and begin their rounds of the cells as I fire up the computer and the kettle. It's all pretty much routine as they drop traps and counts heads, eventually returning to the station to tally their numbers. Once they agree on the total, Thelma calls it into control and we wait for the confirmation.

A short time later, Control calls count correct and Tom and I unlock the unit for another day. Once we finish, I return to the station as crooks begin to line up for the medical trolley that is already making its way through the airlock. The unit is the closest to the medical wing and thus benefits from being the first unit it visits.

The crooks line up and everything begins smoothly. That is until the nurse holds up her hand to a prisoner who's forgotten his ID card. Before anyone has a chance to move, he smashes his fist into the reinforced glass and the sound is not only spectacularly loud inside the tiny airlock, but also very defined as to what else has just occurred. The crook's face goes from a dark fiery rage to a ghostly white in less than a second as he looks at his hand. His legs look shaky beneath him before giving out entirely as he crumples to the floor, clutching his right hand by the wrist, tears of pain welling up. There's a roar of laughter from the other prisoners as I call a code Mike, watching as the crook stares at his hand with eyes as wide as dinner plates.

When we get the report back later, we find that Prisoner Lu has sustained a broken wrist, two broken fingers and a crushed knuckle. Two bone shards were protruding through his skin and a third was threatening to pierce through in another spot while his tiny pinkie was dislocated in two places. His entire hand required wiring and as we watch him wheeled out of the unit still nursing his arm, another crook summed up the thoughts of many.

"Over a fuckin pill. Gonna need more now, dickhead."

It was almost another hour before the unit was back to normal and the med trolley finally finished. Most crooks had gone back to their cells for whatever reason and Tom and I figured it was a good-a-time as any to do our cell searches. He pulled up the random list and much to our delight, found Lu's cell to be one of the three. We headed out and found the first two searches to be pretty much non-events with neither prisoner either complaining about the search or housing any contraband. But when we came to Lu's cell, we couldn't have been happier. Sometimes, on rare occasions, instinct plays more of a part than usual. The cell had a certain "feel" about it and although we found nothing to begin with, our persistence paid off.

I noticed quite a few body building magazines on the shelf above the toilet and during the first pass of the cell, didn't pay them too much attention. They weren't considered contraband and thus focused on the more usual hiding places. But then, once we finished our initial sweep, they came back into my eye and that's when I began to wonder. Lu was as skinny as a broom handle and never entered the gym area. He wasn't what you'd call the physical type and so the magazines looked out of place.

I grabbed the top one and flicked through, nothing appearing out of place. But when I grabbed one from the middle and flicked through, the story changed dramatically. By around a dozen or so pages in, a beautiful breast stared back at me, followed by another and then the unmistakable view of a carefully manicured pubic bush trimmed into a landing strip. Hidden amongst the pages of the body building magazines was an endless supply of pornographic images that had been torn from differing magazines. I grabbed another magazine from the middle of the deck and found numerous lesbian-themed pages, whilst another magazine had gay male porn in it. Pages and pages filled with every porn style you can imagine were contained within the magazine covers.

Tom had been inspecting the bed and was now lying underneath it with a torch in hand when I heard him mutter something. As he shuffled back out from under the bed, I saw something black and rectangular-shaped clutched in his hand. When he got to his feet and showed me his treasure, I grinned, impressed with the find. It was an iPhone. A tiny circular magnet had been glued to it's rear and then had been hidden behind one of the metallic bed beams nearest the wall.

We headed back to the station after locking his cell and grabbed an evidence bag. Thelma had a wide grin as we showed her the find and once we completed our reports, phoned the Sup. I noticed a few crooks standing above the station, leaning on the hand rails as they watched from the second floor of the unit. There was a whisper between them and I knew that we'd found something substantial, both items having significant value within a prison unit. When I looked up at them, they walked away, but not before mouthing something as they turned. 'Fuck' was the word I made out and I knew that they weren't happy. I wondered whether there would be repercussions for Lu once he returned from hospital.

The rest of the day went about quite normal and by the time we walked out, Lu still hadn't returned. The Sup said that he'd more than likely remain in the hospital for a couple of days which I thought was probably a good thing. I hoped that for his sake that the boys would calm a little by then and maybe the repercussions wouldn't be as severe.

Today was a good day.

## WEDNESDAY, OCTOBER 10

I WAS ROSTERED in Admissions today and from the onset, knew it was going to be a good day. I knew this firstly because of the names I was working with, namely Daryl Foster, a fairly new officer that not only had a heart of gold, but also a very funny disposition. The second thing that ensured we were in for a good day was the list of moves for the day. Or should I say the *lack* of a list for the day.

The court moves consisted of just 6 crooks attending court, far less than the usual 30 to 40. Then there were 2 outgoing prisoners, a number normally between 20 and 30. Finally, the incomings were down to just 9 prisoners, and the prison they were coming from meant their arrival would be somewhere well into the afternoon. This left several hours of, well, nothing. It meant plenty of time to find a dark corner and chill or a bright corner to read a book. In any case, it meant for very little work.

By the time I arrived in Admissions, 5 of the 6 court attendees had already been processed. I helped with stripping the last one, then escorted him out and onto the court bus that was waiting out the back. Once he was securely seated in one of the on-board cells, I joined the rest of the crew for breakfast.

Morning count was non-existent for us as our cells stood empty.

We waited for control to call muster correct and once they did, prepared for the two outgoing prisoners who showed up carrying their bags about 10 minutes later. Neither had very much property which meant a quick procession through each of the steps, namely property checks and a quick strip search. Once completed, each was sat in a cell to await their transport buses.

And that was it for the morning. While some people broke off to gather in small groups and talk shit for a couple of hours, I jumped on one of the computers and continued working on my book. There was enough time to get a few pages in and just as I was feeling the onset of hunger rumbles, was pleasantly surprised to see several trays carried past me and into the kitchen.

A function had been held in one of the front offices, some multicultural gathering for visiting dignitaries. There was quite a good deal of food leftover and much to the delight of myself and fellow officers, found several trays of cakes, pastries and elegant sandwiches waiting for our greedy fingers. There are two things officers enjoy above all else; a day off and free food. By the time I walked out of the kitchen, several Danishes and a good deal of sandwiches had been slaughtered by my hand, enough for me to contemplate loosening my belt.

And almost as if pre-planned, a code alpha was called for the hospital unit just as I sat back down at the computer. The run to the unit was not an easy one and I silently cursed every single treat I swallowed with each step. There were several other officers also running beside me and we heard the yelling as we reached the doors.

As we entered the unit, one officer was standing with a chair held out before him while a prisoner stood a few feet in front of him holding a mop out in front of himself. His face took on a look of defeat as he saw the number of officers now piling through the door and quickly dropped the mop, surrendering his hands before him which were subsequently cuffed. It turns out to be a minor difference of opinion between a nurse and a prisoner, with the officer caught in the middle. It's a pretty common occurrence, considering some of the differing attitudes that work within the prison environment.

I return to Admissions and resume my typing. Much to my enjoyment, the final transfers don't arrive until after I leave for home, the late shift taking over from us later that afternoon. I get a great many pages written and with no further codes or excitement, was able to complete two whole chapters.

Today was definitely a very good day.

## SATURDAY, OCTOBER 13

As I have said in previous chapters, weekends have a completely different feel about them and once I head to Thomson East, am happy to see Tom and Scott Jones already in what looks to be a very deep conversation in the staff office. As I enter, they turn to me and share the news that will no doubt dominate that day's topics of conversation within the prison.

"Temple's gone," Tom says and for a moment, I don't catch on.

"Temple?" I ask and almost have a brain fart as I struggle to understand who they're talking about.

"The Gov," Tom adds and then the both of them just stare at me, waiting for my morning-brain to wake up. It suddenly hits me and they both nod as they see recognition wash across my face.

"Gone? How's he gone?" I ask as I stow my gear in one of the cupboards, then popping my lunch in the fridge.

"Apparently he got the tap on the shoulder yesterday afternoon. No-one is saying why but there's a whisper that he applied for another prison. Head office caught wind of it and, well, see ya later, alligator." John Temple had been the Governor of this prison for a number of years and although we never really interacted, seemed like an OK guy. Officers and management rarely mix so it's fair to say that

I didn't really know the man. I do know that this was his first General Manager's role within a prison and am guessing he wanted to take on a prison of a different nature.

"Any idea which one he'd applied for?" I asked but they both shook their heads. I know from previous experience that the transition to a new Governor won't take long, the Deputy Manager taking the reins in the meantime.

We head for the station and once count is called correct, Scott and I head out and unlock the cells. During our trap count, I did notice that Lu still hadn't returned to the unit, his cell still locked and empty. That meant he was still in the hospital and expected back in the unit once fit enough.

The crooks exit their cells and begin the usual routine of breakfast, laundry and hovering around the station with the typical array of questions. The medical trolley enters shortly after and I catch up with Thelma who's the designated trolley escort. She spends the entire time telling me about some rescue kittens she's looking after and almost convinces me to take one. I resist, having several furred friends already and wave her off once meds are finished.

It's all pretty routine stuff and by the time lunchtime count is called, most crooks are already standing by their doors before the announcement is even made. The count doesn't take long to conduct and before long, everyone is eating a lunch of salad sandwiches. Like I've said before, a good day for us is a bad day for you and doesn't make for very interesting reading.

The day runs out fairly fast and although there is a minor altercation mid-afternoon, everything else is smooth sailing. The minor altercation was a prisoner called Jason Mills, who insisted on wearing his hat inside, a firm no-no considering the inability for the cameras to identify him. He was asked several times to remove his hat throughout the day and by the fifth time, Scott had had enough, confronting the prisoner and subsequently locking him into his cell, pending a warning and a Sup's hearing. Being locked up early is generally considered to be punishment enough, with most prisoners opting to learn from the experience and comply with directions.

None of us could ever have foreseen the repercussions that would develop from this minor infraction but would definitely remember it for years to come when the rest of this episode played out in the coming days.

As we walk out after lockdown, the sun still partially visible over the horizon, we joke and laugh at the prospect of the end of another shift.

"When you back on?" I ask my off-siders as we head out into the carpark. Thelma is back the following day, while Scott won't be back until Wednesday. He tells me that he's taken leave tomorrow as his daughter is having her fifth birthday party and he'll be the official security officer of the jumping castle that's been hired. I laugh at the thought and clap him on the back as we part ways, each heading for our vehicles.

Today was a great day.

## SUNDAY, OCTOBER 14

Sundays are always seen as great days to work and although I was looking forward to another easy shift, found myself awoken through the night with severe stomach cramps. Although I won't go into the finer details of my nightly toilet stints, I can say that I didn't venture more than a few yards from the toilet bowl for the next day or so.

Without pun intended, today was a real crappy day.

# WEDNESDAY, OCTOBER 17

I WAS SURPRISED to be back in Thomson East today, not because of the unit, but because I'd been in there a few times over the past week and am more accustomed to getting moved around. Having a variety of places to work in makes for a far more interesting day as opposed to sitting in the same unit day after day.

In any case, Scott Jones was already in the station when I entered the unit and I almost got to him before his face changed as he looked past me. I turned to see Tony Malone coming through the airlock and found all the enthusiasm drop to my feet. If you have been following my journeys through the different chapters of Prison Days, then you will already be aware of the day that lay ahead.

Scott and I shook and when Tony came to the station, offered him a handshake which he returned. I checked the unit muster and found that Lu still hadn't returned. A few other names had been replaced by new ones and the current number of prisoners housed within Thomson East had risen to 64.

While Tony and Scott made their way around the unit conducting count, I jumped on the computer and checked my emails. They tend to pile up quite quickly and if not handled at least once or twice a week, can begin to add up into 4 figure territory. There were the usual ones that didn't concern me, those that discussed daily moves, upcoming events and daily incident reports. The daily reports are of quite a significance as it gives you a run down of what happens in other units in case you are rostered in them. Good to be aware of any incidents that may impact future events.

When the boys return from their rounds, I managed to dwindle my emails down to under a hundred. One had been sent advising of the expected arrival of a new Governor in the coming days but failed to go into much detail. There was another that advised us that Lu would be moving units upon his return to the prison on Thursday the 18th. Due to expected repercussions, he was being moved into protection for the time being. Loddon North would be his home for the following few weeks and would be up to us to empty his cell today, moving his belongings to his new unit.

Count is called correct shortly after we call our number through and Tony and I head out to unlock everyone. By the time we return to the station, the unit is a hive of activity. Scott begins to answer prisoner's requests for various things such as Request Forms, toiletries, account balances and movement slips for various destinations. I grab a bag and head up to Lu's cell to begin the task of bagging his shit up. Although needing a couple of prods, Tony eventually grabs the cell clearance book and follows me to take note of each item, a requirement when clearing a cell for a prisoner that isn't present.

Thankfully, Lu's cell is one that's not nearly as full of property as some of the cells within the unit. Some prisoners can have as much as 3 or 4 large bags worth of items. Turns out Lu only has one. There isn't a lot of personal items considering the porn stack that he was selling or renting, but I figured he was probably being paid with drugs. Junkies rarely have a lot of personal items, more likely to sell things for a quick hit.

Once the cell is cleared of property and locked back up, I take the bag to the office, then call for a general duties officer to come and take it to the new unit. It doesn't take long before they show and the entire process is completed before 9 o'clock. As the GD heads out through the airlock, I check the list of random searches for the day, then take Tony to conduct them before he has a chance to get comfortable in his seat. His groan falls on deaf ears as I head to the first cell.

Out of the 3 cells we search, there is only a single cigarette to be found. I find it wrapped in plastic and hidden in a container of coffee. I call the prisoner to his cell and he admits ownership when I hold it up for him to see. The grin on his face tells me that he was expecting it and he doesn't complain when I confiscate his TV for 72 hours.

The day continues quietly until lunchtime count is called. The announcement is made and the prisoners begin to line up by their doors as the kitchen crew continue to prepare the meal that will be served once the muster is broken off. For once, Tony actually volunteers for something, grabbing the muster sheet and conducting the cell-to-cell count while Scott and I stand in the middle of the unit and conduct stationary counts from where we stood. As Tony passes by above me, I heard him speak to one of the prisoners as he's marking off names.

"Still no TV, Jason? Dam," he said in a gloating tone and I look up to see that the prisoner who he had spoken to was Jason Mills. I'd completely forgotten about the hat incident a few days prior and hadn't checked on the eventual outcome of the Sup's punishment. Turns out that the Sup was having a particularly stressed out day by the time he came to this unit to deal with Jason, taking his TV off him for an entire week. I look at Jason again and see the fury in his face as he stares at Tony, walking away from him as he continued the count.

Muster was called off ten minutes later and the crooks began to line up for their meals. It was a lunch that consisted of fried dim-sims and hot chips and although we were offered our own plates, politely declined. As they ate, I went to the unit log and flicked to the page where the notes were kept of Jason's meeting with the Sup. There was a brief paragraph written, stating that Jason had spat at the Sup when offered a simple reprimand, claiming to have been victimized. He was subsequently locked down that day and lost his TV for a week. It could have been worse, as spitting at an officer can be classed as assault.

I headed back to the station and asked Scott if he was aware of the incident.

"He didn't look too happy when Tony made the remark to him. Maybe he's holding a grudge," I said and Scott seemed to consider. He stood and began to walk out of the station.

"Fuck it, I'll just ask him," he said as he headed for the stairs leading to the upper tier. Shouting suddenly began from the kitchen and I headed there to see what was happening. Two crooks were arguing over who was going to do the washing and as I tried to call to them to settle down, heard a sudden yell from above me. Looking over my shoulder, I saw Jason standing over something. I couldn't see what it was due to the angle, but I noticed that Scott was nowhere to be seen. Jason was swinging something in a wide circle then brought it down in a sudden strike that sounded dull. There was a prisoner standing just behind Jason and he looked white as a sheet. I pressed the panic button on my radio as Tony stood and began to run to the stairs, yelling something into his own radio. In all honesty, I had never seen him move so fast and I sprinted for the stairs fearing the worst.

Half way up the stairs I saw my worst fears as Scott was lying in a pool of blood at Jason's feet who was still swinging something around. He brought whatever it was down on Scott's head, screaming at him to 'fucken die, cunt'. Tony had reached the top of the stairs and had grabbed a garbage bin. He held it out in front of him and charged at Jason. I never paused, running at the prick with all of my 110 kilos. I caught him around the middle as Tony tripped beside me, the bin falling to the floor. Jason first gasped as the wind was knocked out of him, then screamed as he tried to break free from me. Tony was up on his feet and was about to grab an arm when I yelled at him to get his cuffs out. He did and as I struggled with Jason, trying to get on top of him, I saw Scott violently shaking on the floor behind us, the blood pouring from his head. He looked like he was having a fit and it made me sick to my stomach. I was so charged full of adrenalin that I never felt extra hands join in holding Jason down as extra officers finally arrived.

I didn't hear the urgent call for medical help as I sat on top of Jason, dragging one arm behind him as another officer grabbed the other. I didn't hear the other officers call for the unit to be locked down as I grabbed Jason's cuffed arms and helped drag him to his feet. I didn't notice the officer pick the sock up, the pool ball nestled in its base as blood dripped from it, splattering on the floor beneath. I didn't see the officer upend the sock, catching the blood-stained number 8 in the palm of his hand as I watched the Tactical Officers escort Jason from the unit. My legs felt weak, my knees threatening to quit as I watched nurses frantically working on my friend. They had his shirt open and were performing CPR as the blood continued to pool beneath him from his smashed skull.

I could only think of his wife and daughter, going about their day totally oblivious to the fight for his life that their husband and father was currently waging. I cried. I felt the hopelessness of not being able to help him, myself questioning whether I should have stopped him from climbing those stairs. Through thick tears, I looked at Tony as he stood leaning against the wall.

"WHY THE FUCK WOULD YOU GLOAT TO JASON ABOUT HIS TV?" I screamed at him as arms suddenly pulled me back. I hadn't noticed myself taking several steps towards Tony. If I had been able to reach him, I probably would have lost my job right there. One of the officers grabbing me slipped in Scott's blood and we almost went over. But more hands grabbed us from behind and I felt myself dragged away as the nurses screamed for an ambulance. One had already been called, although I never saw it arrive.

I was escorted from the building and taken to the main staff room. There, I was handed a coffee and made to sit so I could settle down. I needed to calm myself, the anger so raw inside me. The Supervisor eventually came and saw me, offering for me to go home once I'd written my report. I'm not usually one to run home but in this instance, I felt that I needed to. It affected me in such a strong way that I was still shaking as I was trying to type my report almost two hours later.

By the time it was finished and emailed to the Sup, my nerves were beginning to calm a bit, my hands no longer shaking. The ambulance had left quite some time before and the word had come that Scott was riding the edge, his head caved in from the impact. The first swing of the pool ball had hit him square in the face, fracturing his eye socket. He was unconscious before he hit the ground, Jason repeatedly hitting him with his weapon until I tackled him away.

As I drove home almost an hour later, having never met his wife or child, I found that they were the only thing I could think of. I prayed that they still had their husband and father. In the coming days I would find out that Scott died on the operating table twice before being resuscitated and stabilized. He would remain in an induced coma for 3 weeks as the doctors debated about how much damage had been caused.

Jason was moved to another prison before the end of the day and eventually charged with a string of offences. He was already serving a ten-year sentence for armed robbery. At the time this book went to print, we are still waiting for the latest charges to be dealt with. I eventually met his wife and daughter during one of my many visits and together we shared our heartache.

Nobody ever said this job was easy. But some days you wonder whether it truly is worth it. Today was a fucking horrible day.

## THURSDAY, OCTOBER 18

REMAINED off work at the request of the Sup.

## FRIDAY, OCTOBER 19

REMAINED off work at the request of the Sup. I also attended a counseling session which I found to be very helpful.

# MONDAY, OCTOBER 22

It's never easy returning to work after a traumatic event so I was relieved to be given a General Duties shift as I came in. It meant that I wouldn't be stuck in any one unit and would keep me busy for most of the day, having dedicated duties at certain times. I did head to the staff room initially to find out any information about Scott and Jason and found out Scott was still in a coma. I also found out that shortly after Lu had arrived in Loddon North the previous Thursday, two crooks had beaten him with a pool cue and before officers could intervene, had picked him up and thrown him off the second-floor walkaway, purposely dropping him head-first to the floor. Word had it that he'd snapped his spine on impact and was now in the same hospital as Scott.

I have no doubt that word would have been sent to the new unit to "fix him". My guess was that he had been tasked with keeping the phone safe for the controlling gang of the unit and once they saw him arc up and punch the window, blamed him for bringing his injury onto himself. Or, if Lu had in fact been feeling threatened by the gang, his punching of the window may have been him attempting to bail from the unit, something that happens much too often. In any case, the word is that he'll never walk again considering his spinal injuries.

My first duty once count was called correct was to accompany the medical trolley to a couple of the units. The nurse greets me with a cheery 'howdy-doo' and we head off towards Murray North. Because of the events in Thomson East, my duties will keep me away from that unit until I feel ready to return. Personally, I've never been one to back away from a situation but in this case, prefer to work elsewhere if the situation allows for it. If management requires me elsewhere then so be it.

The med run goes by quite quickly, each unit sending a second officer to assist with crowd control. A couple of prisoners forget to bring their ID cards but aren't too upset when we send them back to get them. Each unit we attend has a different feel when we enter but each prisoner takes their turn at the front of the line and takes their medicine. It's only during the final unit's line-up that we have a prisoner attempt to divert his pills. As he pretends to swallow them with a sip of water, he turns to the other officer to present his open mouth. The only issue he had was that when he palmed them, he was so slow that both the other officer and myself, as well as the nurse, all saw him slide the pills into his hand instead of his mouth.

We try not to make too big of a deal with it and get the crook to retake them, watching as he first holds the pills between his teeth, then swallow them with water. We all know that if they truly want to divert, there isn't a lot we can do as the prisoner simply heads straight back to their cell and sinks two fingers down their throat, effectively regurgitating the meds in almost complete form. It happens all the time and can not be helped. With harder drugs such as methadone and bupe, prisoners are required to wait a specific time before leaving the dispensing area to reduce the possibility of regurgitation but no doubt it still happens.

When the med run is finished, another officer bumps into me and asks whether I'd mind swapping into the Sally port. It's an area I've always been fond of and agree without hesitation. The Sally port is the perfect place to spend the day, as it has zero prisoner contact, is isolated from the rest of the prison and allows me to spend some time working on my books. It's almost a gift as far as I'm concerned and I don't waste a second getting my butt there.

The afternoon is one of relative peace and quiet as work is reduced to several truck s and busses entering and exiting the prison. It's almost two an hour, leaving plenty of time for me to write. The drivers are friendly as I process each vehicle and all wish me a good day as they exit. I've written about the duties within the Sally port in previous books so won't bore you with the mundane bits.

Today was a great day.

# TUESDAY, OCTOBER 23

As soon as I entered the gates of the prison, I knew something wasn't quite right. There were quite a few officers congregated in several groups and a couple of them were wearing medical face masks on top of their heads. The whole thing looked surreal, like something out of a movie. Turns out that 3 units had been confirmed as housing multiple flu victims. Medical staff were clear that infected prisoners needed to remain isolated. It was about the smartest thing I'd heard that morning.

I was asked to man the Sally port again and due to the outbreak, and the fact that I had children at home, was more than happy to oblige. The problem with infected prisoners who would be isolated in their cells, was that they still needed basic attention. Someone would still need to attend their cells with food and if an entire unit was locked down, there would be a ton of things to do.

It was quite a cool day and I put on my jacket as I entered the Sally port. With the wind blowing through the mesh doors with quite a bit of oomph, it can be considerably colder than outside. There's already a truck waiting to processed and I quickly stow my gear and signal the control room officer to raise the door. It's a vending machine supply truck and I go through the motions of checking it for any hidden contraband. I climb into the back, search the multiple boxes and also check the cabin of the vehicle. I also place the heart-beat monitor on the truck and let it run its check while I process the driver by scanning him for anything metallic. He checks out and a minute or so later, the monitor beeps its 'OK" signal. I gesture to the control room and they open the inner door. As the truck drives out of the Sally port, I hear another pull up at the outer door behind me.

The process repeats itself many times over, with mid-week being the busiest. There are Supply trucks, linen trucks, food trucks, prisoner buses as well as our own escort vehicles that make regular trips to hospitals and other daytrips. Prisoners could have a number of differing reasons to leave the prison including funerals, specialty appointments or specific transfers.

By 10.30, most of the traffic has cleared and I can finally focus on something else. I turn on the computer and check my emails, deleting them as I go. Once done, I open a fresh page and begin working on a new chapter of a fictional story I'm writing. It's called The Final Alibi and I have high hopes for it. Not only will it be my first fictional story, but it will also include quite a bit of the story being played out in a maximum-security facility.

I'm almost 500 words in when the inner Sally port door begins to raise. When it's high enough, I see the Duty Supervisor escorting four prisoners towards me, each carrying their property in clear plastic bags. I can tell from their faces that they are keen to get to the other side of the door behind me.

When they are securely inside the Sally port and the door is lowered again, I conduct a security check on each prisoner. Only once they confirm their ID's do I OK the control room to open the outer door. Unlike previous occasions, there are no police waiting outside; all the prisoners now walking back out into freedom.

As soon as they are gone, I return to my writing and manage another 1000 or so words before I'm interrupted again. Several tradesmen are entering the prison for some maintenance works and I need to not only process each person, but also individually itemize their tools with the tools-register. Things can go south very quickly if a prisoner managed to get hold of a screwdriver, power drill or worse. It takes almost 30 minutes to process the 6 men and their equipment.

By the afternoon, traffic begins to pick up again around 3 as several buses containing transfers arrive. By 5, there's a decent line of regular traffic coming and going and there's virtually no time for writing. My shift ends just after 6 as I'm relieved by a nightshift officer.

Today was a fantastic day.

## THURSDAY, OCTOBER 25

ALTHOUGH I HAD the rest of the week off (yes, four rostered days off. Have I mentioned how much I love the roster?), I decided to make myself available for overtime. I had nothing else planned and aside from writing, would only spend the day sitting around home. I figured that earning a bit of extra coin might ease the stresses of day to day bills.

The call came almost an hour before I was required so was in a mad rush to get ready and into the car on time. Traffic was hectic and I only just made it inside on time. I was given a shift in the Visits Centre and would normally be placed in the back of the building to conduct strips. But the back was already fully manned so I had the interesting task of escorting visitors from the Reception Centre to the Visits Centre. Thankfully, some days can be quieter than others and when I see the list, am happy to read that there are only 34 visits booked for the entire day. There's a huge gap in the middle due to the weekly training schedule. Each Thursday, for a period of 3 hours, the entire prison is locked down so staff can attend various training courses to stay up-to-date with qualifications. These training schedules can be anything from First Aid to X-Ray training. Most of these qualifications only last 12 months and thus require staff to be requalified.

I check the training schedule but already know the answer before I even open the attachment. My name won't be on the list as I'm on overtime, hence would not have been rostered. The roster is the reason the lockdown training days happen weekly. It's to allow all staff to attend, despite their varying roster requirements.

Because I was rostered in Visits, the start time is after count is called correct. It's also a much shorter shift than normal due to the Visits Centre being open for set hours each day. Visits officers work an entirely different shift to the rest of the prison so generally work more days each week to make up their 38 hours.

As I enter the front, I see Mavis Henderson and Sharon Ward sitting at the station. A third officer, Edward Ryan is just coming out from the toilet, clutching a newspaper in one hand. I do a quick walk around of the visits area, a requirement to ensure there's no hidden contraband anywhere before the visitors arrive.

When I enter the station, set up very differently to unit stations in that the entrance is behind a locked door. It's also a little higher than unit stations, giving whoever is sitting in it, a better viewpoint over the tables and chairs.

There's greetings all 'round as I shake with the other officers and when Mavis offers me the list, I say that I've already seen it. The three of them will man the main station, while three other officers will man the back. Once enough visitors have been processed out at the Reception building, I will make my way back and escort the groups here, ready for their family or friends. Just as I'm wondering how long it will take for the first group to be ready, the phone rings and Sharon gives me a thumbs up.

As I enter the rear Reception door, there's a group of around 10 visitors waiting for me. They all seem happy, some of them talking quite animatedly. I also notice a couple of people looking quite nervous, clearly their first time behind the walls. I try and make small talk with them as we walk up the long corridor and one of the ladies tells me about her visit. She is a Mum of a young 18-year-old that was done for speeding. Apparently, he was caught driving at 188km/h in an 80km/h zone. His main mistake was not pulling up straight away, instead trying to run. This meant he added an "evading police" charge which ultimately landed him in prison. I asked if she knew what unit he was in and when she said Thomson East, thought back to the attack on Scott.

The harsh reality is that most times, crimes and age are completely irrelevant when being placed into a unit. For the most part, it's more based on who the unit already houses. I can not imagine how frightening it would be for an 18-year-old to end up in an adult prison, much less the pain and anguish his family must feel. The lady asks me whether it's a good unit and I lie, saving her a little extra and unwanted anguish.

We reach the Visits Centre and I hold the door open as people shuffle in and make their way to the station. The officers begin to allocate each prisoner's visitors a specific table number and I help some find their seats. Only once the visitors are seated, are the prisoners phoned up. This prevents too many prisoners hanging around the area, mainly as prisoners tend to be very impatient and we don't need a crook shouting for his visitor while others are trying to have some quality time.

Almost as soon as all the visitors are seated, the phone rings again and my journey repeats itself, each time escorting a mixture of both confident and nervous visitors. As I hold the door open a second time, I see prisoners already seated at some of the tables, people enjoying chocolate, chips and drinks. It looks like a regular picnic ground and before I have a chance to enter, Mavis gives me the signal to return to the Reception Centre once more.

The process is repeated many times throughout the day, sometimes escorting a single person. It's not only family and friends that come to visit, often lawyers coming to visit their clients. These types of visits aren't normally on the visitors list so the total number isn't really known until the end of the day. Today doesn't seem to be a major "Lawyer Day" as such, saving my legs a few miles here and there.

All in all, it's actually a pretty good day. Far from the major assault that occurred here a couple of months ago where several officers were left injured. I enjoy escorting the visitors back and forth and find the day coming to an end quite quickly. As I return the final visitor to Reception and head back to the Visits Centre, Mavis and Sharon pass me, thank me for the day and head out. The rest of the officers are still sitting around the station and once I grab my bag, we all walk out together.

Today was a really good day and an area I definitely want to work in again.

## MONDAY, OCTOBER 29

Today is the first of a couple of night shifts. I'm rostered in Murray North and when I walk through the doors, am greeted by a jovial bunch of day staff. There are six officers and all of them keen to go home. Two of them are going trap-to-trap conducting count while the other four are sitting in the station talking shit. I shake hands with each then anxiously check the unit muster. Night shifts can be a make or break shift based on who is housed here. One particular name I always check for is Cooper Shelley (see June edition), a serial pest and frantic masturbator.

"It's a pretty good list, man," Rob Guthrie says, seeing me checking. "Should have a quiet night."

"Just the way I like it," I reply, grabbing a chair and jumping on the computer. I check my emails while the boys and girls finish up and once count is called correct, am left alone with 40 prisoners. The unit is fairly quiet for the time being and I take advantage by starting some writing. I'm rostered in here for two nights and know just how bad it can get. I get no more than 50 words into my writing before things kick off.

"Jesse!" one prisoner up on the second-floor yells. "Jesse!" The other prisoner doesn't respond. It soon becomes clear why. "Hey,

Jesse you dog. How was the snitching today?" Jesse Wright is a protection prisoner who was beaten up a couple of weeks ago. Word has it that he lagged on another prisoner who was diverting medication and swapping it for sexual favours. The lagging not only ended the diverting for the prisoner he lagged on but it also caused the prisoner who was handing out sexual favours to be moved into a management unit, effectively isolating him from everyone. It definitely didn't go down well, hence the bashing of Jesse Wright. "Jesseeee!" Pretty soon other prisoners join the first, each calling for the dog to answer, asking if he wanted to be "butt-fucked". Jesse didn't answer any of them.

The burning continued for no less than two hours of constant abuse; shouting that was amplified in the relatively small space. I tried to block it out and continued writing, occasionally pausing to look over the unit. I really only had one duty and that was to monitor the intercom and unless someone pressed it, left me to my own devices. Some officers choose to do nothing more than watch TV while others might read. For me, night time was the perfect opportunity to write, although it was a hell of a lot more perfect when the unit was quiet and everyone was either tucked into bed or just watching TV.

The intercom is fairly quiet, the first call occurring just after 10 when a diabetic asks for his meal which has been put aside for him. I go and find it then walk it to his cell, passing it through the trap. He thanks me and I return to the station to continue writing. The unit is almost completely quiet as the clock reads 1102pm and I heat my dinner in the staffroom microwave. It is spaghetti bolognaise, homemade by yours truly. I eat it while watching some late-night TV although the X-Files episode that's playing isn't one of my favourites.

By 2 in the morning, the unit is almost completely silent and I was quite absorbed in my writing. I nearly jumped out of my skin when the intercom chimed next to my head. As I check the cell number against the muster, I instantly know the reason for the call before I even speak to the occupant. The cell is B14, a second-floor cell on the left side, its occupant being Jesse Wright. Based on the information that I know, as well as the burning from earlier that night, I can almost guarantee that he will try and bail from the unit. And the best way to do that is to wait until everyone else is asleep and then claim to have some sort of pain that will require medical attention.

"Please state your emergency," I say into the microphone, then listen as Jesse breathes heavily into the speaker.

"Boss, I've got chest pains." His voice is hoarse, almost gravelly and I know that my hands are tied when it comes to my own choices of response. Because he's spoken into the intercom, the conversation is automatically recorded. He's also told me that he's having chest pains which means he could be suffering a heart attack. I'm not a doctor and as such am unable to determine whether he requires medical attention or not. And he may well be having a heart attack, but I know he's faking it. It really makes no difference to me to call a code on him and get him a nurse. It will mean all night staff will have to attend the unit, something Sups hate, especially when its known to be a false code but I refuse to jeopardize my job for the sake of a simple report that I will need to write.

The other thing that will happen is the other crooks will know what Jesse is planning, and when the nurse finds nothing wrong with him, will advise the Sup that he will be fine to remain in the unit. The crooks will have a field day with him and the burning will be twice as bad. All of this I already know as soon as the words drift out from the speaker. I decide to offer him a one-time out.

"I'll have to call a code, Jesse. You sure?" He hesitates, then answers as quietly as possible to ensure no one else hears him.

"I need a nurse."

"OK, hang tight," I answer back, then grab my radio and call the code mike. Control responds almost instantly and announces the code to the rest of the staff. The radio comes alive as people begin answering, including the medical team that will attend. I prepare for the influx of people, turn the lights on in the main area and return to the computer to begin typing the report.

As the first people begin to arrive, I point them up to the cell then finish my report. It's already printed and signed by the time the Sup arrives and I set it on top of the bench for him. The nurses arrive shortly after and head straight to the stairs. The cell is cracked and I wait at the station in case I need to activate something.

The scenario plays out exactly as I predicted. Before the nurses are even out from the cell, the other prisoners are already starting the burn.

"Look fellas, that fuckin dog is trying to bail," one shouts under his door. There's hysterical laughing from several other cells.

"JESSEE! RUN BUDDY!" another yells. The unit is now almost completely awake as shouts and heckling come from all corners. Some of the other officers are wearing cheesy grins themselves, knowing what is playing out. A few minutes later the nurses step out from the cell and the door is locked, Jesse remaining inside. The Sup comes to the station and grabs my report, his expression clearly telling me what I already know.

Five minutes later the unit is completely empty again, only myself and 40 crooks left to ride the storm that has awoken. The heckling is relentless and less than an hour later the intercom goes off again. It's Jesse once more and when I answer, tells me he's still having chest pains. This time however, my response changes as the nurses had already seen to him.

"Just have to ride it out till morning, man. There's nothing I can do." He doesn't respond and I break the connection as the other crooks continue burning. It goes on for almost another full hour before they start to tire from the yelling. By 4 that morning, the unit is again almost silent and I manage to return to my writing for another hour and a bit before prepping for breakfast.

Just after 5.30 I begin making the toast for the unit, 160 slices of bread being run through an industrial toaster. They are ready to be handed out by 6 and as the first of the day staff arrive, I begin going trap to trap, handing each prisoner a plate of toast and condiments. By 7, the day staff have all turned up and I bid them farewell, tired from a long night and knowing that I will be back to do it all again in 12 short hours.

Tonight, was a good night.

# TUESDAY, OCTOBER 30

I RETURN to the unit a little before 7, most of the officers sitting in the station. A couple of new prisoners arrived during the day but for the most part, not much had changed. They had listened to Jesse getting burnt a few times but otherwise had a fairly quiet shift.

Once count is called correct and the day staff leave, I flick the TV on and start my night with a couple of episodes of Seinfeld while the crooks hold various conversations around the unit, each yelling to someone from under their doors. A lot of the conversations are far from intelligent and I turn the TV volume up to drown them out. Listening to one crook telling another how he gagged whilst feasting on some chick he picked up at a nightclub because of the stink was not something I really wanted to hear.

The evening played out much the same as the previous night. The intercom went off several times, mostly prisoners asking what movies were due to be shown on the dedicated movie channel. The diabetic called up for his meal around 9.30 and by 10 the unit had fallen silent. I found a Star Wars movie on one of the channels and found myself enjoying it until the final credits started scrolling just before midnight. The burning hadn't been too bad and I was surprised when Jesse called me up again, claiming to need a nurse.

"You know what happened last night, Jesse. I can only get a nurse up here by calling a code. You want that?" There was no answer. "Jesse, you want me to call a code?"

"No, it's alright." I cut the call and jumped on the computer, waiting for the desktop to load after putting in my details. The unit was almost completely silent and it was probably a good thing, because if it had of been as noisy as the previous night, I may never have heard the noise.

Just as I began to type away, I heard what I can only describe as a very quiet moan. It wasn't the kind of moan you'd associate with pleasure, rather one more closely tied to pain. It was an almost grunt and I paused my typing as I tried to listen for it. I heard it again, almost muffled and left the station to investigate. There were close to 50 doors in front of me and the noise could be coming from anyone of them.

I was walking along the bottom tier when I heard the noise again, somewhere from almost directly above me. I frowned a little as I saw Jesse's name on one of the doors up there. I quietly climbed the staircase, then tried to sneak along the top deck as I listened intently. I paused beside Jesse's door then heard the noise again. It was coming from the cell directly beside Jesse and when I looked at the name, saw Dylan Williams. He was one of the new arrivals from that day and when I quietly opened the trap, was hit with the dank and pungent smell of coppery blood.

The cell was completely dark and when I switched the light on, had to stifle a scream that was building in my own throat. Dylan was sitting up in bed, the white sheet completely drenched in blood. He'd sliced his throat with a piece of plastic from one of the disposable plates, the blood pouring through his fingers as he held his hand over the wound. There was a splatter on the opposite wall to him and I scrambled for my radio as he looked at me wide-eyed. I will never forget the look he had in his eyes, the raw fear in them one I had never seen before.

I called the code, yelling for urgent medical help as Jesse asked me something from under his door. I told him to shut-up, instead trying to focus on Dylan. He spoke to me, his voice sounding as scared as his eyes looked.

"I didn't know it would take so long to die, Boss," was what he whispered to me. He was crying, his eyes now filling with tears as he tried to stand, instead falling forward, blood still pouring from his wound. "I need help," I screamed into the radio and control called for an eta on medical. I couldn't open the cell as night staff aren't allowed to have cell keys. It's a requirement as no staff member is allowed to open a cell after hours without just cause. Due to the odd staff member having inappropriate relationships with crooks, as well as some staff smuggling contraband in for crooks, cell keys can not be held by staff manning units alone after hours.

As the first staff began to arrive, I asked for permission to crack the cell via my radio. The Sup on duty gave it and as soon as I had 3 other officers, had one of them open it. The second it was open, we rushed in and began to try and stop the bleeding. We all wore gloves for fear of disease and I held my hand over the wound as someone else searched for a towel to use as a tourniquet. The stench was so bad, not from the blood but from the fact that Dylan had soiled himself, not surprising considering what he had done.

The medical team came rushing in and took over from us shortly after. I was glad to have them arrive and happily made my way out from the stink of the cell. Dylan looked white as a ghost, the blood looking like a massacre on the bed, walls and floor of the cell as the nurses frantically worked on him. He passed out at some point and when he was finally stretchered from the unit, appeared to me to be dead.

But he didn't die, despite losing a vast amount of blood. Dylan was rushed to hospital by emergency ambulance and stabilized by the medical staff. His cell was secured and eventually cleaned by unit billets trained in blood management. For me, seeing the look in that prisoners' eyes is something that I can never forget. He arrived in the unit from a previous prison where he'd been raped by another inmate. Dylan was 23 years old and was in prison for the first time. His charge was attempted burglary but word was that it was an ex-girlfriend that accused him. I don't know how true that is but I do know that the shame of the rape almost cost him his life. I hope he can find the help he needs to get through it.

When I walk out a few hours later, I remember the look in his eyes, the fear that was burnt into them and head home still numb from the experience. It's not something I hope to ever see again but know that with the environment I work in, most likely will.

Today was not a good day.

# WEDNESDAY, OCTOBER 31

ALTHOUGH I WASN'T ROSTERED tonight, I opted for overtime and was pleased to get the call just as I arrived home from my previous shift. It meant that I could get the sleep needed for another night shift. There was a spare spot in the control room and it's one area that I haven't worked very many times before. The role is one of support to the two night control staff that man the numerous cameras, the prison intercoms as well as the Sally port. There is virtually no traffic after lockdown apart from some late prison buses. The other traffic that may come through is a garbage truck throughout the night as well as any ambulances that might be required.

Jason and Jackie are the control room officers and we greet each other as they buzz me in. It's a secure room with access only allowed for specific people. Shortly after arriving, they begin the count, calling for it on the radio. The phone begins ringing instantly with 25 units all vying to get their count called in so everybody can go home. Jackie answers each call and adds the number to the spreadsheet. The process takes around 10 minutes and once the final call is received, the final tally is added up. Much to the dismay of the staff, someone has called in the wrong number. Jason announces an incorrect count and the process is repeated.

Unfortunately, staff are required to remain on duty until the count is correct, regardless of finishing times. The longer it takes, the longer you stay. Incorrect counts can take two differing paths. The first is if the count is short. If it's short it could mean that a prisoner is missing, possibly escaped. It's one of the biggest fears of any prison officer and is something most people try to correct as soon as possible. The other is if the count is over. This could be due to a unit officer failing to write someone out in the log book after leaving for somewhere else. They may not have conducted a proper count, instead relying on the log numbers.

In this case, the count was over by 1 meaning we had too many prisoners. Once the fresh numbers start being phoned in, it doesn't take long to find the culprit. Comparing first count numbers to second count numbers soon reveals the unit responsible. The Sup is sitting in the control room and as soon as count is called correct, phones Thomson East. Each officer on duty in that unit must now write a report for an incorrect count before they can go home. I know the feeling as I have been there before and it's not nice unable to leave on time.

The airlock outside the control room begins to fill as officers begin to drop their radios and keys back to us. I take each and return them to their allocated places. The radios I put into chargers, ready for the next shift. The airlock doesn't clear for almost 30 minutes with a couple of hundred staff all trying to exit at the same time. It's a tedious process but one that can't be changed. I work non-stop with the keys and radio and am glad once I see the last of them.

Jackie selects the movies from the schedule and inserts the first disc, Rambo 3, into the DVD player. We have a TV on as well and can watch the movie if we choose. We can also switch it to normal TV but Jason is happy to keep Sly on.

Once the airlock is cleared and the movie is on, Jason and Jackie begin to complete their own tasks. It is their responsibility to allocate the next day's keys to each officer, as well as update overall systems around the prison. They also answer the intercom calls from unmanned units which begin almost immediately once Rambo begins playing. It would seem that Sly isn't as popular with some of the younger crooks as they request something else. Their voices sound deflated when told that the DVD's are selected by management and must be played as per instructions. In the words of someone much wiser, it is what it is.

For me, it is the start of a night of nothing. There's no spare computer in the control room so writing is out of the question. There's no activity in the Sally port until after 1 the next morning, leaving me with nothing to do except enjoy the movies. There is one thing that I have always enjoyed whilst working with experienced staff and that is the stories. The control room is one of those areas where rumours come to die and truth comes to fruition. They hear everything and am almost knocked for six when I hear them start to talk about Emma Porter. She was an officer from my own intake course. Not one that I ever really clicked with, but would often greet her when seeing her around the traps. Turns out she'd been suspended that day. Apparently Emma had been engaged in some very, how can I say this, extraordinary activities behind closed doors with an inmate. Some of her unit staff had suspected something was going on between her and a prisoner when he continuously hovered around her. Word has it that she worked a night shift not long ago and snuck back into the unit after everyone had left and actually entered his cell, remaining inside it for almost a full hour. Other prisoners had commented on hearing their activities from their own cells. I'm ashamed to say that unfortunately it happens quite often. Lonely women and men who crave the friendship of anyone and will give in to the advances from prisoners looking for mules. I'm glad she was caught and hope she doesn't return.

I'm almost thankful by the time the garbage truck shows up after midnight, happily leaving the control room to process the truck in. When he leaves about half an hour later, I return to the comfort of my chair and pray for morning as I settle in to watch Tom Cruise playing a German officer.

Day staff begin to arrive from 5 onwards and I help staff dish out keys and radios to each. A couple of early buses arrive just before 6 and I process them in, only to be relieved by the day staff as the last one leaves. All in all, it was a good night, with no codes and no painful crooks buzzing up every few minutes like they do some nights.

I'm happy to walk out with the sun coming up over the far horizon, tired from my 3 nights. I think back to the month that was and remember all the craziness that once again has made me realize just how unpredictable this job really is. I think back to the words of someone long ago, who told me that no two days were ever the same. No truer words have ever been spoken regarding this role.

# AUTHOR'S NOTE

THANK you once again for joining me on yet another ride through the dark halls of maximum-security. I hope that the events of this month have opened your eyes to the stark reality of this place. I know from what I hear and see on television, that prisons all across the world have very similar stories. And the supply of newer and crazier stories never seems to end.

I'm already working on the November edition of Prison Days and can share with you some of the things that you will read about. One officer will finally retire after more than 30 years in the job while another begins his journey in the harshest way possible, resulting in him donning the nickname "Shit-lips". One prisoner will attempt to commit suicide in a very public way while another will cause an entire unit to erupt.

As always, I am grateful for your continued Support and look forward to seeing you on my Facebook page @prisondaysauthor or my website at www.booksbysimonking.com

I look forward to seeing you in the November edition, due out on December 1$^{st}$.

Simon

# BOOK 6

# INTRODUCTION

WELCOME to yet another month of Prison Days. As I'm sitting here and pondering just where this series has already taken me, and you for that matter, I truly am comforted in knowing that there isn't a shortage of material that inmates provide me. What I mean is, the events that happen on a daily basis are so varied and intriguing that I could continue to write for a very long time and not run out of subject matter.

Just look at the last hour for example. I'm sitting here in Goulburn West on night shift and it's an hour and a half after lockdown. There have been 2 code mikes already, including one from this unit where a prisoner had shoved a pen into his rectum and made it bleed. He's an IDS prisoner and needs to be kept separated from other prisoners due to his vulnerability.

When I asked him why he jammed a pen into his butt, he said that he felt horny. That prisoner has been shoving things into his anus for as long as I have been a guard and does what he does for attention. The reason, like so many of his kind, is that they have a need to be the centre of attention in order to feel liked. They do this through slashing up, bronzing up, faking suicide and yes, jamming things where there is no logical reason to jam them. It takes up a lot of resources but unfortunately cannot be avoided.

My point is, despite initially believing this series to continue for two or three books, its' now into its sixth, and as long as you, the reader, continue reading them, I am happy to continue writing them for you.

I do have one thing I wanted to share with you. When I first began to write these books, fellow authors advised me not to read reviews, as some may not always be favourable. I do read them though and I thank everyone who has written me one because they do really mean a lot. They were right in that not everyone will be as entertained by these books as most have been and that's OK. That's what makes reading so interesting. If you knew you were going to love each and every book you ever picked up, then there wouldn't be any mystery.

But one of these 1-star reviews stated that my books read like a diary and lacked the emotional side of how these events affect me. The point I wanted to make was that that is exactly what I am aiming for; a real, unbiased look at life behind bars without too much influence from my own feelings and emotions. A true-to-life glimpse into the world beyond the walls so to speak. And that way, I hand the decision on whether something is fair, evil, crazy, cold-blooded or just downright wrong to you, the reader. Make your own mind up about these events and share your thoughts with me on my Facebook page.

But for now, let's not worry what others think. Let's focus on the road ahead as we delve into another month of the unpredictable experiences that are maximum security.

## THURSDAY, NOVEMBER 1

I WAS STATIONED in Thomson West for the first of 2 shifts, as one of the regular officers was away on annual leave for a week. I've never minded working in this particular unit as the officers allocated here permanently are a pretty good bunch. Most of the crooks were OK too, definitely unlike several other units that were generally filled with the "needy" kind.

For some reason I felt off, coming in for the first shift today. I put it down to just something in the air but I had the never-ending feeling of the day ahead going pear-shaped even before setting foot inside the walls.

My two offsiders for this shift were both brand new, barely a couple of weeks out from their training course. Meagan Henry was an overly-enthusiastic pleaser that seemed to have a genuine need to see everyone content before she'd sit down, while David Tansy was the exact opposite; a lazy couldn't-be-bothered kind of guy that favoured sitting in the station rather than actively participating in running the unit.

I'm not one to judge anyone, but being brand new and already lazy with a need to kick back at every opportunity puts the onus on me to set him straight and frankly, I spend enough time needing to set crooks straight without an officer adding to it.

Meagan already has the muster sheet in hand when control calls for count and I follow her around the unit, dropping traps and calling out numbers to her. It doesn't take long for us to add up our tally and call it through. Once control calls count correct, I head to the top deck, while Meagan unlocks the bottom cells, the units' 72 prisoners scrambling for the toasters.

As I step back into the officer's station, the intercom buzzes and David answers the call, listening as a prisoner complains of feeling dizzy. His cell is on the bottom tier and I head over to it to check it out.

The crook is still lying in his bunk when I open his door, not looking well.

"What's up, Jeffery?" I ask and he peers up at me with squinting eyes. I can see he's quite sweaty despite it feeling fresh and he struggles up onto his elbow.

"My head feels all weird," he replies, then without warning, vomits across himself, the retching sounding like gravel in his throat. The rancid stink is almost instant and I have no choice but to call a code mike. Meagan is standing behind me with her radio turned up to almost maximum, the call shouting across the unit. There's a definite groan as everyone is aware of what happens next.

Because a code mike requires the medical staff to attend the unit, they won't enter until all the prisoners are locked away, meaning we have to lock everyone down immediately. I stick my head out of the cell and call out to David who's still sitting in the station.

"Lock 'em down," I call out and with a unified groan, prisoners head back to their cells, some scrambling for bits of bread and other necessities. Others are quickly setting up the washing machines and David looks timid as he tries to get the crooks to move back to their cells. I turn to Meagan and whisper for her to return to the station and announce it over the unit PA as Jeffery launches into another bout of retching.

The nurses are waiting outside the unit within a few minutes as we lock the remaining few prisoners away. Once we finish, Meagan opens the door for them and they wheel their trolley to Jeffery's cell where he's still fighting to get his stomach under control. Several of the prisoners begin to cheer as the nurses enter but it has nothing to do with them. The nurses are both male and the cheering has more to do with the fact that they've finally made it to the cell, the unit wanting to be released so as to continue with morning routines.

As the nurses do what they need to with several officers standing close to ensure their safety, I return to the station and begin typing out my report for calling the code. It's only a few lines of text, stating the main points of the incident. It's only a minor code mike and doesn't require anything too extravagant.

Just as I print it out for the supervisor, a stretcher enters the unit and is taken to Jeffery's cell. He's deemed too unwell to remain and will be wheeled down to the prison's hospital wing. Once there, the nurses will determine if he'll require an ambulance for transport to hospital or simply a bed within the unit there. Either way, he'll be taken out of here for the time being.

We stand by while Jeffery is helped onto the stretcher and once he and the nurses have exited the unit, begin to unlock it for a second time. Most of the crooks thank me as I unlock the top tier and once done, return to the station.

Within a few minutes, the medical trolley arrives and I ask David to help the trolley's accompanying officer with regulating the medicinal dispersion, one officer needed to visually confirm consumption of pills and potions by checking mouths as they finish with the pill room. He actually groans as he stands to go and it tickles me in just the right place.

"Excuse me? Is there a problem with you doing your job?" I ask, Meagan turning to watch. He mumbles something under his breath but heads for the now already forming line by the closed door of the pill room. I look at Meagan and she just shakes her head.

"He was like that on the course as well," she said and now it's my turn to groan.

As the medication line begins to dwindle, I prep the movement slips for those prisoners who are about to head off to morning classes. The prison runs many courses which the prisoners have access to, most creating opportunities with which to better themselves and increase their chances of finding work once back out in the community.

Unfortunately, they are also seen by many as an easy way to increase the chance for parole, never actually wanting the qualifications for what they were intended for but rather a tool to be used when attending court.

But just as I'm about to call for the required prisoners, there's a commotion behind me and when I turn, see a prisoner tumble down the steel staircase. There's no-one else nearby and Meagan is already on her radio to call another code as the prisoner is lying at the foot of the stairs, crying in agony. His left leg is positioned precariously away from him and it doesn't take a second look to tell that it's broken.

I don't need to tell you the response from the prisoners as I make the call for the unit to be locked down yet again. They aren't happy but know that we have little choice so don't give us too much of a hard time.

"Fuck you, cunts," is suddenly screamed from behind me and I turn to see one of the unit billets standing on the top tier.

"What are you doing?" someone yells from the other end of the unit and I see that the billet has an extension cord in his hands. He's the person that does the vacuuming of the unit's carpeted areas and thus has access to the vacuum and necessary extension leads that are needed. He's now holding one of them in his hands, one end tied around his neck and the other end about to be tied to the railing.

"Scott!" I call, trying to get his attention. I see Meagan on the phone and assume it's to control, requesting a second code and asking for back-up.

"Shut up, Boss," he said to me. "I'm not doing this shit for another 20 fucking years." He's crying, snot hanging from his nose as he ties the lead off. Some of the other prisoners are cheering, a couple laughing and this just sets him off some more. "Yeah, fucking laugh about it. I'm sick of this shit," he screams.

I probably need to point out to you, (again if you've been on this ride since the beginning or for the first time if this is your initial entry point to Prison Days,) but some prisoners aren't the brightest sparklers in the sky. Not to say that some of our residents aren't teetering on the edge of genius, but unfortunately for others, not so much.

What followed in the next 5 or so seconds could be put down to either not thinking the entire process through due to the stress of the situation, forgetting some very appropriate and fitting physics lessons or just a simple brain fart.

Scott climbed the railing, precariously balanced on the top one for maybe a second or two, closed his eyes and then calmly said "Later Motherfuckers," before stepping off and plunging into the abyss below. In his mind he may have visualized a scene where he plunged to his death to the gasps of surprised crooks, maybe even shouts of astonishment at his fearless and courageous act.

What actually transpired was that the extension cord which was wrapped around his neck had not been measured correctly. Not only did he reach the end of the proverbial rope only an inch or two above the ground, but his would-be hangman's rope snapped due to the weight difference between the maximum break point of the cord and our unfortunate victim's body weight. He struck the very hard and robust concrete floor with both feet at the same time, snapping both legs in various spots, including one unfortunate shard that now stuck out from his pants in a bloody and grotesque manner. Our would-be-suicide-person was squirming about on the floor as a mixture of shock, pain and embarrassment washed across his white face. The unit exploded into a chorus of laughter, cheers and finger pointing as they howled with delight, drowning out the cries of agony.

Prison isn't really the place for pity and our unfortunate prisoner received none, looking at us officers for escape from the torment. Meagan was still on the phone and I could see her now talking frantically into it. I have no doubt that control was already aware of the situation, in all likelihood witnessing the entire sequence on their monitors.

It doesn't take long for the officers to stream back into the unit, most helping to lock it down. Although it's another disruption to their morning routine, the prisoners seem unfazed at being returned to their cells yet again, most still laughing at the unfortunate soul lying on the floor.

Once the unit is completely locked down, the nurses enter together with a stretcher. But if you think that's the end of the apathetic abuse from the prisoners then you would be mistaken. There are enough gaps and cracks between their cell doors and adjoining walls to ensure none miss out on the show. The goading continues throughout the nurse's assessment and subsequent treatment and hits a fever pitch crescendo as Scott is wheeled out on the stretcher still groaning with pain.

It's another report I need to write and get to it while the nurses are leaving through the airlock, two officers pushing the stretcher for them. By the time the unit is unlocked again, I'm pressing send on my email, the reports finished and on its way to the duty sup.

A number of prisoners make their way to the officer's station, still animated with the 'excitement' of the morning so far.

"Boss, can we go to the gym?" one asks and I phone the gym for confirmation. After confirming that it's OK, I write each of the crooks a movement slip and send them on their way. I also continue with the education slips and once finished, call the appropriate recipients up to collect them. Once the twenty-two leave the unit, there's an instant calm that descends over it, voices only distant murmurs as everyone quietly goes about their daily routine.

With almost 40 prisoners less, tasks become so much easier and I ask David to check that morning's random cell search list. I figure it better to complete them whilst half the unit is out, needing to leave a single officer in the station. As I wait for the list, I consider my options for who to take with me to conduct the searches. I know that Meagan is keen to learn and would jump at the chance, but I also see her as the more confident of the 2, predicting her to be more capable of handling herself if confronted in the station by crooks. David, on the other hand, needs to be kept busy, the one more likely to fall asleep whilst manning the station alone.

"Do you mind holding the fort while we go do the searches?" I ask her and Meagan nods, watching as her demeanour grows in confidence at running the show for a bit. A good side-effect of leaving Meagan in the station alone is that she will be tested by prisoners keen to see whether she's able to be 'bought' or intimidated. Taking advantage of an officer isn't anything new and can be quite confronting and it's probably best for her to experience it early in her career.

"All under control," she said, shooting us a 2-thumbs-up. I wave for David to follow me and make my way to the first cell, a single-outer on the bottom tier. The prisoner is sitting on his bunk reading a book and isn't too fussed when we interrupt him. I wave for David to take the lead and he conducts the strip search, finding nothing of interest.

"Anything in here that shouldn't be?" I ask and the prisoner shakes his head. Once he exits, I close the door and we begin searching.

10 minutes is all it takes to go through everything, finding nothing of interest to us. The crook salutes us comically as we emerge and resumes his novel, something by Stephen King. I close the door and head to the next cell, located up on the second tier. David is grumbling about something as we climbed the stairs.

"Something the matter?" I asked as I reached the top.

"No," was all he managed, looking at the stairs as he climbed. I wasn't sure what the issue was but assumed he really didn't want to be doing anything other than sitting on his butt. We reached the second cell and found it locked. The occupant was one of the "gym" crooks and so we entered without too much of an issue, commencing our search immediately.

Other than a single picture of a naked woman, torn from a magazine, the cell was clean. I crumpled the picture up and put it in my pocket, keeping it for disposal once back in the station. Although technically contraband, it didn't really warrant any subsequent disciplinary action other than a caution upon the occupant's return.

The third cell we search provides a slightly better result as David locates a toothbrush shiv hidden inside the stuffing of the pillow, as well as a single pill which was left sitting on the window sill. Complacency goes both ways, with prisoners sometimes forgetting where they are.

Much to David's disgust, it's up to him to write the report, which he does once we return to the station. I'm amazed by the attitude but know it's none of my business. As long as he continues to do as he's asked, regardless of the mutterings, then I'm happy.

Just as lunchtime count is called over the radio, there's an influx of returning prisoners from the gym. The airlock is filled a number of times as they make their way back inside and head straight to their cells, eyeing the kitchen billets busily preparing their meals as they pass. Once they are all back inside, Meagan announces muster over the unit P.A. system and we conduct count in relative silence.

Meagan takes the clipboard and walks along the cells as David and I take position in the middle of the unit to conduct our own count. I watch as she slowly marks names of, peering into each cell to ensure its occupant is out. Once she's traversed both levels and returns to the station, I yell for the unit to break off and everyone makes a beeline for the kitchen, plates in hand.

Once all 3 of us are happy that our numbers match, Meagan calls it into control and a few minutes later are relieved to hear it called correct, signalling the beginning of the afternoon. It's great to be able to just sit and relax after the morning's incidents, the attempted suicide still the talk of the unit.

I listen to a group of prisoners who are sitting near us talking about it, laughing as one describes the look on the unfortunate Scott's face as he hit the floor. Others soon join in the laughter as they eat, visibly enjoying recollections from different angles. All I can think is that if they are laughing together then they aren't arguing and that's a good thing for us.

I phone the supervisor for a quick chat and find out that Scott had been taken straight to the hospital via ambulance, something I suspected but wanted to confirm. Knowing if a prisoner was returning to the unit is good knowledge to have when it came time for final lockdown.

Once the meals are finished, the afternoon dissolves into several different activities across the unit. There's a game of pool here, several prisoners vying for "unit champion" of table tennis over there, as well as several card games. A game of chess is started near us by two older prisoners and I watch as they silently go about trying to outwit each other over the course of a couple of hours.

About an hour before lockdown, just as the med trolley pulls into the unit for the final time, I come to realise that one particular prisoner is still actively talking about Scott. It strikes me as odd as the laughter around the subject had died off considerably throughout the afternoon, yet he continued to try and drum up an audience with his vocalized story-telling.

As Meagan heads to the airlock to help with the dispensing of the medication, the phone rings. I answer it and listen as the sup asks for a particular crook to be watched until the Tactical boys come to grab him. The prisoner he mentions is called James Dobbs and just happens to be the one still wanting to go on about Scott.

The sup advises me that Scott had made some allegations against James and after reviewing camera footage of the unit, determined there to be sufficient cause for a formal interview with the prisoner. He doesn't elaborate on what the allegations are, other than to say it looked as if Scott had been stood over.

James doesn't argue as the Tactical boys arrive, accompanying them out of the unit. There's a murmur amongst the other prisoners as he is led out but it dies down quickly once he's disappeared out of the airlock.

He doesn't return by the time we lock the unit down for the night, remaining up in one of the admission buildings whilst interviewed by police. As I walk out, I'm glad that the first day of the month is over, but feel a faint flicker in the pit of my stomach about what the rest of the month had in store. I thank my offsiders as we re-enter the outside world and breathe easier once safely back in my car. Today has been an OK day.

## FRIDAY, NOVEMBER 2

As I ENTER the unit for day 2 of my 3-day stretch, I'm happy to see Meagan already in the station going over the muster.

Hey," she calls out as I come through the airlock and I return her wave. "James got taken out of the unit. See? Not on here," she said, holding the muster up. I look and see that his name has been removed. When I check the movement log for the previous day, I point out that he'd been moved to one of the management units.

"Probably found that he'd been doing naughty stuff," Meagan said as I put my bag away.

It doesn't take me long to find out the details of what had transpired the night before, thanks to a quick call to the sup. It turns out that James had not only been standing over Scott but also his girlfriend on the outside, courtesy of another prisoner's brother. The brother had been visiting Scott's girlfriend on a number of occasions, trying to force her to smuggle drugs into the prison when visiting her boyfriend. Scott had tried to resist the pressure, but security footage had shown James entering Scott's cell moments before he tried to hang himself. Police were following up on some leads and it was highly likely that charges may be laid. For the time being, James had been removed from the unit pending further investigations.

David re-enters the unit whilst I'm on the phone and offers us a half-hearted wave. I hear Meagan groan slightly behind me but try to ignore it. I've never been one to enjoy tension between officers. 12 hours of sitting in a tiny officer's station with added tension is not my idea of a good time. Plus, the crooks pick up on it and try and use it to their advantage.

I hang up and share the news with the other two just as control calls for count. Meagan has already grabbed the muster and asks David to help her as I start preparing movement slips for the gym, education and medical appointments. Fridays can also be notorious for visits, but those will be done as they're needed.

It doesn't take long for the unit to be a hive of activity once count is called correct and the day's usual train begins to roll on familiar tracks. Breakfast, gym, education, laundry and early exercise routines all commencing from the get-go. The medical trolley rolls in a short time later and I go and help with the dispensing.

Halfway through, I hear Meagan raising her voice to a crook who's standing in the middle of the unit just grinning at her. He's wearing his hat inside and she's yelling, sounding agitated, trying to get him to remove it. I know that it's nothing more than a test and how she handles it is watched by everyone, not just the prisoner involved. The test isn't so much how she talks to him but more so whether she follows up on his refusal.

"Either take it off or I lock you down," I hear her yell at him and he decides to take it off. The reason hats aren't allowed to be worn inside units is because the cameras have trouble identifying faces in case of an incident. Authorities need to be able to positively identify offenders in case of assaults, vandalism, trafficking or worse.

Once the hat is removed, she turns to sit down, glancing at me briefly. I give her a brief nod and she smiles, acknowledging it. It's the first but probably not the last. Prisoners also have a tendency to get bored, so have a wide variety of things to amuse them; everything from card games, gym equipment, books and officer baiting. It is what it is and we just have to deal with it on a case by case basis.

But knowing that Meagan was able to handle her test doesn't

lower my nervousness thinking about David's. I know it's coming and whether he knows it or not, they will give him a crack before the day is out. If the codes from the previous day weren't so entertaining for them, they would have tested him then. I look at him as he sits in the station, vacantly staring at the computer screen and hope he manages to handle it.

Once the meds are dispensed and the trolley wheeled out again, I return to the station and check the cell searches for the day. 2 of the 3 seem fine, recognizing the names as being of crooks currently studying a barista's course. It's the third name that raises some butterflies for me. Riley Mason is the unit's only IDS prisoner. Because of a current shortage of accommodation around the prison, the unit that houses IDS prisoners is beyond full, requiring some to be spread out to other places. Riley is in this unit because his brother is also here, but much higher functioning than Riley and acting as a sort of mentor. They share a cell together and can normally be dealt with quite easily.

"Let's go David," I say to my offsider and he looks at me over his shoulder.

"Can't Meagan do it today?" he replies and I shake my head.

"Not this one, sorry." I know that apart from being IDS, Riley Mason also has a flag against his name for inappropriate behaviour around female staff. Emails are sometimes sent out when certain prisoners are to be considered more dangerous if left in certain situations and Riley has a history of sexual misconduct when in the company of females.

David groans but stands to follow me and I lead the way to the cell located on the bottom tier. It's closed and David passes me, walking with attitude, obviously pissed off with having to conduct this particular duty. It doesn't phase me much, my only concern being the welfare and safety of officers and if I can avoid a situation then I will. David on the other hand still hadn't figured it out but I knew time wouldn't be on his side.

When living in a unit, there are certain "unwritten" rules that one should try and abide by. Some of these can be put down to nothing more than common courtesy and following them, even by officers, can sometimes avoid confrontations. One of those is knocking on a door. I'm not saying as an officer you should knock and wait to be invited in. That would be silly and stupid as the crook would simply spend a few minutes hiding their contraband while keeping you waiting. But tapping your key on the door before opening the cell door is a courteous cue that you are about to enter. If the prisoner is in a "delicate position" it gives them a split-second opportunity to call out. We still open the door of course but the warning had been given.

The most common "hang on" we tend to get when wanting access to a cell is the unfortunate crook being in the middle of a toilet stop. Personally, I know I don't want to walk in on someone taking a shit but cracking the door even slightly and seeing them sitting on the can is enough to confirm what they're doing, thereby giving us reason not to enter. It's not like we want to stand there watching him wipe.

Unfortunately, David didn't consider the consequences of ripping open a door that stood closed; not locked but just closed for privacy sake. Without knocking or calling out, he simply pulled the cell door open and began to walk in.

There was a table with 5 seated prisoners, located only a few feet from the said cell and when the cell's occupant began screaming insults at the surprised officer, all 5 crooks turned and began to cheer loudly, pointing at the unfortunate Riley Mason who was lying on his bunk bed with half an arm disappearing into his anus while the other was tugging his dick. He was still trying to remove it as I reached the cell and was yelling insults at David with a face the colour of port wine.

When he finally stood and pulled his trackpants up, I waved at the crooks seated at the table to hush a little. There were more coming around to take a look and I pulled the door slightly shut behind me, despite the putrid stink of shit filling the cell. I was about to call for Riley to jump in the shower and "clean" the offending appendage but it seemed David had other thoughts.

"Leave your pants off, gonna strip you anyway," he grumbled at

Riley and before he had a chance to react, instantly realized the error of his ways.

Cells aren't notorious for being huge. Riley wasn't a small prisoner, standing around 6' 1 with a sizeable belly to match. David wasn't small either and so the distance between the two was less than 5 feet, nowhere near enough room to provide enough reaction time if anything was to kick off.

The fist that came flying, was sent with no warning and with the speed of a spooked cat. Still covered with enough shit to paint a mural, it hit David square in the face, sending him backwards into me with the dark smears of Riley's faecal matter wiped across his repulsed expression. The yell of disgusted protest that I felt build in his chest never made it out as I dragged him out of the cell by the scruff of the neck.

"Back," I screamed, pointing a finger at Riley who stood where he had, too stunned by his own success as a grin continued to broaden across his face. He froze in place, that vacant stare watching us as we stepped out into the unit, then disappeared as I slammed the cell door home, locking him inside. The crooks that were still sitting at the table were in gales of laughter as they watched David frantically wipe the shit from his face, one stringy bit dangling from one nostril.

"Hahaha, oh my fucken lord. It's Officer Shit-Lips," one suddenly screams and it sounded like the entire unit erupted into a chorus of cheers, the name instantly catching on. It's a name that will quickly spread around the units and follow the officer wherever he's posted. David is frantically wiping at his face as the deep retching seems to grip him like a vice, his throat gagging in near convulsions.

"Code Alpha, prisoner contained," I call through my radio and control respond by announcing it across the prison. It doesn't take long for help to arrive as David disappears into the staff toilet to attempt to disinfect his face, the retching echoing through the door and out into the unit. As humorous as it may seem to some, there is a real possibility of disease and David will have to subject himself to several tests. I don't know whether any actually made it into his mouth but if it did, then he would need to quarantine himself for up to 3 months from contact with his family. I'm not saying he needs to lock himself in a room but rather cease bodily contact with them by no kissing etc.

Officers begin to lock the unit down and once everyone is back in their cells, remove Riley from his and escort him to the Admissions wing for formal interviews. The police will also be called and Riley will more than likely be transferred to one of the management units. Once he's out of the unit, Meagan heads for the now vacant cell with a bag in hand and proceeds to conduct a cell clearance; itemising items on a list before bagging them, ready to transfer his property into storage.

If Riley *is* transferred to one of the management units, he won't have access to his property until he serves whatever punishment in isolation the supervisor sees fit to impose. That's aside from whatever charges are laid and subsequent sentence from a magistrate. For us, we can only continue with our day. David is sent off to the medical wing to be checked out, not only to remove any lingering turds but to also have his face assessed for injury due to the punch.

To my utmost surprise, he returns to the unit an hour or so later, rejecting the sup's offer to take the rest of the day home. The respect I had for him before the incident just increased 10-fold as I watched him return. He gives me a thumbs up as he enters the station and takes a seat. He begins to chuckle a little and when I turn to look at him speaks just two words.

"Shit-Lips," is all he can manage before breaking out into laughter. It's loud enough for the crooks to hear and to my surprise, no-one responds. I see that he's trying some reverse psychology on the prisoners and I have no doubt it'll work for the most part. It reminds me of a line from Game of Thrones. Tyrion is talking to Jon about being a bastard and Jon is getting all fired up at the name he's being called.

"Never forget what you are and you can wear it like armour," I think is how it goes, or something like it. In other words, accept the name and let it wash over you like water off a duck's back, the insult therefore never hurting you. I think it will work for him. Only time will tell of course but I'm happy he came back to face the horde.

Meagan finished the cell clearance a half hour later and apart from writing a couple of reports, the rest of the day was pretty much a non-event. Good for us, not so for you. But you know from experience that there's always more drama to come, especially in this place.

The afternoon slips by with relative ease and to my surprise, David begins to join in with some of the activities without needing to be asked. By the time we walk out of the gates a few hours later, my opinion of him had turned around completely. I knew that he was posted with myself and Meagan in the same unit tomorrow and am keen to see how he handles the banter which I know is coming.

Although a bit shitty, today was an OK sort of day.

# MONDAY, NOVEMBER 5

Today I was stationed in the medical wing for a shift, surprised as I thought I was due to work in Thomson West again. Although it can be one of the quieter units, things can get pretty hectic in a heartbeat. I was surprised to see Meagan in the officer's station already and soon after greeting her, saw Thelma coming through the airlock.

"Morning Thelma," I said as she waved at us and then proceeded to introduce her to Meagan. The night-shift officer was just returning from a quick bathroom stop before heading out into the bright morning. We all waved her off then began to conduct a couple of morning checks. Thelma jumped on the emails while Meagan and I prepared for count. I grabbed the muster while she went and retrieved the ligature knife from the top draw.

For those unaware, the ligature knife is required to be carried during a muster in case we find a prisoner hanging from a rope or something similar. Because it is essentially a blade within a prison, it doesn't have a sharpened end, only a blade that wraps back on itself to form a u-shape, preventing it from being used as a stabbing instrument.

There aren't too many prisoners kept in the medical wing and our count only takes a little over 5 minutes. We return to the station with a total of 19 prisoners and I call it in once control calls for numbers. It's not too long before they call it correct and we commence our morning unlock.

Although a normal unit would unlock their entire clientele, the medical unit is quite different, the reason being the prisoner's classifications. This is a mixed unit, meaning we house both mainstream and protection prisoners. Segregation is still required and enforced so only one or the other is let out at any one time. This morning, it's protection prisoner's turn for an early let-out. Tomorrow it'll be the other way around, just to keep things interesting.

As I make my way around the unit, crooks begin to emerge from their rooms as soon as they hear the click of the unlock, my key snapping each door open with a short rattle. I'm greeted by a number of them as they come out and I respond back, acknowledging each of them.

Once the 11 protections are out and about, I return to the officer's station where Thelma is checking the morning's transfers. There's 1 leaving us and 2 due to arrive from another prison. We have 14 spare beds and 4 empty observation cells and experience tells us that they can all be filled within hours, particularly the obso's.

Obso's are cells that contain cameras, the feeds of which not only run to monitors on our desk but also back to the control room. There are quite a few obso's scattered around the prison and are normally filled with prisoners requiring monitoring, either on suicide watch or medical watch. The obso's in this unit are some of the most active due to it's location and thus have a very high turnover of occupants. It's rare to find them all empty, like today.

"James, your transferring out today. You want to go and start packing?" Thelma calls to a prisoner who's walking past us. He nods and heads back to his cell, an extra bounce in his hobble, clearly happy to be leaving.

One of the nurses passes us, waving as he heads around the cells to conduct his trap checks. This entails dropping the trap, poking his head in and taking a visual check of the occupants. These types of checks are held every 2 hours, throughout the 24-hour period, night and day. I return his wave and then ask Thelma to print off the incoming list, which gives us the names, details and classification of the new crooks. I check and see that there's one of each, making it easy to place them into the unit.

We have different sized cells in here, most being 4-outers. These contain 4 beds and one bathroom for them to share, much like a normal hospital room, containing shower, sink and toilet. Hanging down from the ceiling between the facing beds are televisions which are housed in a safety box. Although each bed has their own TV, all 4 are linked to ensure the sound is the same. Cell occupants have to agree on what to watch as one remote (held in the officer's station) controls the entire unit. Want to change channel? Buzz the officer and they'll bring it to you.

"Help please?" is suddenly called and I look up to see the nurse standing by one of the locked cells. He's waving for us and I rush to him, Meagan following close behind, calling for the unit to be locked down. Thelma calls the code mike and starts locking them in from the other end, while I peek in through the trap to ensure there's no threat. "He's not responding," the nurse says as I unlock the door and he rushes past me as I hear several other nursing staff heading towards us.

The unit is locked down in under 2 minutes as the nurses begin working on the unresponsive prisoner. He's old and frail looking, skinny to the point of emaciation. It may surprise you to learn that a medical code is called, despite us being in the medical wing, but this is so several things happen. The staff that are on response immediately attend the unit, as well as the duty supervisor. Control puts the code protocol in place which means all non-essential radio traffic ceases. This process makes it easier and more efficient when needing to call for ambulances and extra services and staff.

Nursing staff request an ambulance to be called and the duty supervisor requests one from control who'll make the call and organise its escort to the unit once it arrives. Being a prison, the ambulance still needs to enter via the same access point as any other traffic but isn't subjected to internal searches.

The nurses continue working on the prisoner as the supervisor stands the code down, excusing the extra staff from the unit who immediately leave, leaving Thelma, Meagan and myself to stand guard. The supervisor leaves to organise an officer to accompany the ambulance back to the hospital, as every prisoner leaving a prison must have either one or two officers present to watch them at all times, depending on their rating.

This particular prisoner is a Class-4 rating, the lowest threat possible, requiring a single unarmed escort. If he was a Class-1, then he'd have 4 fully armed officers as well as be completely shackled with cuffs and leg-irons.

Thelma returns to the station to type up the report for calling the code while Meagan and I remain just outside the door of the cell. This particular prisoner is in a single one so thankfully, we don't have other roommates to consider. With the unit locked up for the duration of the episode, it makes it a lot easier for us to deal with the multitude of people coming and going from the unit.

The ambulance arrives almost 15 minutes after the call is made. They arrive with their stretcher, perform a brief check of the patient, then have a team lift him onto it so he can be transferred aboard. An officer carrying a folder and personal bag arrives and escorts the fanfare back to the ambulance, leaving us to return to the usual daily routine.

Once we confirm the ambulance has left the building, I re-unlock the unit to a few cheers, the day back on its usual track. It's not long before the crooks are shuffling around the corridors, some either simply pacing this way and that and others running their errands which can entail changing books by the bookshelf or heading out into the exercise yard, the day a sunny one.

Us officers take care of our duties with Thelma showing Meagan how to add new prisoners onto the muster and finding them a bed in the cell allocation spreadsheet. She's a quick learner and when Thelma offers Meagan the computer to finish the second one on her own, does so with very little guidance. It's a process she will undertake on an almost daily basis and it won't take long to become second nature.

With very little else happening, the next stop on our tour of duty is lunchtime muster, a brief moment of prisoner interaction that is over within a few minutes. Although the unit is run like a hospital wing, it is still technically a prison, a place where both worlds tend to live in relative harmony. The nurses conduct their duties and responsibilities while we take care of ours. Sometimes clashes can occur between the nurses and us, especially when a new staff member commences their duties, inexperience normally to blame.

A new nurse began her first shift just after 10 o'clock and just as control calls for all movement to cease, approaches Meagan to unlock one of the cells to conduct a check. I hear Meagan explain that it's muster but her response is one that doesn't sit well with me.

"I wasn't asking, sweetheart," she said with a thick accent. I looked up to see colour flush the young officer's cheeks, clearly taken by surprise.

"I'm sorry, I can't. Not until after count," Meagan replied, trying her best to sound apologetic but it seemed like this nurse just thought herself a little better than the prison officer.

"Is there a problem?" Thelma asks from behind me and I see the nurse actually roll her eyes.

"Oh look, here comes your back-up," she mutters, eyeing Thelma.

"Excuse me? Did you just roll your eyes at me?" Thelma asks now on her feet. Although standing a little scrape above the 5-foot mark, she has a big set of lungs and the balls to use them. What the nurse doesn't realise is that Thelma has been mixing it in maximum security for over a decade and doesn't shy away from conflict, although not one to go looking for it. What does set her off is when new officers are taken advantage of.

As I watch Thelma home in on the nurse, I see the attitude slowly drain from her face as the much shorter officer closes in.

"There's no movement once the control room calls it. If you have an issue with that, feel free to take it up with the sup. Extension 794 in case you need the number." Thelma locks on to the nurse's eyes, staring her down until she finally shakes her head and turns away. And then loud enough for the nurse to hear, Thelma adds a little fuel to the fire by speaking to Meagan.

"Don't let the inexperienced try and dictate to you, sweetheart. Takes time for them to realise where they're at." The nurse doesn't turn around, instead making a beeline for another nurse standing in their windowed office. They both begin to whisper to each other, looking like a couple of high-schoolers, glancing sideways at us every so often.

I remember back when I first began, I too had a run in with a nurse. She ended up phoning the sup who rightly put her in her place, explaining that we weren't there to make life difficult for the medical staff, instead trying to keep them safe. But unfortunately, some people struggle with a lack of perceived authority and that particular nurse never spoke to me again, eventually transferring out of the prison a couple of years later.

Count is called correct a short time after we call our number in and the same nurse approaches me to accompany her to her previous destination. She speaks the bare minimum to me and I don't get a thank you when I close the cell door upon her completion. I'm not too fussed, having more serious matters to manage.

Apart from a code mike in Tambo West, there's no other excitement to speak of and when we head out a short time after lockdown, wish each other a good night. Today was a good day.

## TUESDAY, NOVEMBER 6

I PASS Thelma on my way in and she tells me that the prisoner from the previous morning had passed away just as he arrived at the hospital. He was 82-years old and convicted for "tampering" with his neighbour's daughter. I wish her a good day and continue on to my shift in the Visit's Centre.

There are already 3 officers seated in the back and after greeting each of them, make my way through to the front where I'm welcomed by 2 more. A third joins us a few minutes later, an old guy called Joseph McDonald. Joseph has been an active correctional officer for over 30 years and the grin on his face tells me that there's more than just the sunshine cheering him up.

"You all good, Joe?" I ask as he throws his bag in one of the cupboards that line the inside of the station.

"You haven't heard?" Tom Grady said from behind me and I turn to shake hands with him.

"Heard what?" I ask, confused.

"Well, let's just say the cake in the fridge isn't for his birthday," Chris Upton chirps over his shoulder.

"Joe?" I ask, looking at the old man, his cheeks flushing a little.

"It's my last day today," he said, the happiness sounding more like relief as he speaks.

"Holy shit, man. That's awesome." I shake hands with him, congratulating him with a hearty slap on the back. He coughs comically and Chris tells me to take it easy, otherwise the old man might fall over before his final holidays even begin.

The average life-span of an active officer is less than 3 years, so seeing one make it past 30 and into retirement earns pretty high praise in my book. By lifespan, I don't mean actually alive; I'm referring to their lifespan as an active officer before quitting or being asked to leave.

"And just to make it even more fun," Chris said from his seat at the computer, holding up a piece of paper he'd just printed off. "Here's today's list, people." Tom grabs it from his fingers and immediately chuckles into his hand, holding the page up for all to see.

It's blank, the columns devoid of their usual names and times.

"What?" I ask, unsure of the meaning.

"It's a legal day," Chris said, saying it more like a question as if speaking to a child. I nod, finally understanding. Legal days are when prisoner's legal councils can visit with them. It's no different than normal other than the fact there can be a lot more allowed, due to the rest of the centre being empty. It'll still be a fairly active day, but nowhere near as busy as when we have a list of keen family and friends wanting to see their loved ones.

Lawyers have never needed to make an appointment, able to simply turn up. Once they are comfortably seated in the centre, we contact the unit to send the specific prisoner up for their visit. The sessions aren't really timed either, giving their legal counsel a relatively stress-free visit. But prisoners in prison are already under stress, often strained by not only the environment, but also by the constant fear of a pending court case. When they meet with their legal representative, crooks only really want to hear one thing; when they'll get out.

There are of course those that know they won't be getting out anytime soon. Those that have been in and out of prison know the way things work, understanding that sometimes they need to serve the time for the crime they committed.

Our phone rings and Chris answers it, looking at me as he's talking. Just as he thanks the caller, he flashes me a thumbs up and I take the cue to go and collect whoever is waiting at the front door, ready to be escorted to the centre.

When I open the reception airlock, I see 2 men and a woman, all dressed in their finest suits and carrying leather folders. I greet them and they follow me back to Visits, none bothering to talk to the lonely officer. Once back, they head to the desk and speak to Tom who collects the names of the lucky prisoners, then assigns each lawyer to a private visit's room, which are located across two of the centre's walls. Chris phones the appropriate units and our day begins.

The visits proceed with relative ease, prisoners coming and going throughout the morning, the 9 rooms almost filling completely at one point. We hear yelling a few times but when we approach the windowed doors, are waved away by the visitors like flies being shooed.

It's not until we find one poor soul who's practically pinned to a wall that we intervene. This particular prisoner is facing a murder charge and has been extremely vocal about his innocence. When we hear the voices begin to rise, 3 of us hurry to the door, the yells rising to almost fever pitch by the time we reach it. The unfortunate lawyer, a middle-aged man who looks to struggle in a strong wind, is standing with his back to one wall. The prisoner had picked up a chair and pushed the legs against the man, pinning him like mouse in a trap.

We push through the door and grab the crook, dragging him from the room and to the back of the centre while he's continuing to abuse and threaten his rep.

"Get me the fuck outa here or I'll send someone after your kids. Fucken do it," he screams, struggling against us as his pale-faced lawyer stays standing there with a panicked grin on his face.

Once we've isolated the crook in the back with the three of the officers there, we return back to the room where the man is still standing, visibly shaking from his experience.

"Well that was rude," is all he says to no one in particular before finally packing up and waiting for his escort back to the front. He doesn't speak until we reach the final airlock where he offers me a whispered thank you before heading inside, clearly relieved to be leaving.

Lunchtime muster comes and is finished without a hiccup as we begin our afternoon stretch. It gets quite hectic at one point when we have 8 legal reps turn up at once but all the visits finish in record time and before it hits 3 o'clock, our unit is down to dribs and drabs as 1's and 2's come and go. Some visits are nothing more than a minute as the prisoner is simply required to sign some form the lawyer wishes to lodge with whichever court is required and these are simply walk in and walk out affairs.

The only incident that occurs during the afternoon run is one lawyer, a young guy feeling especially important, getting himself a blood lip courtesy of a swift backhander from his chosen crook. Their visit seemed to have gone without a hitch, both emerging from the room with smiles less than 10 minutes after entering. The prisoner had asked the lawyer when he would get his mother's signature as he walked out behind the rep. The man had replied with a carefree tone that didn't sit well with the crook, a large islander with a short fuse.

"When I get around to it," he'd said. The crook made an "oi" sound and when the unsuspecting guy turned to look at his client, felt nothing more than his head snap to the left as a backhanded slap struck him so fast, it was over before anyone realised what had happened. We were on our feet in a second but the prisoner was already standing aside with his hands held out in front of him, ready and waiting for the cuffs. The lawyer stood with a shocked expression on his face, a sliver of blood running down the side of his chin, as little droplets began to adorn his silver suit like tiny red beads.

Chris was the first to reach them, cuffing the crook who was grinning at the surprised expression on his lawyer's face while Tom called the code Alpha.

"Don't speak to me like that, Bro," he simply said before being led away. The man looked at us dumbfounded, trying to make sense of what just happened. Officers begin to enter but with the prisoner already cuffed and fully compliant, there's very little for them to do.

It'll mean an extra assault charge for the crook, already facing two for a bar fight. He's a regular visitor to our establishment and is what you'd call an "easy-timer", a prisoner who sees prison as nothing more than a bit of rest and relaxation.

We are all required to write reports which takes a good half hour, given the lack of computers to go around. But once we finish, the phone calls from the front had completely ceased, our slapped visitor the final one for the day.

With a half hour to go before the end of our shift, one of the tables is slowly filled with all manner of food, snacks, cakes and sandwiches. Cups and bottles of juice are also added and before long, like ants finding a dropped ice-cream cone, officers begin to pile in for the free feed, courtesy of our retiree.

Beginning his prison career back in 1986, Joe had worked at 3 prisons in total, ours being his longest and final one with 19 years. During his time in service, he'd witnessed several riots, numerous stabbings and countless assaults. He'd seen colleagues attacked, injured, spat at and targets for faecal missiles. But Joe had made it without ever suffering an attack himself. He was an honest officer who understood what "duty of care without prejudice" really meant and always followed it, as far as I know.

Numerous officers come and pay tribute to him, many of them shaking his hand for the final time, including me. They tell war stories throughout the rest of the afternoon, continuing as I head out with Chris and Tom, leaving Joe to enjoy the rest of his final shift as an officer.

Today was an awesome day.

## WEDNESDAY, NOVEMBER 7

After having such a great day yesterday, I jump at the chance to work in the visit's centre again when offered it. I know that both Chris and Tom will be there and am surprised to see Kon sitting out the back as I walk through the airlock. We shake hands and I ask him about the weekend he'd just had. He told me the previous week that it was his 25$^{th}$ wedding anniversary on the Saturday and had arranged to take his wife away for the night. The smile on his face told me more than his words and I clapped him on the back, congratulating him on such an amazing milestone.

Scott Jones suddenly comes through the far door and I shake with him as a third officer arrives through the airlock. The face is unfamiliar to me and when I introduce myself, find his name to be Lee Harrison, a young lad from the recent graduates.

"Leave you to it, boys," I said and head towards the front where a full crew is already waiting for the first phone call. I see that Daryl Foster is the escorting officer today, leaving me to take a seat by the phone, officially running the station. By having one officer take care of phone calls, seat and room allocations and notifying units of visitor arrivals, leaves the rest of the crew to focus on the visits taking place, monitoring the tables and rooms either directly or via the monitors on our desk.

It doesn't take long for the first phone call to come through and I give Daryl the thumbs up to head to the front and collect the first round of visitors. Chris turns the monitors on while Tom continues to read his emails. Within a few minutes, the centre is alive with activity as a number of small children begin to tear the play area apart as the grown-ups patiently await the prisoner's arrival.

Once I have the names ticked off my list, I proceed to contact the units, advising the names required to attend. It doesn't take long for the majority to arrive, keen to meet with their loved ones. It's a cycle that will continue throughout the day, only pausing once while changing from mainstream to protection.

The phone rings and when I answer, am told that a visitor for Prisoner Ascot has tested positive for cocaine and has accepted a box visit. Random visitors are given a drug swab upon entering the prison and if traces of drugs are found, have to submit to a strip search. They can refuse but are then subject to a 12-month ban on attending the prison. If they do submit to a strip search and pass, are then offered a box visit. If drugs *are* found upon their person, they are confiscated and both the drugs and visitor handed to police.

This particular visitor had submitted to a strip search and passed and has also accepted the box visit as a final option. I know from experience that the crew in the back are the ones tasked with advising the prisoner in the change of plans, the notification being one of the most common times for things to get volatile.

But when the prisoner turns up, he accepts the change with very little fuss, knowing that the onus is on the visitor. But his calm demeanour doesn't last long as he challenges his girlfriend the instant the door is shut.

"Why the fuck you taking? You said no more," he's heard to scream through the glass. Chris does a walk-past to ensure the room isn't being damaged and stays within close proximity. The voices soon calm and the visit continues without incident, Chris eventually returning to his post.

When he returns 40 minutes later to give the couple their 10-minute warning, he finds the woman standing with her top lifted and her hand down the front of her pants while the prisoner is sitting back in his chair and masturbating his exposed dick. Both seem to be having a wonderful time and aren't too pleased when Chris begins hammering on the door. But timing wasn't in his favour, the crook shooting just as Chris bangs on the door for the second time. The woman flashed him a grin of accomplishment while the prisoner puts his dick away, waving at the officer. In the adjoining cubicle, a prisoner continues his box visit with his wife and 2 small children.

Chris heads for the bathroom and grabs a handful of paper towel, returning to the room and handing it to the crook to clean. He does so as his girlfriend watches on, giggling as her man is made to wipe his cum off the walls and floor. There will be a six-month ban imposed on the girlfriend which neither seem too fussed about and we find out why later when the prisoner's wife turns up with their 3 children to visit with him.

You've already read plenty of stories from the visit's centre and I won't bore you with more non-eventful happenings. The afternoon flies along as we process prisoners and visitors both in and out, until the last finally leaves just before 5. There's very little to do once the centre is empty and I'm happy to end another shift as we walk out mere moments later. Although the day is extremely unpredictable in the centre, it's still one of my favourite places to work.

Today was a great day.

## MONDAY, NOVEMBER 12

RETURNING after a 4-day weekend is never easy but I would never say no to one. The days away give me plenty of quality writing time and I often surprise myself with how many pages I get through by the time I return to work.

Today I'm rostered in Yarra North, happy to be working with Meagan and Kon. From the moment I see her step through the airlock, I can tell that Meagan's confidence has increased dramatically. It's a positive sign and I greet her as she enters the station.

"How's work been?" I ask and she explains her previous day to me, an overtime shift in Murray North where she was introduced to the work ethics of one Tony Malone. I nod my understanding, having experienced his ethics personally on many occasions.

Kon arrives halfway through the story and when he hears some of its contents, mouths the name "Tony" at me questioningly. I nod a second time, Kon firing up the computer while brandishing an understanding grin on his face. Meagan finishes her war story and breathes a sigh of relief.

"Glad to get that off my chest," she said, putting her bag away.

"No transfers for us," Kon says, continuing to brows his emails. It's one less thing for us to take care off. Transfers in or out create a wake of extra duties, mostly concerning cell allocations. If a prisoner transfers out and happens to vacate a single cell then the flow-on effect it leaves can lead to conflict and headaches from prisoners and staff alike. The struggle for a single cell is never ending.

As I'm about to grab the muster board, Meagan beats me to it, leading the way towards the first door. I drop each trap, greeting those prisoners that are awake, while rousing those that aren't, calling out the numbers as we proceed around the unit until we have our final tally.

Meagan adds her numbers while I check my emails, checking gym times, education and medical appointments. These can often change throughout the day but it gives us somewhere to start. Being a protection unit, all our prisoners are escorted wherever they need to go and just as Meagan calls in her number to control, our fourth officer arrives into the unit. It's David, the officer with the very unfortunate nickname that still seems to be sticking just as its namesake.

"Hey," I call as he enters the station. He offers handshakes all 'round and then asks if we have any moves yet.

"After unlock. There'll be a few moves to begin with," I said, showing him the computer screen. He peers at it, slowly nodding through the names.

Count is called correct moments later and Megan and I head back out to release the horde into the day. Several make a beeline for the station to ask a question I already know is coming. Kon is there to greet them and as I see him shaking his head from side to side, know what the curious few were wanting to know; whether there were any transfers out. The look of displeasure on each of their faces is enough to tell me just how disappointed they are. I couldn't imagine what it would be like to have to live with one of these inmates 24/7, listening to every bodily function and enduring every aroma throughout each day and night.

David has his first group, 17 methadones, ready to rock 'n roll a minute later and they head out through the airlock with animated excitement. They return within 20 minutes, a little ahead of the med-trolley that's slowly making its own rounds. As Kon calls for medications over the PA system, a line begins to form in front of the dispensing window. Nearly the entire unit is lined up, the queue almost as long as the length of the bottom tier. As each prisoner reaches the front, they flash their ID card, recite their prison number and then patiently wait for their cup of goodies, some filled more than others.

27 pills are the most I've ever seen in one cup, the prisoner almost eating a meal of pills. 27. They half-filled a drinking cup and looked full of jelly beans, the prisoner simply drinking them down in 3 large swallows, paid for by the taxes from you and I.

It's almost 30 minutes before the final pills are dispensed, Kon giving the unit a final call as the last of the prisoners head back to their cells. There's a hive of activity outside in the exercise yard with several prisoners giving the washing machines a workout.

It's just normal day to day stuff as the morning's activities play out as they do most days. David returns, sometimes with crooks and sometimes without, each time leaving within minutes to deliver a new prisoner to some exciting destination. While I print off the list of random cell searches, Meagan is busy sorting out an issue with bedding. 3 new arrivals from the previous day had been locked up without any bedding, spending a fairly fresh night sleeping fully clothed.

There's a sudden commotion from one of the upper-tier cells and when Kon and I approach, are confronted with a prisoner lying face down on the floor, his face dripping blood. As he slowly turns to look up at us, I can see 2 teeth lying on the floor beneath him.

"Bradley, what the hell man?" Kon asks, squatting down to help the crook up. He's a young guy, in for suspected rape and murder and our initial thoughts are that he's been attacked in his cell.

"Fell off my fucken bed," he tries to tell us. It's a 2-outer and Bradley occupies the top bunk. "Was trying to change the channel," he continues, pointing at the TV sitting on the desk which sat on the opposite wall. I call a code Mike and wait for the medics to arrive while Kon returns to the station to call control. They'll rewind the camera footage and see if anyone entered or exited the cell in the previous hour or so.

By the time the nurses leave with an injured prisoner, control calls Kon to confirm that no one had entered or exited his cell at all. From what we could gather, he'd tried to lean across the 4-foot gap between bed and TV and lost his grip, tumbling to the floor face first and knocking out two of his teeth plus cutting his lip. Both Kon and I write up our reports and email them to the sup. By the time lunchtime count is called correct, we begin the afternoon side of things with a clean slate.

As the hours tick by, the only person really doing anything is David and before I have a chance to swap with him, find Meagan already ahead of me as she calls for a couple of names to escort to the medical unit for their appointments. She leaves the airlock with the prisoners in tow as David grabs a seat in the station, heartily chomping down on a block of chocolate.

The prisoners begin to settle into the afternoon with various activities on offer around the unit. There's the usual pool game, table tennis play-offs, card games and chess tournaments. The gym also attracts a few partakers and out in the exercise yard, several prisoners are perfectly happy just pacing back and forth in the sunshine.

The three of us enjoy the quiet time, mixing it up with war stories, jokes and bits of gossip heard around the traps. The gossip consists mainly of who is seeing who and who's been walked out over allegations. The latter is normally for either sleeping on the job or trying to smuggle cigarettes into the prison, a sad reality of the environment we work in. But every now and then, a juicy piece of gossip will do the rounds, told with deep enthusiasm by the sharer of said news. David tells us that he heard that one of the women had been walked off for being caught in a crook's cell after hours.

The unfortunate truth is that it actually happens a lot more than people realise, the average of two females being sacked each and every year. But when David tells me the name of the latest discovery, I'm shocked beyond belief, not because of the act but rather who the person is. Her name is Gail Humphries and it's a real shock to me because the lady had been an officer for as long as me, having been on the same intake course together. She was always so anti-crook, often going out of her way to ensure that any breach of rules was dealt with swiftly and harshly. She was also married with 3 children, all teenagers.

The prisoner she supposedly visited, was in for a string of robbery and drug offences, by no means a stranger to the inside. His prisoner number was of someone first into the system last century, when he was still in his very late teens. I was floored beyond belief.

"Wow, you just never know," was all I could manage.

"Fuck off, cunt," suddenly came from one of the tables near the front. A game of poker had been slowly proceeding and it looked to have just blown up over a difference of opinions.

"Guys," Kon called out.

"Boss, we both got 2 8's. Who wins? I say it's a tie and we replay the hand," one of the crooks calls out.

"Your next highest card is played," Kon replies and one of the other crooks begins to cheer, holding up the ace of spades for all to see. The first crook throws his cards down in disgust but remains at the table, not wanting to be labelled a sore loser.

The afternoon continues with very little excitement, the unit cruising through the final med trolley, dinner and final muster with relative ease. Once the unit is locked down and our prisoners are all tucked in, we head out into the fading light, happy that another one is done and dusted.

Today was a pretty good day.

## TUESDAY, NOVEMBER 13

I'M BACK in Yarra North again and to my surprise, see Kon already in the station when I enter. But his expression isn't one of happiness, a frown of anger on his face.

"Hey, everything OK?" I ask as I near him. He hesitates for a moment then turns to me.

"I found a joint in Nick's room last night," he said, almost whispering. Nick is Kon's 9-year old son.

"Oh man, I'm sorry." Kon hesitates again, then slowly nods.

"Dope," he says awkwardly, the heaviness of his voice now so low that I strain to hear the rest of his words. "Told me he'd only tried it a couple of times, but." He paused, gazing at me with a look I knew to mean I already knew the answer. "My kid's a drug addict, Simon. He's just 9-years old and a junkie," he said now losing control of his emotions as Thelma came through the airlock. Kon rose and went to the staff toilet, giving Thelma a brief wave as he passed her.

"What's wrong with him?" she asked but I just shook my head.

"That he'll have to tell you himself."

"Oh, that bad, huh?" she asks and I nod at her.

"Yeah, that bad."

Kon emerges from the bathroom just as Thelma and I finish our count. She tallies up the number then calls it in as Kon returns with 3 cups of coffee, holding one out to each of us. When we sit and wait for count to called correct, Kon shares his news with Thelma who is just as shocked as I was. We sip our drinks as we discuss the options open to Kon, a parent who's always been there for his children.

Thelma is just as stunned, more-so by the young age of the child in question. Her advice is to visit with his school and find out who he's getting it from. I'm totally floored, having young children myself. It appears there's no hiding from the drug epidemic that seems to be gripping the world.

Count is called correct just as I finish my coffee and follow Thelma out to help with the unlock. It's not long before the familiar shuffle of feet and excited voices fill the air as freshly unlocked crooks jostle for positions at the toasters, washing machines and officer's station.

"Anyone leaving?" asks one.

"Gym today, Boss?" asks another.

"Where's my name on the single cell list?" asks another. Just as Kon pulls up the list of transfers, Chris Upton comes through the airlock, our escorting officer for the day. The prisoners keen for their morning methadone dose instantly surround him like flies around a discarded bone. Once the final call is made and no one else appears to want to join the field trip, he leads the pack out of the unit, leaving us to deal with the crowd before us.

"Turner, Lazenby. Go pack your things, lads. You're out of here," Kon tells the crowd. There's an instant holler of voices as the group realise both transfers occupy single cells, opening up 2 vacant possibilities. Thelma chuckles a little as the voices gain definite excitement; the all important single-cell list finally produced.

"And the winners are," Thelma begins, glancing over the group who instantly hush. She pauses for dramatic effect, locking eyes with each of her audience in turn.

"Come on, Miss," one finally says, breaking the silence of the rest. Thelma holds her hand up for silence and only once she gets it, reveals the next 2 names on the list.

"Gavin Maher and Richard Huggett." There's a split second of hushed silence as the names appear to be considered and then the wild commotion restarts as cries of disagreement and objection begin.

"But I was here before Gavin. How come he's ahead of me?" one starts but they all know Thelma well enough. The names stick and the list is swiftly returned to its hiding spot in the bottom drawer.

The excited winners of the single cells hurry back to their homes and begin to pack, an entourage of onlookers following them, hoping for any handouts that may ensue during the moving period. Gavin is the first to emerge from his second-tier cell, slowly descending the stairs while carrying a single bag of possessions. He stands beside the door of his new cell whilst its current occupant finishes his own cleanout.

It's not long before both of the transfers are waiting patiently by the airlock, quietly awaiting Chris's return. When he does, he doesn't bother coming inside, simply waving for the crooks to come out to him. He shoots me a wave to confirm the transfer and continues about his duty while I head to the computer for the day's cell searches.

One of the cells to be searched turns out to be offline due to a leaking toilet, saving us a bit of time. The second cell is for a lifer on the bottom tier who's been in the unit for close to 10 years, easily the longest serving in Yarra North. To my surprise, the third cell is one that had only just been vacated, now occupied by Gavin Maher. I show the list to Kon and he chuckles a little at the last cell on the list.

"Is what it is, I guess," he says and he follows me as we head straight to Gavin's new home.

"Guess what?" I say as I knock on the open door, watching as the crook is placing some t-shirts on a shelf.

"Huh?" he mumbles, turning to me.

"You're up for a search, Gavin."

"What? Are you serious, Boss?'

"Sure am. Just leave your stuff, man. Easier for everybody." He agrees and although not the start he was hoping for, reluctantly strips for us and once given the all clear, exits the cell, leaving Kon and I to go fishing.

We weren't really expecting to find anything, and we almost didn't, but just as we were about to leave, I dropped to the floor and peeked up under a lip of metal under the bunk of the cell. To my surprise, there was something sticky-taped there, wrapped in paper for protection. As I reach up and pull it free, I can already feel what the find is and once I'm back on my feet and peel back the top layer, confirm my suspicions.

There is a wad of about a dozen tailor-made cigarettes, all held together by a sheet of paper towelling, then carefully sticky-taped together.

"Good find," Kon says as I hold the durries up to him. He opens the door and beckons for Gavin to join us. As soon as he enters and sees what I'm holding, his face changes instantly, holding both hands up before him.

"Whatever that is, it's not mine. Fuck man, I just got here."

"But it could have been the first thing you did," I said, holding the package on the palm of my hand.

"A-ah, nope, no way. I'll go back to my old cell if I have to. That ain't mine, Boss." I look at Kon and he shrugs his shoulders, his gesture confirming my thoughts. There's no proof either way.

"Alright, Gavin. Leave it with us," I said, walking out and back to the station.

"Probably Greg Turner's stash," Kon said as we get back and I call the Admissions staff to see whether he's still there. They tell me he is and I phone the sup to tell him of the find. He agrees to question Turner and will call me with the outcome.

When the sup calls back less than an hour later, I'm surprised to learn that Turner had owned up to the package. The sup had simply told him that Gavin would be charged with the stash. Turner knew he was transferring out and although the sup could have phoned his offence through to his next jail, said he wouldn't once Turner accepted responsibility without needing to be coerced. I let Gavin know once I hung up the phone and was glad to put the matter to rest.

And apart from a brief code mike early in the afternoon, there is little else to share. The code mike was for a swollen ankle which we saw happen right in front of us when a crook tripped down the last couple of stairs leading from the top tier. He hit the deck quite hard, his ankle having rolled quite painfully.

Some days, it's just not worth going on and on about meaningless routine which is exactly what the rest of the day was like.

Today was a great day.

## SATURDAY, NOVEMBER 17

FIRST NIGHT SHIFTS are always the hardest on the body, especially when you have a cold. That's me tonight. Stupid cold and 12 hours stuck in Murray South. It's not a bad unit really, but no unit is great when you'd rather be in bed relaxing. But there's little I can do about that as I slowly make my way to the unit.

The day staff are tying up loose ends and already conducting final trap musters as I enter the unit, greeted by Vicky Temple who is manning the book.

"Oh boy are you lucky," she told me as soon as I enter the station.

"Huh?" I reply, clueless.

"Toby Manning has just been transferred to Murray North. Little prick bronzed up in 44. It's offline till a cleaning billet fixes it." I instantly realized that the faint fragrance that greeted me the second I stepped inside was shit.

"Oh my God, thank fuck for that," I said, totally agreeing with my offsider.

"First one?" she asked as I sat down, watching the others continue their count.

"Yeah, first of 3. Ugh." The others soon join us and as Robert tally's up the numbers, the rest begin to pack their stuff, readying themselves to sign off for another shift. "Any excitement today?" I ask and most shake their heads.

"Nah, not even a single code. So quiet on the radio." Weekends sometimes feel exactly like they should, even in prison.

It takes the day crew less than 10 seconds to vacate the building once control calls count correct. Their overly-loud conversation fades from my ears as they exit the airlock, a couple of them shooting me a final wave as they disappear from view.

I stand by the station for a few seconds and take in the sounds of the unit. Most of the lights have been turned off and the few that remain lit, struggle to contain the shadows in the corners. Less light reaches the upper tier and there are several patches of darkness in between the few overhead lights that are still lit up. Several TVs are on and I can make out a number of different programs, one being an American comedy, the laughter track unmissable. It's probably Big Bang or something similar, the viewing crook occasionally laughing at whatever funny line had just been delivered.

A toilet flushes near me, somewhere overhead, the trickling of the water sounding crystal clear amongst the other sounds. There's a cough further along and somewhere near the other end, someone is singing along to "Radio Ga Ga".

I head over to the store room and begin my only duty for the night, other than to keep an eye on the unit itself. It's to restock the supply cupboards inside the station. There are certain items that prisoners are entitled to on a daily basis and these are kept close at hand so as to reduce travel time. Tubes of toothpaste, replacement tooth brushes, sponges, detergent, toilet paper and garbage bags are just to name a few. Each item has an allocated shelf in one of the four cupboards and I restock them to acceptable levels to ensure they meet the next day's demand.

Once I finish restocking, I turn my attention to the staff TV, setting it up and scanning the channels for something suitable. An old episode of MacGyver briefly grabs my attention, but it doesn't hold it for long, the remote working overtime to find something more interesting. My finger suddenly freezes in mid-air as Darth Vader's helmet fills my screen and I instantly know I'm set, a Star Wars marathon just the ticket to help me stay awake.

There's a brief moment of excitement when a crook buzzes me at around 2am, but the emergency he needs solved is resolved with the handing over of a toilet roll, a disaster averted in the blink of an eye.

To stay awake in the small hours of the morning, I turn to my writing, punching out pages at a pretty decent rate. There's a second buzz up when a prisoner asks for a piece of fruit at around 5. He's a diabetic and feels his blood sugar-level crashing. I manage to scrounge him up an apple and an orange and he thanks me when I pass them through his trap.

Other than that, its's a pretty bland night shift that was made a little more enjoyable courtesy of the force. Once a couple of day staff arrive, I bid them farewell, knowing that I will return before they finish their shift.

It was a great night.

## SUNDAY, NOVEMBER 18

The second of my nights in Murray South and Vicky greets me again as I come stumbling through the airlock. I say stumbling because I'm walking like a man on the tail-end of a 12-hour shift cutting trees with an axe. My nose is leaking like a prison tap, my back feels like there's a screwdriver lost in it somewhere and my whole body feels like it's giving me the finger.

"You look like shit," Vicky snorts as I drop into a chair next to her.

"Oh yeah, laugh it up, lady." She takes my advice, practically splitting her sides at my expense. When I embed a tissue into my nostril and leave it hanging there while sighing, she laughs even harder.

The others soon join in and I'm ready to walk out with them, given the chance.

"Anything new?" I ask and she shakes her head; a very good sign for me. If the day was fairly quiet then hopefully the night would follow suit and I could be left to my own devices again.

It doesn't take long for the Deja vu to return as count is called correct and the group of happy campers exit through the airlock, sending me a final wave as they round the corner.

The buzzer goes off almost immediately and when I ask what the issue is, am greeted with loud groaning, sounding like a cow with a broken leg. Once I'm able to ascertain the issue, a toothache, I phone the sup to OK an after-hours medical move. I don't really want to call a code and the sup agrees, asking me to contact the nurses. Unfortunately, they don't want to attend the unit, so I call for a couple of staff to conduct a move, taking the crook to the medical wing for some pain relief.

The prisoner is back in his cell with 20 minutes, happy to have swallowed a couple of tablets. I thank the three staff that turned up for the move and they leave the unit giggling at my unfortunate red nose and croaky voice. We part company with the flash of a finger and the words "fuck you" mouthed through the window.

Once the unit is settled again, I finish restocking the supplies then flick on the TV and begin searching for something worthwhile. It's another good night for a TV marathon as I spot Indiana Jones playing on one of the movie channels, the first of the planned 3. It suits me fine, not in the mood for writing due to my diseased head.

I struggle through the wee hours of the morning by pacing around the unit, walking with a slow and steady pace. Although my keys jingle a little, the crooks don't seem to mind as I circumvent the unit several dozen times. The intercom goes off a little after 5 and it's the crook with the tooth problem. I try and get the nurse to attend the unit and this time he accepts, the other option being me calling a code.

I call for an escort and have two volunteers within seconds, both heading to the medical unit to pick up the nurse. Things run so much smoother when people are a bit more forthcoming and I thank the nurse once the crook has been dosed. He returns my handshake and even hangs around for a few minutes to talk a bit of shit but due to the escorting staff having other duties, cut short our conversation.

I don't hang around very long once the day staff arrive a couple of hours later and breathe a sigh of relief as my head hits the pillow a short time later.

When it comes to nightshift, it was an OK sort of night.

# MONDAY, NOVEMBER 19

WITH 2 SHIFTS DOWN, I push through and arrive for my last night shift a little early, catching up with a couple of officers who are heading the other way. There's a bit of gossip regarding an officer caught handing a prisoner a bag containing white powder, the idiot passing the drugs over right in front of a camera. He was walked off the site pending an investigation and will most likely be charged by police.

It's great to catch up, but when I hear the 15-minute warning till lockdown, head for my unit. I find Chris manning the station while the others are already locking the unit down by conducting their trap muster. It's not long before the usual sequence of events is finished and I'm left to my own devices for another 12 hours.

My cold seems to be easing its hold on me and I breathe a lot easier as I restock the cupboards and answering a couple of intercom calls for toilet paper. The TV is set up shortly after but tonight I find that my urge to write is back with a real hunger, words and phrases circling my brain until I release them onto a page.

As the night passes 10 o'clock, there's a code in one of the other units and I listen as the chatter passes back and forth on the radio. It sounds like a code Foxtrot in the unit next to mine, although no details are passed over the airwaves. Fights between cell mates are fairly common, occurring maybe once or twice a week. The issues range anywhere from a disagreement over what to watch on TV, a bowel movement after lockdown or even something as trivial as eating too loud.

The code is stood down about 10 minutes later and the sup calls me a short time later, asking if I have a spare cell. I check the muster and find nothing available, one cell offline due to having no running water. She thanks me and continues her hunt at other units across the prison.

It's a fairly easy shift and for once, am happy to have a triple go by with relative ease. There's one final buzz up just after 5 from my toothache guy and he's dealt with the same way as previously, the nurse happy to give him a house call.

When staff finally turn up an hour or so later, I practically skip out of the unit, knowing that I have 6 whole days to myself. Although night shifts can be hard on the body, officers tend to look forward to them, knowing there's almost a full week off after them. A whole week's holiday as part of your roster.

Today was an awesome shift.

## MONDAY, NOVEMBER 26

BACK AFTER A WHOLE week off and my inbox is filled with almost 400 emails. I try and get through the bulk of them before I head to my allocation today, which is in the prison kitchen. I don't mind the kitchen so much, the place running more like a place of employment as opposed to a prison unit.

If you can look past the prison uniforms, the knives all chained to the benches and the metal detectors used to scan everybody out, then you could be forgiven for mistaking it for a civilian place of work.

Because the kitchen begins long before the prison is unlocked, my 3 offsiders and I have to go around to each of the units to collect our workers. There's a list of names to carry and we split into two teams, each visiting four units and bringing a total of 22 prisoners to work. The process takes about half hour and all the cells we crack have ready and waiting workers inside.

Once back in the kitchen, the prisoners start by getting into their work attire while one of the civilian chefs makes everyone breakfast. One of the huge burners is turned into a lavish breaky buffet, frying up bacon, eggs and mushrooms. The fryers have hash browns cooking and there's juice available on one of the benches. We tuck into the food for a good 20 minutes and then begin our shift in earnest, the crew preparing to create several meals at once.

The kitchen has been known to turn over staff quite regularly due to the temptations it holds. Crooks can't seem to help themselves, often attempting to steal some delicious treats any way they can. I've personally caught several, notably one guy that tried to hide almost a dozen or so sausages down the front of his pants, the evidence clearly visible. Some have tried to steal coffee rations by hiding them in their mouths, or sugar rations up the butt. In any case, the enticement just proves too great for some and so the working crew has quite a regular turnover.

The crew works diligently until lunchtime and once we finish with our 12 o'clock muster, release the workers to eat, the civilian chefs again cooking a pretty decent meal of fish and chips. I did notice one particular prisoner repeatedly go to the bathroom but checking on him showed nothing out of the ordinary.

Once lunch is finished, everyone returns for the afternoon stretch, the planned dinner that day being spaghetti bolognaise. A huge vat filled to the brim with the sauce smelt amazing, almost to the point where I wanted to try some. But I've always had a rule when it came to prison food. I know that some people believe prisoner's food to be the best because no one would dare mess with it, but I figured you just never know.

The shift continued into the late afternoon, the kitchen a hive of activity in every corner. People were starting to assemble the unit trolleys, filling the shelves with large containers of the various meals on offer. The bulk of the meals were the spaghetti bolognaise, but there were also vegetarian salads and some kind of curry thing.

As I stood watching the team prepare the bolognaise containers, something caught my eye from near the back of the work area. There was a long row of unit trolleys, each standing with their doors open and shelves empty, waiting for the trays of food to be placed inside. Each unit required a set number of trays and several crooks were in charge of preparing the trays while others placed the trays inside.

I was standing in one of the offices and the window looking out was quite tinted, preventing anyone from outside to look in. As I stood watching over the kitchen, I noticed the crook that had been actively back and forth to the bathroom throughout the day. I could tell he was up to something because he was doing something with his hands and all the while looking around to make sure no one was watching him. I couldn't quite make out what he was doing because I could only see him from the chest up, the trolley nearest him covering the rest of him. He was preparing the sauce trays, ladling the bolognaise into trays and then putting a lid on while another crook would come and take the tray and walk it to a trolley.

It was while the crook was walking the tray to the trolley that the other one was doing something. The only way I could really see what he was up to was if I exited the office, walked out through a side door and circled to the other side of the building. There was another door almost directly behind him and although hardly used, could provide a viewpoint if I was careful.

I did just as I said, quickly running to the other side of the building undetected. The windows that lined the walls of the kitchen were set too high to look out of so I knew I wouldn't be spotted. Once at the far door, I quietly put my key in the lock and slowly turned it, carefully trying to remain as quiet as possible.

It worked and I cracked the door ever so slightly, no one inside the wiser. The prisoner who I'd been watching had his back to the door and a large rack of clean trays blocked the door from the rest of the kitchen. I watched him continue with his job, looking like he was doing everything right.

As soon as he filled a tray, another crook came with a lid and popped it on, then walked it to one of the trolleys and checking it off his list. And then without warning, while the other crook was walking the other way, the prisoner with the ladle, Sam I think his name is, slips his hand down the back of his pants and rummages around for a bit. He then spoons some more sauce into his current tray and then for some reason runs his hand through the sauce, the hand that he just had down his pants.

I'll be honest with you, I thought I was about to uncover a secret drug distribution network, my mind racing almost as fast as my heart. I watch as he jams his hand down his pants again and again, each time running it though the sauce and then wiping his hand on a towel to clean it. The other crook returns, waits for the tray to be filled and then takes it to another trolley, seemingly unaware of what was happening.

But just as I think I've seen enough to warrant closing this little cartel down, Sam does something that changes everything. He jams his hand down the back of his pants, rummages around for what seems like forever and then removes it. But instead of running his hand through the new tray, he brings it to his face and smells his fingers. I can see the brown stain of shit on one of them and then watch as he plunges the fingers into the tray. I suddenly realize what he's been doing and no longer keep quiet. I open the door, charge through and knock over a couple of the trays, the crash sounding deafening in the small space. The other crooks in the area turn to see what was happening and Sam finally becomes aware of my presence, a goofy grin on his face.

"What the fuck are you doing?" I shout, which brings my colleagues rushing over. Everyone is standing still, waiting for someone to enlighten the crowd.

"What?" Sam asks and I shake my head.

"Do you know how long I been watching you? I've seen everything." I turn to a couple of the civilian chefs that were still working nearby, unfazed by the ruckus. I wave them over and when they get close, point at the tray of sauce. "This bloke's been sticking his fingers in his arse and then wiping it through the sauce." Every set of eyes suddenly turn on him, the prisoners glaring at him with rage. Sam simply looks at the floor, the same stupid grin still smirking at us.

"Why?" the chef asks but there's no answer. One of my offsiders cuffs Sam while another calls the sup. One prisoner spits at Sam as he's walked past and he begins to laugh while another tries to take a swing. When it comes to prisoners, there are 2 things you never ever want to mess with; their medication and their food. Several begin to shout at him but he's not listening, walking briskly as he's led away.

The chef begins to rip the trays from the trolleys, telling crooks to dispose of the lot. They begin to empty the trays while several are tasked with beginning another meal from scratch. They are forced to cook fish and chips, the only other thing available at such short notice.

As I return to the office to write my report, I suddenly think back and wonder whether Sam had been doing the same thing for previous meals. Just as I approach one of the chef's, a prisoner approaches me.

"He's got diarrhoea, boss. He's my cellie. I told him not to come today but he insisted."

"Why would he do that?" I asked, pointing at the trays waiting to be emptied.

"He had a fight with a few of the boys yesterday. Maybe he wanted to get 'em back." I thank the prisoner and head to the chef, asking where Sam had worked for the lunchtime meal. He tells me that Sam was helping fill the trays of salads that went out to the units and it's enough for me to contact several units.

Four out of the seven units I call have a couple of ill prisoners, most with diarrhoea. I call the nurses and although they tell me that the effects can take days to take hold, agree to start monitoring for symptoms.

Sam was taken to Murray North and locked down, pending an investigation. Camera footage showed that he also tampered with some of the lunchtime salad trays but not all. Although they couldn't identify the specific units, the salads did make it to 9 units according to the footage.

By the time our shift ended and we were heading out, 9 prisoners were suffering symptoms of food poisoning, 1 transferred to the medical wing for observations. Although it could have been much worse, the cases were relatively isolated and thankfully contained to the trays of salads. I knew there was a reason why I didn't eat prison food and this just confirmed it for me.

Today wasn't a very good day.

## TUESDAY, NOVEMBER 27

I CAME in for a shift in the kitchen again but was sent to the medical wing instead. There had been several more cases of food poisoning overnight and one of the regular officers had to escort an ambulance into town. I didn't mind, the unit one I quite enjoyed working in. And to my surprise, Meagan was sitting in the station as I came through the airlock, grinning from ear to ear.

"Someone looks happy," I said as I came around to her side and she nodded enthusiastically.

"Can you keep a secret?" she asked and I looked at her curiously. "No, seriously. Can you?"

"Yes, of course," I replied, trying to sound serious. She paused, looking at me with eyes that seemed to try and decide if I were being truthful.

"I'm leaving," she whispered, looking around to make sure no one was eavesdropping.

"Leaving? Like going sick?" I asked.

"Leaving as in I got another job."

"What? But you just got here," I said.

"I know, but I applied for the police long before this job and I've just been accepted." She sounded genuinely pleased and I was happy for her. A girl as young as she was deserved to begin an interesting career, even if it was far more involved than this was.

"Oh wow, hey congratulations," I said, giving her a hug. "That's awesome news. When do you finish here?"

"Next Thursday is my final shift. I can't wait." I was really happy for her, as well as a little jealous. Anyone leaving to start their dream job is fulfilling their life goals. I've always wanted to be a writer and for me, I hope that one day I can afford to leave this job so I can write full time. But until that happens, I'll just have to continue these books and share the experiences you can only witness in a place like this.

The unit is practically filled to capacity as we conduct our morning trap muster and once count is called correct, unlock the 9 mainstreamers for their early runout. The weather isn't too bright today and they all elect to remain indoors, sitting around and talking shit. One sits on the bike and begins pedalling while another jumps on the treadmill. The TV is on, McHale's Navy playing through an episode from yesteryear.

It's a really quiet morning, the prisoners relaxing while the nursing staff quietly go about their business. Meagan is flicking through the newspaper while I go through my emails, slowly working my way through 1200 that are cramping my inbox. Most I have already read and so delete the majority with a simple flick.

An argument begins to ensue between biker and treadmiller, both wanting a channel change on the TV. With only a single television out here, it's a tough call to make but Meagan offers to go and sort it out under my watchful eye. She tells the crooks that as there's only one TV between them, they can either decide via a coin toss or go without entirely.

Both reluctantly opt for the coin toss and once Meagan has announced the winner, hands him the remote. The loser does what so many have before him, telling the other guy to go fuck himself, before hopping off the bike and returning to his cell.

I know it's not really the excitement you're hoping for but that was the highlight of that shift. With quite a few food poisoning cases in the unit, as well as several injuries and a couple of cancer sufferers, no one is in the mood for too much action, most opting to remain in bed, trying to sleep through whatever battle they're currently fighting.

The day seems to drag for the most part, seeming to just go on and on forever. I begin to yawn a little before 4 and by 5 am struggling to keep my eyes open. I end up doing several laps around the unit, checking open doors and strolling through the exercise yard where four crooks are busy pacing up and down.

By the time our shift finally ends, I am well and truly ready to go home, thankful for another easy day. I wish Meagan all the best in case I don't see her again and she gives me a brief hug, thanking me for my help.

Today was an Ok sort of day.

## WEDNESDAY, NOVEMBER 28

I WAS ROSTERED in Murray North today and as I enter the unit, see Chris and Salesh in the station. Salesh is a lovely man who I've seen around the place but never really worked with before. I think he's been working at the prison for a little over a year, mostly down in the factories, an area I hadn't spent too much time in personally.

"Good morning, guys," I said as I neared the station. They both wave and shake hands when I am close enough.

"Thank fuck that cretin from the kitchen is getting moved today," Chris tells me, pointing at one of the cells on the upper tier. He's talking about Sam and I ask what's been happening with him. Turns out that several prisoners have offered rewards to have him killed, he's had faeces sprayed under his door on 3 separate occasions just yesterday and the burning through the doors is relentless throughout the day.

Another 3 officers come through and enter the station; Harry, Mick and a new officer who I don't recognize. He introduces himself as Stan and he shakes everyone's hands with frantic speed then heads for the back. I look after him curiously and Harry tells me that Stan has a decent commute to the prison and normally makes the toilet his number 1 stop.

Mick and Chris take the muster sheet and start the trap count as I check the day's movements. I'm still waiting for the computer to fire up when I hear the code called on the radio.

"Code Mike, Murray North." I look up and see the boys looking through one of the traps, shouting for the ligature knife while Mick calls for the sup on his radio. He requests permission to crack the cell and once the door is open, disappears inside while me and the others begin to bound up the stairs. There's a sudden commotion from within the cell and when we finally round the doorway, are surprised to find a different scene to the one we were expecting.

The occupant of the cell, a long-termer named Dallas Lincoln, is wrestling with Mick and Chris. Chris is desperately trying to restrain one arm, blood already pouring from a gash above his right eye. There's some sort of metal bar in the crook's hand and he's desperately trying to break the arm free, his body convulsing like a fish out of water. The hand suddenly breaks free and the metal pole connects with Mick's jaw, sounding like a dull chink as hits. He yelps in pain and is thrown backwards, his head striking the edge of the toilet bowl. As I throw myself on top of the crook, I grab the pole, punch his forearm and manage to wrestle the weapon loose, still unsure of what the hell was happening.

Salesh finally ends the struggle by slapping a cuff onto one of Dallas's wrists and painfully twisting it sideways, the crook instantly screaming in pain as the metal bites into his wrist. We manage to turn Dallas over and he finally submits, holding his other hand out for us to restrain. Once he's cuffed, we walk him out onto the tier, the cheers from the other cells now sounding like a mob gone wild. I turn back and see Mick lying unconscious on the cell floor, blood dripping from the back of his head. I call for nursing staff to attend a downed officer but they are already climbing the stairs as Dallas is led down them.

Mick comes to a few minutes later and is lifted onto a stretcher and wheeled down to the medical unit. He's eventually taken to hospital by ambulance and assessed with mild concussion and a laceration to the back of his head that required 4 stitches. He also suffered a broken jaw during the ordeal.

Chris suffered a fractured eye socket and a broken finger, the finger breaking when we rolled Dallas over onto it. Both officers are given several days off and both return to work the following week.

As for Dallas, he'd been wanting a transfer to another prison, one where his 2 brothers were being held. Because the department of corrections had denied him on several occasions, he decided to initiate a move himself, knowing that by striking an officer, the move would be automatic. He'd pretended to hang himself, tying a torn bedsheet around his neck and then sticking the other end under his mattress. He could hear the officers' approach and then held his breath, turning his face blue and then simply waited for them to crack the door.

Dallas was eventually transferred out of the prison later that day. But he wasn't sent to the prison he wanted to, instead facing charges much more serious than the ones he was in for. He was being held on remand for breaching a restraining order. Now he's facing several assault charges, the sentences of which could run into years.

The only other excitement from today was when Sam finally transferred out of the unit. The 55 crooks that lined the bottom and top tiers all began to cheer under their doors, calling for the dog to be killed. Although Sam was still wearing the same goofy grin he had when I first caught him, the colour now flushing his cheeks told a different story. He was scared, the fear clearly showing in his eyes. He knew that it didn't matter where he went; this episode was going to follow him for a long time to come.

As for the rest of our shift? We ended up receiving 2 new officers for the remainder of the shift. Movements had been suspended for the day and that left all the crooks in their cells for the most part. Several were still allowed out to make their allocated phone calls but other than that, the unit remained locked down.

When we walk out at the end of our shift, I remind myself that any shift you can walk out of the prison under your own steam, is a good shift. But a couple of my friends were hurt today, and that can never be a good thing.

Today was not a good day.

## THURSDAY, NOVEMBER 29

WAS CALLED in for overtime today and after the stress of the previous shift, am grateful to be given a role in the gymnasium. It's the first time I'm ever stationed in there and feel like a fish out of water from the onset.

My offsider is Kate Hunter, a 7-year veteran and also a personal trainer outside of the prison. She's been running the gym for almost 2 years and loves her job. She greets me with a warm smile when I come through the door and shows me where to stow my gear. After a few basic pleasantries, she shows me the list of activities for the day and I'm surprised that physical activities aren't among them.

The gym will be used as a make-shift holding yard for the day as a couple of units are being given the once-over. Normally, ramping a unit means searching every single cell, nook and cranny that a unit has and locating all the things crooks hope to keep. The unit is emptied of prisoners and brought to the gym where we will supervise them until their unit is cleared for their return.

Within 20 minutes, the gym is filled with 80 crooks, all jostling for cups of coffee, gym equipment and the toilets in one endless and noisy parade. We have to replenish the coffee, sugar and milk supply repeatedly until we finally call it quits, knowing that most of it is ending up in the pockets of the more selfish in the group.

The crooks keep busy with shooting hoops at one end of the gym, congregating into little scattered groups and chatting, or using the gym equipment that's spread around the outside of the hall. When their units are finally finished, they are led back out through the doors and down the corridor to home.

The process repeats four times, four units targeted this particular day. They are Tambo East and West, Thomson east and Avoca. Units are chosen either at random or based on intel that's been received. Intel can come from officers, prisoners and civilian contractors that may have come into some information.

But ramping of units is a very good thing, often uncovering a vast array of contraband which will ultimately lead to a safer environment for all. As the prisoners are taken back to their units, those that have had things found in their cells, are separated and then interviewed plus given the opportunity to own up. If warranted, most will face a governor's hearing where the punishment will be handed out, most of it kept in-house.

I check my emails just before the end of shift and find a new one, sent moments before. It's from the Governor, thanking everybody involved for a job well done. He says that the search was deemed a complete success, having been initiated after the intel unit had received some key information regarding the influx of contraband.

Found in the four units were-

14 home-made shivs

32 x pills (14 in one cell)

3x make-shift tattoo guns

4x bottles of home brew

1x cell phone

3x cell phone batteries

THE RAMPING PROVES to be a very successful undertaking and I'm always grateful to see the shivs confiscated. I know that there are always some missed and there will no doubt be more made to replace the ones removed. But it's a start and one I'm always happy to help with.

As I walk out of the prison that evening, I look forward to a long weekend with my family, happy to be walking out under my own steam. It has been another eventful month and wonder just what the next one has in store.

Today was a great day.

Ready to go further?
Prison Days Book 7 is available right now.

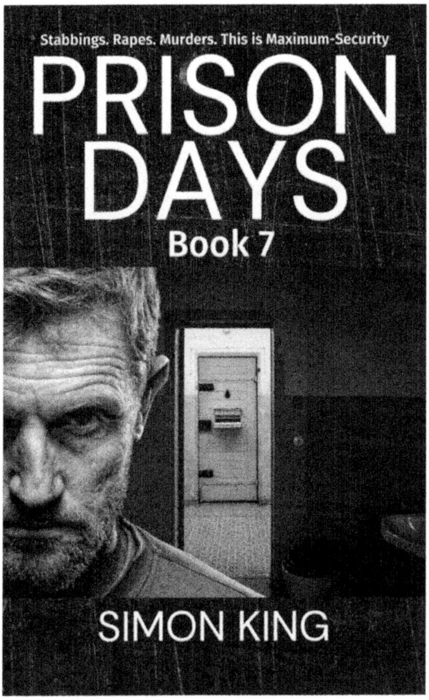

Stabbings. Rapes. Murders. This is Maximum-Security
PRISON
DAYS
Book 7
SIMON KING

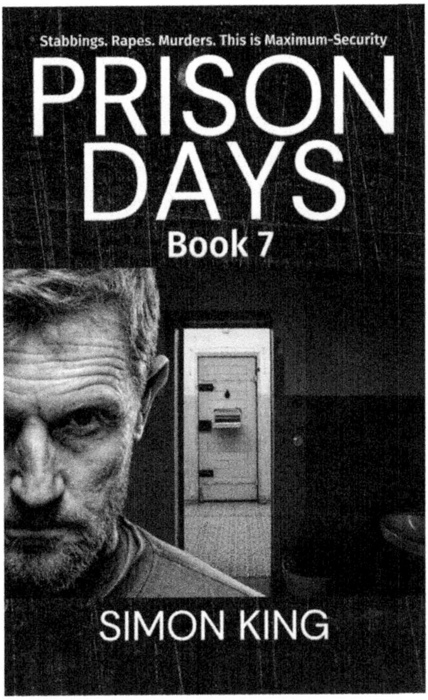


Book 7 is available now

# AUTHOR'S NOTE

THIS MARKS the completion of my 6th book in the series and proof that these books are far more popular than I ever had imagined when I first began, and for that I thank you personally. There are several other projects that I hope you would consider, each further exploring my experiences in maximum-security.

I'm currently working on an off-shoot series, titled "Prison Days: Inmates" that I hope to begin releasing next month. These books will focus on specific prisoners that I have had dealings with and I believe their individual stories will shock and surprise you.

The other new project I am hoping to begin is another new series called "MAX". This series will be a fictional one based in a maximum-security prison but will be as true to real-life as I can make it. Think "Orange is the new black" but set in a men's jail.

Plus, I'm also working on the second installment to my first novel, "The Final Alibi" released last month.

As you can see, I'm really pounding the keyboard trying to keep you entertained. I hope it's working for you and look forward to hearing your thoughts on my Facebook page at https://www.facebook.com/prisondaysauthor

Don't forget to subscribe to my website at www.booksbysimonking.com for all the latest updates, announcements and give-aways.

Thank you again for your continued support.

Simon

Printed in Great Britain
by Amazon

77914206R00263